Hilary Hoge, MD

Women's Stories of Divorce at Childbirth
When the Baby Rocks the Cradle

*Pre-publication
REVIEWS,
COMMENTARIES,
EVALUATIONS . . .*

"In this elegant book, Dr. Hoge focuses on a study of women whose marriages collapsed following the birth of a child. Transition to parenthood, considered by some to be a developmental phase and transforming event, draws upon childhood roots that can strengthen or doom the beginning of parenthood. The multiple conscious and unconscious forces at work constitute a significant personal and interpersonal challenge that, for one or both partners, can at times be overwhelming.

In the first part of her book, Dr. Hoge, utilizing both the experiences of her study subjects and a helpful literature review, traces many of these factors that normatively or pathologically underlie pregnancy, birth, and early parenthood. In later sections she discusses the major psychological and economic effects of divorce on parents and children, tracing the possible lifelong and intergenerational reverberations. She makes a significant distinction between normal grieving and severe traumatic reactions when the divorce is one-sided and comes as a surprise. Dr. Hoge's last section on clinical management and implications is very useful.

This volume is full of facts and clinical insights and is highly recommended to clinicians at all levels, including pediatricians and family physicians."

Alan Gurwitt, MD
*Faculty, Boston Psychoanalytic Society and Institute;
Co-chair, Parenthood Study Group*

More pre-publication
REVIEWS, COMMENTARIES, EVALUATIONS . . .

"**H**oge takes up the side of parenthood that we most deny—that, as a transition to a new phase of life it can be a joyful and fulfilling time, but it can also be traumatic. It can bring ghosts from the past to haunt new parents and it can be accompanied by loss and pain. Dr. Hoge shatters many myths of perfect families and lives and, through her clinical eye, she sees the complexities of this life experience and the long-term consequences when marital disruption is an outcome. She synthesizes a substantial body of literature and presents a clear picture of some of the heartbreaking experiences of those she has interviewed."

Carol Cooperman Nadelson, MD
Clinical Professor of Psychiatry,
Harvard Medical School,
Brigham and Women's Hospital,
Boston, MA

The Haworth Clinical Practice Press
An Imprint of The Haworth Press, Inc.
New York • London • Oxford

Women's Stories of Divorce at Childbirth
When the Baby Rocks the Cradle

HAWORTH Marriage and the Family
Terry S. Trepper, PhD
Executive Editor

Women's Stories of Divorce at Childbirth
When the Baby Rocks the Cradle

Hilary Hoge, MD

The Haworth Clinical Practice Press
An Imprint of The Haworth Press, Inc.
New York • London • Oxford

Published by

The Haworth Clinical Practice Press, an imprint of The Haworth Press, Inc., 10 Alice Street, Binghamton, NY 13904-1580.

PUBLISHER'S NOTE
Identities and circumstances of individuals discussed in this book have been changed to protect confidentiality.

Excerpts from S. Fraiberg, E. Adelson, and V. Shapiro, Ghosts in the nursery, *Journal of the American Academy of Child Psychiatry,* 14: pp. 387-421, 1975. Reprinted with permission.

Excerpts from J. S. Wallerstein, The long-term effects of divorce on children: A review, *Journal of the American Academy of Child Adolescent Psychiatry,* 30(3): pp. 349-360, 1991. Reprinted with permission.

Cover design by Jennifer M. Gaska.

Library of Congress Cataloging-in-Publication Data

Hoge, Hilary
    Women's stories of divorce at childbirth : when the baby rocks the cradle / Hilary Hoge.
      p. cm.
    Includes bibliographical references and index.
    ISBN 0-7890-1291-X (alk. paper)—ISBN 0-7890-1292-8 (alk. paper)
    1. Divorce—Psychological aspects. 2. Parenthood—Psychological aspects. 3. Parent and child. I. Title.

HQ814 .H675 2002
306.89—dc21   \
                                      2001039708

To Wendy, Ben, Leslie, and Nicholas

ABOUT THE AUTHOR

After graduating from Dartmouth College, **Hilary Hoge, MD,** attended the University of Virginia Medical School and completed her psychiatric residency at Massachusetts Mental Health Center, a Harvard teaching hospital. She helped found the Trauma Recovery Program at Westwood Lodge Hospital and is currently a candidate at the Massachusetts Institute of Psychoanalysis.

Over the ten years she has been in private practice, Dr. Hoge has had extensive experience with patients undergoing difficult divorces. In addition, she has helped many clients with their transition to parenthood. She is currently in private practice in Brookline and Milton, Massachusetts, where she specializes in long-term psychotherapy.

CONTENTS

Preface

Childbirth and divorce are words that do not seem to belong together. Drawn from separate dictionaries of love and ire, they are rarely used in the same sentence. Surely, we think, even in our society where divorce is common, new parenthood must buffer such decisive action until many chapters later. Although they are drawn from different lexicons, however, divorce and childbirth do collide, perhaps more often than we would like.

As a psychotherapist in private practice, I became interested in the subject of divorce at childbirth for two reasons. First, as I worked with men and women of childbearing age, I witnessed their frequent struggles with transition to parenthood and noticed that, although some weathered this transition with relative ease, others found it especially difficult. Among this second group, even those who had greatly desired children sometimes found themselves in unexpected turmoil that did not quickly resolve. I began to wonder what forces, from within and without, could make transition to parenthood so stormy.

The other avenue that led to my writing this book involved witnessing the very destructive nature of some divorces. Both in my professional work and in my observations elsewhere, I realized that a subset of divorce exists in which at least one party is unable to grieve the marriage's end. I referred to this as "traumatic" divorce, to distinguish it from that under more ordinary conditions. What causes such divorces, I wondered, and how can therapists best help people heal?

To answer these questions, I needed more information than provided by my clinical experience. By designing a study of parents who had separated or divorced within one year of childbirth, I hoped to gain windows into both the nature of difficult transitions to parenthood and traumatic divorce. I was not attempting to generate a random sample or to obtain results that would generalize to a large population. Rather, I was hoping to hear people's stories, in all their subjectivity, about this difficult time in their lives. I realized my inquiry would generate more questions than answers and hoped these questions would in turn generate further research.

Description of the Study

At the onset, I placed notices in several magazines inviting readers who had experienced separation or divorce within one year of childbirth to participate in a study and contribute their stories to my book. During in-depth semistructured interviews, I focused on the following six questions:

1. What do you think caused your marriage to end?
2. What were the effects of the breakup, short-term as well as long-term? What was most difficult?
3. How did the breakup affect your capacity to parent? Did you notice any effects on your children?
4. How has your relationship with your former spouse evolved, following separation?
5. Reflecting on your and your former spouse's own family history, was there any information you thought relevant?
6. What helped you cope with this difficult time? How have you attempted to heal?

Seventeen women participated. Some responded directly to my ads; others heard about my work indirectly and contacted me from different parts of the country. All respondents were Caucasian, with an average age of 33.5 years and average time since final separation of 2.5 years. Most were college educated, were middle income, and held professional jobs before divorce. Many were interested in having their stories told, not only as tales of trauma, but of resilience. Consequently, these women may not be representative of others in their situation, as those with fewer initial advantages might fare considerably worse.

To ensure privacy, I changed names and other identifying features sufficiently so that none of the women or their husbands are recognizable. Although in some cases I shortened the stories to highlight points relevant to particular chapters, in making these changes, I tried to stay true to each story's original meaning.

These accounts, of course, are subjective. None of the respondents wished their husbands to be interviewed or thought the latter would be interested in participating in the study. As a result, some of my interpretations are based on secondhand reports, information that may be considered one-sided. Furthermore, all of the information about the women's former spouses, their own families, or the families of their former spouses is alleged and included solely to illustrate the points I make in the book. Although I cannot vouch for the "objectivity" of these accounts, nonetheless, I do believe they illustrate issues that commonly arise with new mothers and fathers. They should be read, not for their absolute accuracy, but as illustrations of common themes among new parents whose marriages suddenly nosedive.

Although my study solicited both men and women, only one man responded. Sadly, as the issues concerning divorce, child support, and custody become gender polarized, some men may not have trusted a female interviewer. I hope that those experiencing difficult transitions to fatherhood, as well as traumatic divorce, will let their stories be known. Meanwhile I appreciate the courage of the one father who did participate. Although I did not include his story because I felt uncomfortable drawing conclusions based on a single interview, it did illustrate that men as well as women can experience unwelcome, traumatic divorce during this vulnerable time.

Grief versus Trauma Responses

This book portrays separations and divorces that were unusually traumatic in nature. Just as in the physical sciences a law is applicable only under certain conditions, so in the social sciences is our understanding of how people react valid only within a certain range of circumstances. Newtonian physics breaks down in the core of a star. Similarly, the way people behave under extreme stress does not always correspond with how they behave ordinarily. I do not believe, however, that this discontinuity has been fully recognized for the situation of divorce. My impression is that well-meaning mental health professionals as well as many legal scholars apply a similar set of assumptions to all divorces, traumatic or not. This, I think, may be a mistake.

But are not all divorces traumatic, my readers may ask? Does not everyone who has been through the breakdown of a marriage suffer permanent scars?

Yes and no, I would answer. Certainly divorce leaves its mark on almost all who undergo it, but ordinarily, under good-enough conditions, people are able to grieve the loss of their partners, and as we will later see, such grief is the key to letting go of a marriage while retaining some internal representations of a former spouse as good and worthy of respect. Under more extreme conditions, however, this process breaks down. If one partner unexpectedly, unilaterally exits the marriage at a vulnerable time, the other may not react with grief but suffer trauma. Even those initiating divorce may experience trauma if they felt forced to do so by the others' behavior.

Unlike one able to grieve, a traumatized spouse becomes numb to any fond feelings about the former partner. Previously cherished memories become partitioned, with little or no emotional access, as they are just too painful to bear. Because such memories are walled off, a traumatized spouse is unable to reflect on them, to "decathect" gradually, to grieve. Large areas of the inner world, including thoughts, feelings, and internal representations, are blocked.

With this in mind, I posed a couple more questions as I interviewed these women: What causes a person to end a marriage in a traumatic way, creating extreme-condition divorce? What helps people grieve? These are complex questions and could never be fully answered on the basis of my interviews, but hopefully these stories, for the most part about survival from traumatic divorce, will shed some light on the matter.

Outline of the Book

This book has three parts. In Part I, I explore the nature of difficult transitions to parenthood, drawing on both sociological and psychoanalytic literature to explain why some couples experience an unusually stressful time. Translating psychoanalytical concepts into ordinary language, I focus on how childbirth can activate previously dormant issues, creating apparent personality transformations. In Part II, I discuss the consequences of unexpected divorce at childbirth. Its emotional as well as economic sequelae are portrayed as relevant, not only to this event, but more broadly to all unplanned divorces involving young children. In addition, I include findings from recent infant research to suggest how divorce might affect the youngest in these stories. In Part III, I return to my original six questions and summarize the findings of my study.

Intended Audience

As I struggled between wanting to write a book that would be clear to nonprofessionals but also of interest to clinicians treating individuals, couples, or families, I realized some sections may appear too obvious to therapists or too murky to nonprofessionals not already familiar with psychodynamic language. Yet I decided to include these different pieces, in what may occasionally read as a mosaic of languages, to reach both important audiences.

I do hope that, for many readers, I got it right. May this book help clinicians as well as prospective parents understand the forces childbirth unleashes and assist those parents already suffering divorce at this time in healing.

Acknowledgments

Of the many people who helped me write this book, I wish to thank in particular the women who bravely shared their stories with me. Even though doing so was painful for them, they trusted that relating their experiences could help others recover from similar divorces. Without their willingness to tell their stories, this book could not have been written.

My Massachusetts Institute of Psychoanalysis (MIP) classmates—Anne Waters, Valerie Palms, Mike Reison, Kyra Montagu, and Rheta Keylor—also deserve a special thanks for their unwavering encouragement and support as I led a double life, writing this book at the same time I was in psychoanalytic training. Mike's sharing with me his doctoral thesis on transition to fatherhood was especially helpful. For excusing me from photocopying duty, as well as for our lively class discussions, to all I give my warmest thanks.

I am also deeply grateful to Judy Huizenga, Alan Gurwitt, and the other members of their study group for reviewing my first three chapters and offering invaluable advice. To David Doolittle for his careful reading of Chapters 4 through 6, I am indebted. Dan Jacobs, the first person to whom I dared show my book proposal, encouraged me to continue. Gaston Blom gave me many suggestions for readings in the area of attachment research, which I would have been unlikely to find without his guidance. I would also like to thank Mal Slavin, Gerry Stechler, Barbara and Stuart Pizer, and all my other teachers at MIP, many of whom unwittingly gave me ideas for this book through their many excellent seminars.

Nonpsychoanalytic colleagues included Jim Lindsley, who generously read and critiqued my ideas from a broader stance. His sharp mind helped to clarify my thinking and remove the cobwebs from some of my murkier concepts. Carol Peckins, besides always being there as a friend, immeasurably deepened my understanding of grief and trauma.

Terry Trepper, my editor at The Haworth Press, deserves special thanks, as he offered not only steadfast assistance with my writing of the manuscript, but also technical support that pulled through my old Mac Performa. Amy Rentner, copy editor, and Peg Marr, senior production editor at The Haworth Press, not only fixed the commas, but always produced the right word and spared my readers the worst of my metaphors. My agent Sally Brady as well as my colleague Ron Levant offered much-welcomed encouragement. My secret editor, my mother, contributed her skill, wisdom, and well-tuned ear.

Finally, I wish to thank my family, whose enormous sacrifices encompassed more than the usual. Their belief in me and this project never wavered, even when it could have, and their faith helped me keep mine.

PART I:
CAUSES OF DIVORCE
AT CHILDBIRTH

Amy never thought she would become a divorce statistic. At thirty-three, she felt her life was in place, as she balanced a successful musical career with a happy, intimate marriage to Bill, who expressed not only his love for her but also his eagerness to be a father. Soon after she became pregnant, however, he began an affair and, against her protests, left when his son was only three months old. Almost a year later, Amy is still in shock, trying to piece together what happened to her marriage.

Amy's story, to which we will return, is hardly unique. While many couples hope that a baby will bring them great happiness, this may occur only if they are able to overcome childbirth's multiple challenges. When they fail, so may their marriages. What causes new parents to undergo such stress?

The answer to this question might appear straightforward. Childbirth, after all, turns life upside down. Whereas previously the couple had to nurture only each other, now they are part of a triad. Their entire balance of forces must be recast. Furthermore, this must be negotiated at a time of sleep deprivation, physical exhaustion, and economic pressure. No wonder couples have difficulty.

This is the traditional answer.

As we will see, it does not always suffice. Amy's story opens the door to a number of questions that have been insufficiently addressed. Her story also begins to sketch several themes, which may be helpful to list, as we will return to them later:

1. Transition to parenthood is more difficult than commonly supposed. Even previously well-functioning couples may enter a crisis that leads to divorce.

2. Traditionally, this crisis has been considered to be a *couple's* crisis. In other words, divorce at childbirth has often been thought to result from long-standing, maladaptive patterns in how a couple relates, further exacerbated by the additional stress of childbirth. Yet, in Amy's case, divorce was precipitated not so much by difficulties in the *relationship,* as by her husband entering an internal state of profound, *personal* crisis.
3. The nature of the personal crisis triggered by childbirth varies but may include activation of old fears and scripts, character traits, or trauma. Although in some cases these problems may have been intentionally hidden from the other partner, in others they may have remained deeply unconscious until childbirth.
4. When couples have had difficulties for many years, divorce at childbirth may be foreseen. In other cases, however, it may occur unpredictably; at least one member of the couple, and sometimes both partners, may be taken completely by surprise. Although in retrospect, the "reasons" for divorce may become clear, identifying these factors ahead of time with sufficient accuracy to make predictions may be difficult.
5. When surprised by divorce, new parents often feel traumatized. Emotional stability, parenting skills, and economic survival may be severely compromised, and recovery may take years. Grieving, in the traditional sense, may be difficult.

In this "transformation" model of divorce at childbirth, I am departing radically from many popular, as well as standard clinical narratives that emphasize a more transitional nature of divorce at this time. These narratives use a paradigm of additive stress, in which the baby simply adds one more weight to an already burdened couple. Furthermore, they make an implicit assumption: partners who live intimately in each other's interpersonal fields must certainly sense each other's moods. Neither member of the couple, accordingly, should be *too* surprised by divorce; they both should have seen it coming. When such couples enter therapy, they are often implicitly encouraged to take mutual responsibility for knowledge of the marriage's flaws. The unstated value judgment is that if one partner was truly surprised, this reflects, at best, a large investment in denial and, at worst, a lack of psychological sophistication.

On the one hand, this standard narrative does illuminate the dynamics of many failing marriages, in which either both partners are aware of serious problems, or a system of mystification perpetuates their denial. Within this model, many family and couples therapists have worked successfully to ameliorate the leaving party's guilt, usefully confront the "surprised" party's maladaptive defenses, and help children caught in the conflict not to fixate blame on one parent.

Although this model applies to many divorces, in some it fails. It does not take into account how pregnancy and childbirth can trigger deeply buried issues and fears, causing one partner to enter an unexpected personal crisis that explodes the marriage.

To frame our understanding, we will begin by exploring, in Chapter 1, why transition to parenthood can be difficult. After reviewing sociological studies on how couples adjust, we will turn to psychoanalytic concepts of parenthood, as both a developmental phase and a developmental line, to understand how couples can be out of sync at this critical juncture. In Chapter 2 we will discuss how parenthood may precipitate a personal crisis by activating previously dormant fears, trauma, or both. In Chapter 3 we will compare and contrast these two models, *transformation* versus *transition*. Although both are relevant to divorce at childbirth, I have chosen to emphasize the former, as I believe it is less recognized.

Now let us return to Amy's story, for although her husband may have recognized his vulnerability, divorce took Amy by surprise.

Chapter 1

Transition to Parenthood:
Why Might It Be Difficult?

Amy believed she knew Bill well. Introduced in their early twenties by a mutual friend, they had dated for several years before marrying. In addition to enjoying a good romantic life, Amy felt they were best friends; sharing many activities together, such as hiking and volunteer work, they seemed close in every way. As over the years Bill had demonstrated his love and loyalty, she had no doubts about their future together.

Both Amy and Bill wanted children. As a mutual decision, they stopped using birth control. They both spoke enthusiastically about the joy children would bring them, while at the same time preparing for the accompanying lifestyle changes. Bill hoped he would be able to take some time off from his job in a busy Chicago law firm while Amy, looking forward to raising their children in an atmosphere of love and respect, never imagined anything was wrong.

Amy was a well-educated, insightful, and intelligent woman, one who could look squarely at difficulties and not avoid unpleasant conclusions. If Bill had given her any reasons to doubt his commitment, she believed she would have picked up on these. But her radar—as far as she knew in good working order—received no warning signals. She entered pregnancy feeling fully secure about her marriage.

Although Bill had been eager for her to conceive, after she did he seemed strangely uninterested. He became more distant, worked longer hours, and stayed out late at night. Although Amy was concerned, during much of her first trimester she was too nauseated and tired to worry much about Bill's behavior. Counseled by her friends that he was simply adjusting to fatherhood, she understood her pregnancy could be a hard time for both of them; after all, it was taxing for her physically. She tried to spend extra time with him, and as her pregnancy progressed, he reassured her that he loved her and was excited about the baby.

Exhausted from her seventy-two-hour labor, Amy appreciated Bill's attentiveness in the hospital. As he doted on her and their newborn son, they appeared to have the perfect family.

Once home, however, Bill's attitude changed dramatically: he ignored both her and the baby. Sleepless from breast-feeding every three hours, Amy noticed he never helped with child care. Complaining that he was not receiving enough attention, he refused to do household chores, as his former cheerfulness shifted to disgruntlement.

When Bill began staying out until 3 a.m., Amy could ignore his behavior no longer. Even though it had been inconceivable to her that he might be having an affair, she began to feel alarmed—and finally confronted him. During this conversation, while repeatedly denying his infidelity, Bill answered the ringing phone. It was Margie, a much younger woman he knew from work. Agitated, he began telling Margie that no, he did not love Amy, but only her. Extremely distraught, Amy begged him to go to couples counseling. He refused. In fact, he denied the liaison and told Amy she was imagining everything.

In desperation, Amy hired a detective. Through his photographs she learned that Bill's younger girlfriend had long, curly amber hair similar to hers at an earlier time. The image of this younger, glamorous woman stung Amy. Even though she too was an attractive redhead, she compared herself unfavorably. Realizing she had been preoccupied with both her pregnancy and the baby, she thought if only she had been more attentive to Bill, he would not be leaving. Begging him to stay, she promised to give him more love. But there was no stopping Bill. Explaining he was repulsed by her postpartum figure, he left when their baby was three months old, before he did much bonding.

Although Amy initially blamed herself for Bill's departure, over the next months she discovered some aspects of his character she had not previously fathomed. For example, she had always respected his honesty. When she appeared in divorce court, however, Amy discovered that Bill's financial statement revealed a monthly payment for child support—but not to their son! Never had he mentioned that he was already a father.

Other aspects of his character came to light, as well. Although she had known he did not handle money well (he had entered the marriage with significant credit card and school loan debts), she had not known about his past declaration of bankruptcy, nor was she prepared for how he handled money during the divorce: during the next three months he ran up over $10,000 on credit cards, his expenses including expensive restaurants, airline tickets, and exotic trips. During their marriage, Amy had taken responsibility for their finances. As her salary was higher, she had helped him with his school loans, which, in fact, she had just finished paying off when he left.

Through these revelations, Amy became aware that her husband had had a hidden side, which he had purposefully kept secret from her. She also wondered whether, in order to have a life with her, he had kept these sides hidden from even himself. Perhaps under the stress of fatherhood, he could not maintain this false front. Perhaps, she mused, they had both shared an illusion that he was someone he was not.

After leaving Amy, Bill was initially quite amicable, telling her they were now "best friends" and having the "best divorce." But within a few months he turned on her viciously. Angrily blaming her for everything, he dragged her to court many times over money and visitation before the divorce was finalized.

Divorce did not end their legal battles, however, as Bill continued to contest visitation arrangements. Before the divorce, when it became apparent he took improper care of his infant, the court had ordered his visits supervised. He had shown little interest in his son at that time. Afterward he suddenly demanded him every other weekend (Friday through Sunday) as well as one night during the week, while refusing to disclose his address or telephone number to Amy.

Amy had a number of concerns about his visitation proposals. Perhaps if he had paused long enough to bond with his son before leaving, it would have been worth destabilizing his environment to ameliorate missing his father. But since this did not happen, Amy thought it preferable to wait until her son was older before shifting his residence back and forth so frequently. In addition, Bill's rage and rigidity worried Amy, to the point that she feared he might even try to kidnap their son. Yet Amy wanted her son to have a father, and though she herself wished to have nothing to do with Bill, she struggled with the complexity of what was best for her child.

It is now eleven months since Bill left. In addition to worrying about visitation, Amy continues to puzzle over what happened to her marriage, vacillating between thinking something is seriously psychologically wrong with Bill and wondering whether some other party, such as his family, is fueling his anger. Very close to his parents, who continue to live in a nearby Chicago suburb, Bill was always their shining star. When he left Amy, they were initially furious at him. More recently they have turned against her for resisting his visitation demands. She is sad, as for years she felt part of his family. Now she is losing them. Even so, she keeps sending them cards.

Further reflecting, Amy recalls that Bill told her that his father left his mother many times; after each occasion, though he remained involved with another woman, she took him back. He was more like a pal than a father to his son. Amy wonders if Bill, who identified strongly with his father, adopted this model of marriage as his own.

Bill, however, had very different explanations for the divorce. When Amy asked him why he left, he confidently explained he had *always* been unhappy with her—adding that she had not been loving or sexual enough, had not made him feel welcome, and had been too obsessed with money. Amy was perplexed. He had not raised these issues before conceiving a child with her but, rather, had repeatedly spoken of his contentment with their relationship. Nor had she sensed that he was unsatisfied sexually; in fact, he had seemed pleased with their romantic life until late in her pregnancy. Now, it seemed, he was rewriting history.

Profoundly rejected, Amy felt she was living through a nightmare in which a vision of someone she loved and trusted shimmered for an instant, then transformed into that of a torturer. She was unable to sleep, lost a lot of weight, looked like a skeleton, cried incessantly, and could not tolerate being alone. She could not focus on her baby and knew that her mothering was impaired. She wondered, what had she done so wrong to deserve this treatment? Although she tried to attend to her baby, she was preoccupied, as over and over Bill's complaints replayed in her mind, like a movie reel that would not end.

Also, she blamed herself for not having foreseen the divorce, for not having "read" Bill correctly. In giving me permission to publish her story, she knew that some readers might question whether she had ignored earlier signals that Bill had serious problems. As she reviewed her marriage prior to pregnancy, however, she could not recall any ominous signs. Perhaps because he himself had disavowed the importance of his issues, he had been able to present to her an illusion with few, if any, cracks—an illusion in which they had both wanted to believe.

Fortunately, Amy has emotional support from friends and family. Gradually, she is understanding that neither the divorce nor her lack of foresight were her fault. Although these insights are beginning to turn the tide for her, she remains traumatized that someone who seemed to love her could turn on her so quickly, without warning or cause.

Although earlier she still loved Bill and would have considered reuniting, she no longer feels this is a possibility. Her love, faith, and bond with him are dead. Worse, she feels so shaken by seeing him that it takes most of a day to recover. Wondering how best to raise a child with someone she now hates, Amy remembers her own good childhood, in a stable home where both mother and father kissed her goodnight, where both were there for her day in, day out—not just because they loved each other, but because neither could have conceived of living apart from her. She had assumed her children would have this security. She yearns for it for her son. What would have been the happiest time of her life became the worst, and her son's permanent loss.

As prevalent as divorce is in our society, marital breakdown within a year of childbirth still startles us. We wonder how couples who loved each other enough to have made two major commitments— first to marry, then to raise a child together—find their relationships deteriorating so quickly after achieving pregnancy. Unlike divorcing couples with older children, it would seem there had not been time for their marriages to unravel, and certainly not time to give up on them before attempting repair. As suddenly as a tornado destroys a summer's day, divorce at childbirth shocks us, as it seems to strike unpredictably, discontinuous with our emotional landscape.

Divorce at this time is also shocking because of the vulnerability of infants and their mothers. The physical challenge of pregnancy as well as the biological storm of giving birth make a woman especially dependent during this period. No matter how equal her relationship was with her spouse before pregnancy, toward its end she may well be physically hindered, require time off from work, and rely economically on her husband for the first time. Postpartum hormonal shifts and exhaustion make new mothers especially vulnerable to depression; uncontrolled weeping, known as "baby blues," affects a majority even under the best circumstances. Given the biological vulnerability of infants and their dependency on their mothers, it would appear a most imprudent time to separate or divorce. Why would a postpartum mother leave her husband, or, conversely, what would motivate a husband to leave the mother of his newborn?

To understand the forces involved, we need to review what is known about transition to parenthood. Although a complete survey is beyond the scope of this chapter, an acquaintance with some relevant studies will help frame our understanding. After examining how parenthood affects a couple's relationship, we will look at how it affects each spouse separately. Comparing traditional psychoanalytic concepts with those of contemporary infant research, we will elucidate some of the challenges parents face as they rework old issues while trying to incorporate their new babies.

EFFECTS OF CHILDBIRTH
ON COUPLES' RELATIONSHIPS

Traditionally, childbirth was thought to increase marital satisfaction. Delight in one's newborn, fulfillment of one's role as parent, and deepening awareness of the life process were all expected to bring couples closer together. Recent research, however, shows that parenthood does not necessarily make marriages happier. On the contrary, many couples—even some who were previously well-adjusted—experience a crisis after having a child. Several authors have tried to assess the degree of this crisis and have questioned whether it is already nascent in troubled marriages, or if it arises de novo from the stress of childbirth.

After reviewing numerous studies on transition to parenthood, Goldberg (1988), for example, concluded that about 20 percent of couples experience a true crisis—a time of great psychological upheaval—whereas the majority experience a less tumultuous time of transition. Goldberg and Michaels (1988) also found consistency between couples' functioning from the pre- to postpartum period: the baby does not jolt but rather nudges them toward further problems.

Klinnert et al. (1992), summarizing the literature, also found that a new baby has a modest but predictably negative effect on marital happiness. Similar to Goldberg and Michaels, they noted that, overall, couples' satisfaction before having children correlates with that afterward; most happy couples remain happy—if a little less so—and most unhappy ones show a predictable deterioration. A few couples, however, show sudden, unanticipated changes. A happy marriage can thus turn sour, and an unhappy one can occasionally be improved by the birth of a child.*

Similarly, the Cowans's (1988) literature review revealed that childbirth often triggers an increase in marital stress and dissatisfaction, and in their own work they found that, following the birth of a first child, many parents, discovering they have different child-rearing styles, complain of feeling distant. Although the Cowans found that most parents decide their new babies are well worth the extra stress, for a few couples the transition is extremely difficult. Of seventy-two expectant parents followed over two years, 12.5 percent not participating in a support group separated or divorced by eighteen months. Looking at what predicted marital breakdown, the Cowans found that couples are more likely to remain together if both spouses have positive memories of their own parents' marriages; if they have more negative memories, they are more likely to divorce. Interestingly, these memories affect marital satisfaction only after the birth of a first child, suggesting that internal factors formerly of lesser consequence now rise to the foreground. Birth of a first child can be a watershed event.

Another factor contributing to difficult transitions is the emergence, sometimes for the first time, of spousal conflict over precious resources of time and energy. Interviewing couples three, six, and nine months after childbirth, the LaRossas (1981) found that parents argued extensively over who earned "downtime" from child care responsibility. Noting that conflict between parents can escalate without sufficient resources, the LaRossas stressed the need for more child care options and greater job schedule flexibility.

Overall, these researchers found the transition to parenthood to be difficult. Moreover, not only socioeconomically disadvantaged parents, but even those with unusual educational and economic resources, often had difficulty incorporating their new children into preexisting family structures (Lewis et al., 1988).

---

*Klinnert et al. (1992, pp. 340-341) noted that in general, studies show an increased rate of divorce after a premature or handicapped child is born. This result was not born out in their own study, however; other stresses such as number of children, spacing of children in years, and external pressures on the couple added linearly to predict marital satisfaction. Their study stressed the linear, additive nature of stresses rather than a "threshold" or nonlinear relationship. They contrasted this with Lewis's (1988) finding that some distressed couples experience a sudden, nonlinear change—even an improvement—in their marriages.

In summary, transition to parenthood is troublesome for even the best-adjusted couples. Sleepless nights, continual demands for infant care, and conflicts over precious downtime stress most couples, no matter how happy their marriages. Differences also begin to emerge in couples' child-rearing styles, differences with roots deep in their own pasts. Although the new arrivals bring unimagined joy and fulfillment, they also turn their parents' lives topsy-turvy. Alternating between ex-altation and despair, new parents may experience a deterioration in the quality of their marriages and, in some cases, enter crises.

Although the degree of most couples' dysfunction after childbirth can be anticipated from that shown previously, some couples, such as Amy and Bill, show little apparent continuity. For these parents, child-birth transforms their relationships in ways at least one partner may not have divined. To further understand how parenthood can be a water-shed event—changing lives toward the unimagined—we will turn to a psychoanalytic understanding of how parenthood affects individuals.

PARENTHOOD AS A DEVELOPMENTAL PHASE

What is meant by a developmental phase? The term refers to a time of life, with a wide but finite window, in which certain psychological challenges are addressed. If they are not well met, or if severely com-promised solutions are formed, the result may be a failure to thrive. Optimally, people work through new life challenges satisfactorily; if they are unable to do so, or if they flee, their psychological growth may be impeded. As in the acquisition of language, there is room for later repair, but this will become more difficult once the sensitive time frame has passed.

We do not know, for Amy and Bill, how each will address this phase, as my interview took place early in their son's life. So let us turn to the following story, which portrays two opposite approaches to the developmental phase of parenthood.

Karen and Raymon: Out of Phase

Karen, a thirty-three-year-old graphics designer, separated from Raymon af-ter seven years of marriage. Conceiving their daughter shortly thereafter, they traversed opposite paths through parenthood.

From the beginning, Karen knew that Raymon would not make an ideal mar-riage partner. Having just graduated from college, she met him while traveling abroad. Although they quickly fell in love, she was well aware of their differences;

he had only a high school education and, unlike her, was restless and hesitant to put down roots. But Karen loved him, and as he did want to move to the United States, she agreed to marry, knowing this would help his immigration process.

During the first years of their marriage, Karen enjoyed their traveling lifestyle. Still young, she exhilarated in exploring the world, as Raymon's restlessness still appealed to her sense of adventure. Although they were developing separate circles of friends as well as conflicting values, for the most part she felt they had a good marriage.

When she was in her early thirties, they returned to live near Portland, Maine, and although earlier she had loved traveling, her dream began to change. Now she wanted to settle down, finish her master's degree, buy a house, and start a family. While she worked days, Raymon worked nights; their lives were becoming more separate. Furthermore, Raymon made it clear he did not share her dream. Even after he lost his job, he did not look for work. Instead, he stayed out late at night with his friends, going to nightclubs and discos.

When Raymon forgot her birthday, Karen became suspicious he was having an affair. A few weeks later, she confronted him, and he admitted he was in love with another woman. Karen had known that he had had occasional affairs, but she had thought she could tolerate these, as long as they were not serious. In fact, as part of a mutual understanding, she had had a few flirtatious flings herself. This time, however, he seemed emotionally involved, which in her mind was very different: he was in love with someone else. Extremely upset, Karen decided to move out.

Although initially in favor of the separation, after his girlfriend broke up with him, Raymon had second thoughts about ending his marriage. He reapproached Karen. She, however, was skeptical. Much as she had loved him and had tried to believe in their future together, not only was she terribly hurt by his passion for another woman, but she also realized they had different long-term goals. Yet Raymon was not deterred. One night they went out to dinner, and although not heavy drinkers, both consumed more than usual. Raymon accompanied her home and spent the night. After they had sex, he left, and she did not see him for awhile, as he reunited with his girlfriend.

Stressed and drained, Karen began feeling ill. Although when she missed her period she wondered if she could possibly be pregnant, she tried to put this thought out of her mind. By the time she did confirm her pregnancy, it was too late to consider an abortion. In retrospect, she thinks she may have unconsciously wished to have a child. Having just ended a ten-year relationship, she needed something to remember it by: she did not want to be alone. Nevertheless, during her pregnancy, she did not eat well or gain adequate weight. With her inner and outer lives in turmoil, she had difficulty just getting through each day.

Meanwhile, Raymon and his girlfriend moved into a condo he had just bought. As a favor Karen had cosigned his mortgage application so that he could qualify for a loan. Despite her earlier help, he did not now reciprocate. On her own without much money, Karen had not foreseen the economic difficulties she would encounter as a single mother, and she worried how she would support herself and her baby. She felt forced to hire a lawyer, who gave Raymon three choices: pay Karen's rent, buy her a condo, or give her the one he had just purchased. By now comfortable in his new home, he was loath to give it up, so instead he offered to buy another for her. Although his intentions seemed good, he never came through, as he simply could not afford another downpayment.

Hoping to settle some of these issues, Karen invited him to couples counseling. She wished for an amicable divorce, and for Raymon to remain involved as a father. He, however, was not sure what he wanted. On the one hand, he felt divorce was too cold a solution; on the other hand, he was determined to stay with his girlfriend. Little progress was made.

After Abbie's birth, Karen blossomed as a mother, taking endless delight in her newborn. Raymon, by contrast, avoided fatherhood; by the time his daughter was ten months old, he had seen her only twice. Telling Karen he would like to stop by more often, he complained that his girlfriend, afraid of losing him if he became too attached to Abbie, forbade him to visit. Eventually, Raymon gave Karen his condo and then left the country with his girlfriend, after which Karen did not hear from him for many months. As pleased as she was to be a mother, she was sad he was not more involved.

Although Abbie was a beautiful, easy baby, the practicalities of being a single mother made life difficult. Realizing she had to return to work, Karen placed her two-month-old in family day care. Initially promising, this situation rapidly turned into a nightmare. First, Karen noticed that the provider's live-in mother (absent during the initial visit) smoked nonstop around Abbie. Second, the provider herself became pregnant, so that the grandmother took over watching Abbie and the other children—and watching was about all she did, as they stared at the television and ate junk food all day. Desperate for another affordable situation, Karen searched for over a year before finding good-quality day care within her budget.

Meanwhile the divorce became final. Still abroad with his girlfriend, Raymon was wary about marrying again; he later told Karen that marriage is "too legal . . . lawyers can tell you what to do, how much money to pay." Although he was frightened of this commitment, nevertheless his girlfriend did become pregnant. Unwed and without health insurance, she returned to the United States while he followed some months later, arriving just in time for the birth of his second daughter. A few years later, he left again—this time alone.

Because Raymon was not often present during Abbie's early years, he did not truly bond with her. Even during the period he was most present—after the birth of his second daughter—he would just occasionally drop by to pick up Abbie to take her to her half sister's. Sometimes Abbie did not want to go, and she was forced to do so, crying. Later, as her father moved back and forth across the ocean, she learned that she could not count on him at all. Now that she is twelve, Raymon is once again living nearby. Suddenly wishing to be an involved father, he is bitterly disappointed that she does not respect him. "You didn't raise me, so you can't tell me what to do," she says. This is very painful for him, and as a result, he avoids both daughters. Although he is supposed to take them Saturday nights, he usually has other plans, as his social life continues to thrive.

Karen has stayed single. Although after her divorce she dated occasionally, she has had only one long-term relationship. Her decision to break up with her boyfriend, made because she could not uproot herself to move to the city where his career was centered, was hard not just on her but also on Abbie. "Finally you're with a man who feels like a father to me, and now he is going away," she said. Blaming her mother for first allowing her to bond with him and then casting him out of their lives, Abbie cried inconsolably.

Karen has avoided bitterness about her situation. Although angry when Raymon betrayed her, she had known all along he was a Peter Pan. Like a child, he had always needed her care. Recognizing his limitations, after the divorce, Karen found her ire subsiding into disappointment that Abbie missed out on a father and family life.

Karen revealed some of her own family history. Because her paternal grandfather was severely alcoholic, his wife divorced him, went to work, and gave her son—Karen's father—to her own parents to raise. Surviving a difficult childhood, Karen's father later became a successful businessman and married. He was unfaithful, however, and after having five children with Karen's mother, he left. As he then had little contact with his children, she was forced to take him to court for money, which remained tight. Karen and her siblings had to do most of the housework, and due to their mother's long work hours, they basically raised themselves.

How did Karen's childhood help her later cope with single motherhood? The first year after Abbie's birth was the most stressful. Up several times a night to breast-feed, she barely had the strength some mornings to rise and go to work. Not until Abbie was two did Karen realize she was not exhausted all the time. Pulling her through the difficult years were her strengths: intelligence, ability to sustain a career, and support from friends. In addition, she drew on memories of her own mother's courage. "If my mother got through this with five kids, then so can I with only one child," she told herself. Many years later, Karen feels she has survived the breakup of her marriage, re-gained hope for her future, and raised her daughter well under difficult conditions.

While Karen entered a new realm of love and commitment, Raymon, unable to traverse the developmental phase of fatherhood, chose to flee. To be fair, he had not planned on having a child with Karen. In the turmoil of their separation, he most likely viewed her pregnancy as an accident. He probably did not feel ready for fatherhood under any circumstances, for, as Karen noted, he seemed young for his age, more committed to personal freedom than to the sacrifices of family life. Parenthood was thrust upon him at a time when he was neither psychologically nor economically ready.

Nor did he seem much more prepared the second time around. By then approaching forty, perhaps he reassured himself that he was still sufficiently young to have more chances, should he wish, to father children with women toward whom he might be more committed. Should this occur, he might be seen as a late bloomer, whose entrance into fatherhood was simply delayed. But here is the catch: by then, the opportunity to raise his first two daughters will have passed. Not only will they have lost a father, but also he will have lost them, as well as the risks and rewards of reworking with them his own history.

Karen and Raymon portray a couple whose developmental phases were out of sync, a factor that may have contributed to their marital problems and divorce, as well as to their subsequent divergent paths through parenthood. The survival of many marriages, such as theirs, depends on these phases being in balance. Although Karen's marriage was in trouble even before she became pregnant, for other couples, if the fulcrum is the baby, the marriage will topple.

What do we know about developmental phases? Traditionally, they were thought to be organized around the vicissitudes of libidinal energy, particularly in childhood. Later theorists expanded the concept to include psychosocial stages extending into adulthood. As examples, we will consider the ideas of Erikson, Benedek, and Nadelson.

Erik Erikson

Erikson (1980) envisioned a number of psychosocial stages, progressing from infancy to old age, through which one passes with various degrees of mastery. Rather than narrowly defining the tasks of each stage, he stated them somewhat broadly, with a wide range of possible solutions. For example, in discussing "generativity versus stagnation," he defined generativity:

> [It is] primarily the interest in establishing and guiding the next generation, although there are people who, from misfortune or because of special and genuine gifts in other directions, do not apply this drive to offspring but to other forms of altruistic concern and of creativity, which may absorb their kind of parental responsibility. (p. 103)

Although he did not directly name parenthood as a developmental stage, he elaborated:

> The principal thing is to realize that this is a stage of the growth of the healthy personality and that where such enrichment fails, together, regression from generativity to an obsessive need for pseudo intimacy takes place, often with a pervading sense of stagnation and interpersonal impoverishment. Individuals who do not develop generativity often begin to indulge themselves as

if they were their own one and only child. The mere fact of having or even wanting children does not itself attest to generativity; in fact the majority of young parents seen in child-guidance work suffer, it seems, from the retardation of or inability to develop this stage. The reasons are often to be found in early childhood impressions; in faulty identifications with parents; in excessive self-love based on a too strenuously self-made personality; and finally (and here we return to the beginnings) in the lack of some faith, some "belief in the species," which would make a child appear to be a welcome trust of the community. (pp. 103-104)

As Erikson noted, parenthood is neither necessary nor sufficient for psychological growth; those who decide to remain childless often find other, equally successful, roads to generativity. Once entered, however, parenthood must be successfully navigated. Failure to do so, whether by becoming a dysfunctional parent or by fleeing one's responsibilities, may lead not only to one's children's but also to one's own failure to thrive.

Therese Benedek

Benedek (1959) was the first psychoanalyst to write explicitly about parenthood as a developmental phase. Describing how each critical period of a child's development revives in parents their own earlier conflicts, traumas, and joys, she believed that those who successfully rework these challenges achieve a new level of psychological integration. One result can be "intra-psychic reconciliation" (p. 396) with their own parents.

Benedek also believed that parenthood creates internal transformation. In the first months after childbirth, the new mother is faced with certain tasks, which, if successfully met, not only allow her infant to thrive but also support her own maturation. As she meets these challenges, she makes the gratifying connection: good-thriving infant equals good mother. Gaining not just confidence, but also a fresh sense of being good, feminine, and beautiful, she develops new psychic structure by fulfilling her maternal ideal. While earlier clinicians emphasized that the infant matures by internalizing experiences of the mother, Benedek appreciated that it is also the mother who grows by internalizing interactions with her infant. Similarly, the father looks to his infant, who can either reflect back his goodness or, alternatively, confirm his worst fears of being ugly and unlovable:

> The imitating child holds up a mirror image to the parent. Naive and completely intuitive as the child's gestures are, they are also unmistakably true. Thus the parent responding to the mirror image may recognize and even say to the child, "This is your father; this is me in you." . . . If the child's imitative behavior expresses positive aspects of the parent and positive attitudes between them it shows that both parent and child are lovable. (p. 407)

Since Benedek wrote these lines, we have realized that infants do much more than simply imitate their parents. Nonetheless, I believe, in a sense, every new parent asks "Am I fair?" to the demanding, new little mirror. The affirmative answer builds confidence in one's goodness, as old wounds are erased by the tide's fresh treasures. The negative answer, if too sustained, pulls like a rip current to the point of past trouble.

Carol Nadelson

Later writers further discussed parenthood as a developmental stage. Nadelson et al. (1984), for instance, believed that marriage involves six stages:

1. Idealization
2. Coping with disappointment and disillusionment
3. Productivity and parenting
4. Career resolution
5. Redefinition, child launching
6. Reintegration, postparenting

After resolving the disappointments of the second stage, greater commitment is possible as couples enter the third, but if phase two has not been resolved, problems may arise as roles shift and parents must give up their own "child" positions. For example, a father may become anxious about his wife's increased dependency and vulnerability, fearing he will no longer be able to meet her needs, nor she his. Nadelson believed that, as in other developmental stages, parenthood presents challenges that, if not mastered, may lead to regression and fragmentation rather than to growth and integration of one's personality.

These three writers were among the many who held in common the notion that parenthood (or, in Erikson's words, "generativity") is a specific phase of life, which, if entered, must be successfully navigated. Notwithstanding, these ideas have been poorly absorbed into our culture. While much attention has been focused on the effects on *children* of ill-equipped parents, little has been given to the effects on *parents* if they do not meet the psychological challenges of this stage. Perhaps because our culture views life as long, with ample second chances to rework missed opportunities, we are reluctant to admit that the window can shut on sensitive periods of psychological growth.

As we reread Karen and Raymon's story, accordingly, we may feel as much sympathy for him as for her. While Karen struggled with the hardships of single motherhood, she also discovered, in Benedek's words, her internal mother-ideal. Over time, she became a more complete person, with greater access to her inner world; she felt more womanly, more beautiful. Raymon, on the other hand, while retaining his freedom and youthful lifestyle, and never lacking a girlfriend, seemed to drift. Since I did not have the opportunity to interview him, we do not know how he felt. Perhaps he found other ways to be generative. We do know that many divorced men later regret not having been more involved with their children and feel, many years later and despite considerable other compensations, that they missed the greatest opportunity of their lives.

Although the concept of developmental phases has come under fire for being too rigid and linear, parenthood does appear to be a critical period (Parens, 1974). Requiring reexamination of childhood relationships, it is a one-way street: after having children, this reworking cannot be avoided without losing one's way.

PARENTHOOD AS A DEVELOPMENTAL LINE

As with the concept of a developmental phase, that of a developmental line is useful in understanding different responses to childbirth, particularly those based on gender. First, let us consider what we mean by a developmental line.

Anna Freud (1965), who first used the term, gave several examples: from dependency to emotional self-reliance, from egocentricity to companionship, from play to the ability to work. By attempting to trace the origin and vicissitudes of a specific trait over a lifetime, a developmental line thus differs from a developmental phase. Though sometimes criticized for setting up false norms, the concept of a developmental line may yet be useful if dissociated from narrow prescriptions for "healthy" results. Attempting to answer "Where do we come from? What are we? Where are we going?" these lines, as with Gaughin's questions, must allow space for ambiguity and open-ended answers.

Is there a developmental line for parenthood? If so, it might shed light on the origins of both the desire to have children and differing parenting styles. It might also shed light on what can go wrong.

Early Psychoanalytic Writers

Observing that the wish to parent may begin in childhood, early psychoanalytic writers described pregnancy fantasies in both sexes between the ages of two and four. Freud, for example, interpreted a girl's wish for a baby as compensation for lack of a penis; a boy's parallel wish he attributed to innate bisexuality. A boy gave up his pregnancy fantasies, Freud thought, as he identified with father and, rather than yearn to be similar to mother, came to desire her as a love object. Later writers questioned the compensatory nature of the girl's desire for a baby, emphasizing instead her "primary femininity" (Stoller, 1976). But although they explained their observations differently, these psychoanalysts agreed that the young of both sexes have fantasies of bearing children.

Kestenberg

Kestenberg (1980), summarizing her work in the 1960s and 1970s, also believed that the wish to parent begins early in childhood. Observing a "maternal stage" common to boys and girls between ages two to four, she noted that children of both sexes may develop elaborate pregnancy fantasies. Kestenberg thought these were partially fueled by children's mourning their own lost infancies.

While a girl's desire to bear children is consistent with her future possibilities, a boy's course is more complicated. Attempting to trace a developmental line for fatherhood, Kestenberg et al. (1982) hypothesized that whereas nurturing aspects of fatherhood arise from early mirroring between a boy and his mother, "provider-protector" aspects develop through later identification with the father. Through early positive maternal interactions, the boy acquires the ability to relate warmly; later he adopts his father's more distant role as protector of the family's frame. Further evolution of paternal attitudes occurs during adolescence, when he forms new identifications with peers and teachers.

In this model it is not the father, but the mother, who lays the groundwork for a boy's future development of tender parental attitudes. Furthermore, some clinicians believed that the boy must disidentify from even this nurturing to establish male gender identity (Greenson, 1968). Fearing he will not be a "real man" if he harbors a capacity to caretake in a warm, tender fashion, the boy may disavow his earliest experiences of love as a basis for later ones.

Herzog's Study: Fatherhood As a Developmental Line

Expanding on these ideas, Herzog (1982) designed a retrospective study of 103 fathers of premature firstborns. He discovered that men who bonded well with their infants had also been emotionally attuned and empathic toward their pregnant wives, while those who bonded less well had been poorly attuned.

Herzog also discovered that during their wives' pregnancies, all men in his study relived aspects of their own early development. First, during the early months of expectant fatherhood, they experienced reawakening of emotions similar to those they might have felt during their own infancies. Poorly attuned men, for instance, relived experiences of deprivation; angry, frustrated, and self-centered, they complained about not getting enough attention from their wives. Well-attuned men, by contrast, were able to enjoy the early stages of their wives' pregnancies. Over the next few months, expectant fathers reenacted slightly later aspects of their childhoods, which corresponded to Kestenberg's (1980) maternal stage. Identifying with the feminine role, well-attuned men became aware of gastrointestinal sensations and felt increasingly preoccupied with their insides, as though they themselves were pregnant, while poorly attuned ones felt no such sensations and remained emotionally disconnected from their wives. Next, between fifteen and twenty-five weeks, expectant fathers reworked earlier disidentification from their mothers, as they searched for male role models, often turning to their present-day fathers for guidance. Well-attuned men, finding positive models in their own fathers or father substitutes, became preoccupied with providing and preparing for the baby, but poorly attuned men were unable to do so; having had inadequate male role models or actually lost fathers early in life, they often compensated by becoming promiscuous or turning to "hypermasculine" pursuits. Finally, toward the end of their wives' pregnancies, both groups became more angry and aggressive, possibly reworking old frustrations concerning competition for their mothers' love. Interestingly, while well-attuned men had *fantasies* of harming their babies (but after childbirth became nurturing and supportive of their wives), poorly attuned men actually made *attempts* to hurt their wives emotionally and, after birth, angrily avoided them.

To summarize: Herzog (1982) thought that during their wives' pregnancies, men rework their own developmental lines toward parenthood. Early in expectant fatherhood, those who experienced early maternal deprivation feel frustrated and distant. Later on, if they lack the critical variable of a good-enough male role model, they tend to act out in anger, subsequently bonding less satisfactorily with their newborns. Although I am not certain that all expectant fathers rework their childhoods so linearly, I do believe Herzog's study was important for focusing on the complexity of reactions among prospective fathers.

Chodorow's Version: Motherhood As a Developmental Line

Turning from fatherhood to motherhood as a developmental line, we observe an interesting phenomenon. Whereas post-Freudian analysts criticized the view that women desire children to compensate for lacking penises and emphasized instead the primary, instinctual basis for motherhood, some recent theorists have reinstated the notion that maternal attitudes are largely due to environmental factors, albeit different ones than suggested by Freud.

As an influential representative of this movement, Chodorow (1978) deserves attention. Basing her theory on a traditional family in which the father is absent much of the time and the mother assumes the larger share of child care, Chodorow noted that mothers not only have more direct influence on their young children but also relate differently to sons than to daughters. This second phenomenon, she believed, arises from sharing the same gender: mothers experience their daughters as less psychologically separate than they do their sons, who themselves must disidentify to establish male identity. As a result, in such traditional families, girls have more experience than boys in maintaining comfortable closeness; they remain more identified with caretaking, more invested in connection, and more interested later in life in assuming the greater share of child care. Boys, on the other hand, grow up conflicted about emotional intimacy. They define themselves as more autonomous and less directly caretaking:

> . . . growing girls come to define and experience themselves as continuous with others; their experience of self contains more flexible or permeable ego boundaries. Boys come to define themselves as more separate and distinct, with a greater sense of rigid ego boundaries and differentiation. The basic feminine sense of self is connected to the world, the basic masculine sense of self is separate. . . . Masculine personality, then, comes to be defined more in terms of denial of relation and connection (and denial of femininity), whereas feminine personality comes to include a fundamental definition of self in relationship. (p. 169)

Motherhood, accordingly, is not an instinct but is "reproduced" as a cultural pattern of asymmetrical parenting.

Problems do exist with Chodorow's argument. First, the obvious: informed by the dynamics of traditional families, which are becoming less prevalent, Chodorow's reasoning may not apply in the new millennium. Fewer wives now stay at home as full-time mothers, and many more married fathers participate directly in child care. Nevertheless, considering the divorce rate and the large proportion of American children who live in single-parent families headed by women, I suspect this part of Chodorow's reasoning may hold; in spite of liberalization of gender roles, father absence may be on the increase.

The main problem with Chodorow's as well as Kestenberg et al.'s (1982) reasoning, however, is oversimplification along gender lines. Although some daughters may feel less urgency than their brothers to separate from their mothers, and thereby develop more empathic skills through continued close connection, these developments are actually complex and multidetermined. Much depends on the personality of the mother: Is she overly remote or engulfing? An opposite argument could be made: boys' innate biological differences may allow them to identify comfortably with many aspects of their mothers, without becoming confused about their own masculinity. Girls, on the other hand, already sharing gender with their mothers, might be more inclined to delineate aggressively their separateness. Contemporary therapists do observe that some boys maintain healthy close emotional connections with their mothers, whereas some girls, feeling too ensnared, withdraw from such suffocating orbits.

PARENTHOOD AS A UNIQUE
PSYCHIC ORGANIZER: STERN

Whereas traditional psychoanalysts explored notions of parenthood as a developmental phase and a developmental line, contemporary infant researchers have drawn on a large body of observational work to further define parenthood's early stages. Stern (1995), summarizing years of research on mother-infant pairs, considers parenthood not so much a developmental phase as a unique psychic organizer. For women, he refers to this as the "motherhood constellation":

> With the birth of a baby, especially the first, the mother passes into a new and unique psychic organization I call the motherhood constellation. As a psychic organizer, the constellation will determine a new set of action tendencies, sensibilities, fantasies, fears, and wishes. (p. 171)

Stern stresses that the mother then becomes preoccupied with three conversations, both internal and external: that with her own mother, one with herself, and another with her baby. As a result, a new "psychic triad" is created, temporarily dominating her psychological landscape—and it does not involve her husband. Stern believes this maternally oriented relationship axis is the one toward which a new mother turns.

This new orientation has at least two effects. First, to help guide her through the uncharted territory of nurturing her infant, a mother seeks current support and advice. Knowing the stakes are high, nothing less than her baby's physical and emotional survival, she points her compass toward those people most equipped to model the necessary skills. She concerns herself with four main questions: Can she maintain the life and growth of the baby? Can she emotionally engage? Can she elicit the necessary support network? Can she transform her self-identity? (p. 173). When she looks for adults to meet her needs, she is focused on finding those who can help her answer these four questions in the affirmative. To the extent her own primary parent was female (Stern draws on Chodorow's [1978] notion of asymmetric parenting patterns), she will seek women, not men, as navigational guides (p. 180).

The second effect of this new orientation, according to Stern, is that mothers rework and reorganize childhood memories, especially those relating to their own maternal figures. Here Stern reflects the ideas of many psychoanalytic writers, but rather than use the words "internal representations" or "issues," he uses "schemas-of-being-with," which he defines as "representations of interactive experiences, either real or imagined (fantasized)" (p. 19). These map the topography of human interactions. For example, a woman's schema-of-being-with regarding her own mother might include representations of how she felt as a baby, as well as how she thought her mother felt as a parent (p. 181). Referencing Edelman's (1989) theory of memory, Stern notes that recovery of such representations depends on current triggers. As a powerful remembering context, a new baby has the potential to evoke maternal schemas-of-being-with, some of which may be "actual memories," some fantasies, often bringing these into awareness for the first time (Stern, 1995, p. 181).

Stern's work informs our discussion about why transition to parenthood might be difficult. Early parenthood, at least for mothers, is a time of intense change—not only in external circumstances, but also in internal psychological organization. As old representations, or "schemas," are unexpectedly activated, mothers may be overwhelmed by the dual tasks of caring for their babies at the same time they are experiencing profound inner realignments. No wonder that, during this transition, what they primarily desire, according to Stern, is nurture and guidance from other women. In fact, these needs are so strong that marital problems may result if husbands feel pushed to the side. As new mothers appreciate their husbands more as fathers, providers, and protectors, they may become less interested in them, temporarily, as lovers or sexual partners (p. 172). As a corollary, when couples must manage without an extended support system, fathers may face too much pressure to fulfill roles traditionally held by women (pp. 177-180). All these factors may strain some marriages that previously functioned well.

Although Stern limits his discussion to a "motherhood constellation," I believe one might also exist in relation to fathers. Although Stern may be generally correct that new mothers experience the most profound disruptions, many fathers also enter emotional crises upon the birth of their children. We recall that Herzog (1982) found that some expectant fathers experience activation of problematic schemas as they attempt to orient toward positive male role models, in a process parallel to that which Stern describes for women. In the next chapter we will look at this more closely.

Accordingly, parenthood can trigger sudden, unexpected marital problems in at least two ways. The first is by activating previously dormant internal issues, in either parent, that lead to destructive behavior patterns. The second is by changing the configuration of needs as the family shifts from a dyad to a triad, with partners developing new expectations and demands. Either process may erode a marriage.

PARENTHOOD AS TRIADIFICATION

When a couple has a first child, the structure of their relationship shifts from dyadic to triadic. With this shift come new opportunities for growth and well-being, as a state of "being together as a family" emerges, yet there also come possibilities for competition, for two against one, for favorites, for imbalance. Some mothers, for example, become so engrossed in their infants that they fail to make room for their husbands, who are pushed to the periphery. They continue to relate dyadically, but by replacing their partners with their children.

Compared to dyadic systems, triadic ones are more complex. As they involve interactions among three variables, not two, not only do triadic systems have more complicated sets of solutions, but these may be less stable than those for simpler equations. Before the infant's arrival, a couple may have developed guidelines for balancing each other's needs, guidelines that may have been relatively straightforward. After the newcomer arrives, however, these may be upset, as rapidly oscillating states unfold, each a temporary solution to the new triadic puzzle. Some couples may lack flexibility to accommodate these changes and become overwhelmed by interactions that seem at times chaotic.

Clinicians disagree about the extent to which a new mother is tightly dyadically bonded with her infant. Winnicott (1956) referred to a mother's near total absorption as "primary maternal preoccupation," which Stern similarly considered part of the normal motherhood constellation. For both Winnicott and Stern, the mother-infant dyad is primary, with the father assuming a supportive role as protector of the family's frame. By contrast, other clinicians underscored the direct importance of the father from the very beginning—not just as a support for the mother, but as having his own unique, separate relationship to the baby. In either case, for the family to function well over time, both parents must bond with their baby not just individually but also jointly. They must learn to take turns, to support each other, to tolerate being left out, to find a way back in. If they fail, so may their marriage.

To measure triadification, researchers (Corboz-Warnery et al., 1993) have devised a type of interview in which parents are observed interacting with their infants under four different situations: mother playing with baby and father as the third party; father playing with baby and mother as the third party; both parents interacting with the baby; and the parents interacting with each other, with the baby as the third party. By videotaping these interactions, Corboz-Warnery et al. were able to determine how families transitioned between modes. Those having difficulty switching roles in a smooth, synchronous way were thought to have infants who were more disorganized and disengaged.

Accordingly, infants as well as parents are sensitive to three-person interactions. Klitzing et al. (1999, p. 76) found that measuring parents' "triadic capacity," which they defined as "the capacity of fathers and mothers to anticipate their future family relationships without excluding themselves or their partners from the relationship to the infant," during the last trimester of pregnancy predicted how well infants could enter into three-person interactions four months after birth. In fact, the authors discovered that fathers' prenatally assessed triadic capacity had the highest correlation with the success of four-month-old infants' triadic play. Fathers who believed in their importance to their infants from the very beginning, and who had had good relationships with their own father figures, were able to form sufficiently positive internal pictures of family life to incorporate their babies into new family triads. Their infants, as early as four months, seemed to know the difference.

SUMMARY

Transition to parenthood is more difficult than traditionally thought. While couples might hope that a baby will fix their marriages, contemporary research, as supported by cases such as Karen's, reveals that childbirth often adds just one more stressor to an already strained, sometimes broken marriage. Furthermore, in cases such as Amy's, childbirth may stress a marriage that previously appeared stable, at least to one member of the couple, to the point of rapid breakdown.

Why does this occur? To begin to explore this question, we have reviewed concepts of parenthood as a developmental phase, as a developmental line, as a unique psychic organizer, and as a process of triadification.

As a developmental phase, parenthood presents many challenges. Sleep deprivation, difficulties reconciling child-rearing styles, conflict over downtime, and a sudden shift in responsibilities are only some of the obstacles couples face. As they reconfigure their relationships from dyads to triads, they may also discover that stable solutions to equations with two variables no longer apply with three. During this upheaval, stresses are enormous.

Parenthood, however, requires something more than adjustment as a couple. It requires the reworking, individually, of one's own childhood—a reworking that can lead to greater integration and vitality, or to a sense of failure and despair. A phase in the present, like a wormhole linking two universes, it is also a tunnel to the past.

Yet in forward, real time much happens between past and present. Models of developmental lines for parenthood show that the desire to parent begins early in life and undergoes many vicissitudes. The type of parent we become is constructed not only during the formative years of childhood but also during adolescence and beyond.

Some writers have emphasized gender differences in this process. Chodorow (1978), for example, believed that, due to the asymmetrical pattern of parenting, women grow up better equipped than men to form close, nurturing bonds with their children, and Stern observed that new mothers orient primarily toward female role models, needing their husbands less as romantic partners than as protectors of their families' frames. Although both statements are sometimes true, I do not think they can be used reliably. Elucidation of how men and women develop nurturing parental attitudes involves a more complex mosaic of influences. Karen, for instance, did not enjoy a close, nurturing relationship with her mother, who was rarely home due to working long hours to support her children, yet she knew how to nurture her infant and blossom herself, identifying with, not her mother's tenderness, but her mother's strength in surviving her own divorce. Amy's devastation after her husband left was a reaction to losing him not only as a provider-protector but also as a romantic partner, who now implied that, once a mother, she was no longer attractive. Although women need women after childbirth, they also need men, specifically their mates, to reassure them concerning a primary vulnerability: in spite of their inner and outer changes, they must know that they have not irrevocably lost their attractiveness.

Although it may be true that, in our society, men are first asked to disavow their nurturing sides and then pressured to fill roles for which they are not equipped, they are not culturally doomed to become distant fathers. It is not only culture—but also personal, internal crisis—that results in men and women fleeing parenthood.

Chapter 2

Parenthood As a Personal Crisis

In the last chapter, we saw that transition to parenthood can stress couples, often more than imagined. As the baby joins them, couples must open their dyadic bonds to incorporate the newcomer, a process that involves a basic reconfiguration of their relationships. If partners are out of phase developmentally, they might find parenthood particularly difficult to traverse together.

A number of the women I interviewed felt that, in addition to precipitating a couple's crisis, parenthood also precipitated a personal crisis in either themselves or their partners. In fact, it seemed just such a personal crisis that led to difficulties with triadification. The following story illustrates one mother's struggle.

CAROL:
MOTHERHOOD'S MAGNIFYING LENS

A twenty-nine-year-old elementary school teacher, Carol had always wanted children, but although she had been happily engaged to Thomas when they conceived their first daughter, after they married and had a child together she abruptly left him. Her story is unique in this book because, on the brink of divorcing, she turned back.

Carol and Thomas had known each other since kindergarten. Remaining friends, they later attended the same high school, where both were popular and academically successful. After graduation they enrolled at the same teacher's college in Ohio and began to date. Several years later they bought a home, in which they lived while both taught at the same school. Carol and Thomas loved each other and felt certain they should be life partners. While preparing for their wedding, they had a pleasant surprise: Carol was pregnant. They both felt very fortunate.

As happy as she was, after the wedding, Carol nevertheless found physical adaptation to her pregnancy difficult. Exhausted during her first trimester, she left work early each day in order to sleep. She also felt isolated, as her peers, not yet parents, were unable to give her much advice. Although Thomas tried to do more things for her, such as having a hot bath ready when she returned from work, at times she experienced his hovering attention as oppressive.

After the baby was born, Carol continued to have trouble adjusting. Whereas previously she had taken pride in her self-reliance, now, overwhelmed by infant care, she could no longer maintain an illusion of independence, nor could she find comfort in her husband's attentions. Knowing she was fatigued, Thomas tried hard to help. The more perfectly he managed the house, however, the more inadequate she felt—as though he were saying to her, "This is how it *should* be done." Why could he not just accept her as she was, she wondered. His attentions began to feel less like help than pressure. In addition, under the stress of parenthood, some of their differences began to surface. Thomas had grown up in an orderly household, where his mother had served three regular meals a day; he was the type of person who wanted the unopened Campbell soup cans organized on the same shelf. Carol, who had grown up in a household with a looser structure, did not care so much about being methodical. She felt that Thomas was becoming critical, and the more he tried to help, the more she felt put down.

Carol had had a difficult childhood. Her mother, suffering from clinical depression, had required caretaking much of the time; although she had taken medication, her illness had remained poorly controlled. From a young age Carol had felt responsible for her mother. Nonetheless, Carol had always been a model child. It had been important to her not to cause more problems for her parents, but, rather, through her considerable achievements, to make them proud. Carol developed the sense of being a "perfect" caretaker of her mother, a daughter who would excel in school, manage her own life, and not cause trouble—in other words, function autonomously. After her own daughter was born, as her energy waned and she felt overwhelmed with still trying to be perfect, she increasingly felt not good enough—for her parents, her husband, her baby, and herself.

Over the next six months, as spring led into summer, she became progressively more unhappy. Not knowing why she was so sad, she was aware only that she was building up enormous resentment against Thomas. In stark contrast to how she had felt about him previously, she was annoyed now by every little thing he did for her. In fact, she wondered whether she should leave. To sort this out, she began individual therapy, while she and Thomas also started marriage counseling. Although Carol's friends wondered if she could be suffering from postpartum depression (they could not believe she would leave Thomas, as she had seemed so happy), her counselor did not agree. Remaining neutral about whether Carol should end her marriage, the counselor encouraged her to discuss her conflicts concerning independence and autonomy. As Carol did so, she became increasingly defiant and began to think that others perceived her as weak, needing help, and unable to manage alone. In her mind, these were signs of deficiency, signals she might be similar to her mother, whom she had tried not to model. The breaking point came when Thomas told her she needed him as a husband. Enraged, she whispered to herself, "I'll show him." No one was going to tell her she could not be independent! After renting an apartment for herself and the baby, she left, singing "Ha, ha, I'm leaving you," as she backed out of her driveway, angry but liberated. Free at last, she felt she had won a battle for control over her life.

Devastated, Thomas could not fathom what had gone wrong. Before his daughter's arrival, he had thought he was happily married. Also shocked was Carol's father. Supporting Thomas, he remained puzzled over what had happened. Carol's mother, on the other hand, sympathized with her daughter's decision. "Good for you," she said. "You're strong." Perhaps not recognizing her own need for care during periods when she was truly debilitated from illness, she had sometimes complained to her daughter that her own husband was overly controlling.

Thomas tried to reconcile with Carol. Over and over, he asked her to come back. She did not appreciate his pleading, however. Feeling coerced and pressured, she simply asserted her independence more adamantly and began divorce proceedings. At the pretrial conference (a meeting between the couple and their two lawyers), Thomas remained dumbfounded that Carol had turned on him; he was beside himself, crying. In contrast, Carol felt on top, in control. "Finally I got him," she gloated—not that she did not feel sad. Deep down, she still loved him. She had decided, however, that they could not live together and was glad to have won her freedom. Now she was the strong one, the one in control, and Thomas seemed weak and helpless. With this flip of the mirror she had reasserted her old coping mechanism, saving her self-esteem but sacrificing her marriage.

As it turned out, leaving Thomas did not help Carol as much as she had anticipated. Her symptoms of decreased appetite, weight loss, insomnia, poor concentration, and a sensation of her head spinning only worsened. Although earlier it was questionable whether she was in need of medication, by now it was clear she was suffering from depression. In fact, when medication was prescribed, it was very helpful.

After Carol felt better, she began dating other men. Reluctantly, Thomas stopped asking her to return; he also began dating other women. Carol could not help noticing that he was working out and looking attractive. She pictured what it would be like to have him fall in love with another woman, remarry, and raise their daughter in a stepfamily; the more she thought about it, the sadder she became. As the divorce approached, her reservations grew stronger. One day she let down her guard and started talking to him. They began to feel close again, as in the old days. She realized that Thomas was trying to help, not criticize. Establishing her freedom began to feel less important than saving her marriage, and eventually she called off the divorce.

A few months after reuniting, she and Thomas conceived another child. Carol's second pregnancy went smoothly; now over a year later, they have two children they both treasure. Carol is glad she returned, and not only for the opportunity to keep her family intact. Realizing neither one of them is perfect, they have an open dialogue and a deeper understanding of each other.

Trying to understand her actions, Carol believes that to avoid causing more trouble for her already burdened parents, she had tried to be the perfect, independent child, while adopting a caretaking role toward her mother. This had served the dual purpose of allowing her to maintain a bond but not be like her mother, whom she perceived as weak and helpless. Through this reverse mirroring, she disidentified with her mother. After Carol's first daughter was born, however, she could no longer live up to this task. Unable to go to the bathroom without her baby crying and with no time to herself, she often felt burned out. Although desperately needing Thomas's help, she was unable to accept it, as she feared it might lead to the collapse of her image into her mother's. Paradoxically, when she left Thomas, she reestablished her old sense of autonomy while lessening the pressure on herself: "I'm not perfect; I'm not going to have the best kids or the best house; in fact, I'm going to be very imperfect by leaving my husband," she effectively announced. To divorce was her first truly independent decision, she thought, as in the past she had tried so hard to please other people. Divorcing against the advice of friends and family—seemingly under her own steam—felt liberating.

At the end of our interview, Carol mentioned another factor. In addition to trying to be flawless, she had long harbored a dread of becoming depressed, as had her mother, whose illness had worsened after childbirth. Carol secretly worried that she, too, might be vulnerable postpartum. Never did she want to be so depressed, so dependent! No wonder she panicked when she felt overwhelmed after the birth of her first child. Fearful of following in her mother's footsteps, she had been terrified that the source of her own depression might be internal and, rather than face this anxiety, focused on her marriage being the problem. Pointing her bow at Thomas, she released the arrow and fled. Later, with the help of counseling and medication, she realized that her mother's problems need not be her own, and only then could she return to work out the problems in her marriage.

Carol had one last reflection. When she had backed out of her driveway, she had thought she was making an independent, even defiant decision. Later she realized that she might have been influenced by her mother, who, rather than suggesting to Carol she first work on her marriage, had communicated approval of her leaving a controlling man. Perhaps unconsciously, Carol acted out her mother's unrealized ambitions to get the upper hand in her own marriage. Although she did not recognize it at the time, Carol's flight to divorce may have spoken more to being controlled by forces from the past than to being liberated from them.

As couples enter parenthood, their family structures suddenly shift from dyadic to triadic, and this may create conflict, even for those fortunate enough to have previously experienced little. Stressed and strained by the addition of the third, many struggle with the opening up of their two-person bonds to the complexity of new, three-person configurations. In many cases, husband and wife gradually adjust by making mutually adaptive changes, forming a cohesive, well-functioning family. For these, a new state of contentment may arise, as they enjoy participating in a system greater than the sum of its parts. Yet others are unable to achieve this happy result. Their difficulty may be caused by inflexibility on the part of both spouses, but Carol's story illustrated that it may also begin as a personal crisis. Although she and Thomas had some wrinkles to smooth out in their marriage, the driving force behind her departure was not marital conflict, but her own inner turmoil.

Carol was unable to let Thomas help her with child rearing, to allow him to form a triad with her and their daughter, because for Carol any dependence signified weakness, imperfection, a state of disability, which reminded her all too much of her own mother. By becoming her mother's reverse image, Carol had developed self-esteem, but along fragile, easily shattered lines that childbirth confronted. Overwhelmed by the reality that she could no longer be either perfectly strong or completely independent, she became terrified that she could no longer maintain the integrity of her mirror. In fact, she worried she was becoming like her mother—depressed, needy, deficient. Carol's representation of her parents' marriage as her father strong and controlling, her mother weak and subservient, may have further informed her interpreting Thomas's helpfulness as demeaning. It is possible that she would have left, no matter to whom she was married.

Before childbirth, Carol had enjoyed many happy years with Thomas, during which these issues were relatively inactive. Although it had been important to her that she function well—almost flawlessly—at school, work, as a girlfriend and then as a wife, she had been able to do so relatively successfully within a dyadic framework. Before motherhood's challenge, she had been able to maintain a sense of independence, while also feeling quite close, emotionally and physically, to Thomas. On the surface, she would have appeared to have had few major problems with intimacy, not because they did not potentially exist, but because their fault lines were not yet stressed. For people such as her, parenthood can precipitate internal crises by reawakening old issues that were buried, sometimes deeply, until the birth of a child.

PARENTHOOD AS CRISIS: WHY PANIC?

Motherhood's Disequilibrium

Psychoanalytic writers have explored how pregnancy and childbirth can trigger such significant inner turmoil as Carol's. For example, in her study of pregnant women in a prenatal clinic at Beth Israel Hospital, Bibring (1959) found that, similar to puberty and menopause, pregnancy engenders profound biological and psychological changes:

> [We should] consider pregnancy as a crisis that affects all expectant mothers, no matter what their state of psychic health. Crises, as we see it, are turning points in the life of the individual, leading to acute disequilibria which under favorable conditions result in specific maturational steps toward new function. We find them as developmental phenomena at points of no return. (p. 119)

The expectant mother confronts new tasks, which lead both to revival of earlier unsettled conflicts and to loosening of inadequate past solutions. Noting the unidirectional nature of pregnancy, the disequilibrium it can cause, and the continuation of the crisis beyond delivery, Bibring et al. (1961) concluded that incomplete reorganization of the mother's psyche is a frequent problem in early mother-child relationships. It might also contribute to couples' difficulties.

Later writers, such as Lester and Notman (1986), also viewed pregnancy as a type of psychological crisis in which a woman's mental representations undergo significant shifts and realignments. Pregnancy may mean, among other things, renouncing separateness, autonomy, or a sense of control over individual destiny. As she experiences her body taken over by a process of nature not always kind (consider the possibility, historically quite high, of dying in childbirth), the expectant mother may regard the new life within her, not only as a gift, but also as a type of parasite usurping her body, destroying her figure and sexual attractiveness. Dreams of dense overgrown jungles may occur, as she both marvels at life's proliferation and fears its potential malignancy.

Reading these accounts reminds me of a current children's science fiction novel that describes an invasion of sluglike creatures from outer space. These intruders, after entering their human victims' brains, take over their hosts' thought processes, but in such a way that the latter remain unaware. Gradually the humans' own fantasies, wishes, and goals are usurped by those of the alien slugs. Some women, at the same time they regard pregnancy as a much desired event, may also experience it, in modified form, as just such a science fiction fantasy.

Nonetheless, Lester and Notman believed that most new mothers accommodate to pregnancy and grow to love their babies as welcome additions, who are perceived neither as narcissistic extensions nor as alien threats. These clinicians also believed that the course of pregnancy is significantly influenced by a woman's prior experience with her own maternal figure. To guide her through pregnancy's normal crises, she needs sufficiently positive internal representations of her own mother's navigational skills.

Biological Factors

Psychological issues are not the only sources of disequilibrium at childbirth. Other researchers have emphasized that new mothers experience major biochemical and hormonal changes, making this a time when they are especially vulnerable to biologically determined psychiatric illness. Fedele et al. (1988) reviewed research on postpartum depression, the best known psychiatric condition affecting new mothers, and discussed three of its varieties: baby blues, nonpsychotic depression, and psychotic depression.

According to this review, 50 to 70 percent of new mothers are affected by "baby blues," characterized by a downcast mood that may occur unexpectedly after the arrival of even a much-desired baby. Of these mothers, almost one-half experience intense sadness, weeping, insomnia, and often thoughts of regret, such as that the baby has ruined one's life. Though time limited, this condition may last for several weeks before responding to rest, reassurance, and the baby's smile.

More serious is true postpartum depression, which affects up to 20 percent of new mothers. As with the baby blues, it is accompanied by sadness, crying, and insomnia, but it may also involve severe weight loss, decreased ability to concentrate, hopelessness, and inability to enjoy anything—including the baby. Suicidal feelings and suicide attempts are not uncommon. Unaware that her depression has a biological basis, a new mother may instead blame circumstances and try to cure herself by leaving her husband, baby, or both. Unlike the baby blues, postpartum depression is not always time limited. Some mothers never truly recover but drag through their children's tender years still afflicted. Fortunately, it is usually treatable with antidepressants and psychotherapy.

Of even greater severity is psychotic postpartum depression, a rare disorder affecting between .01 and .02 percent of new mothers. Those who experience it lose touch with reality. They may develop delusions of being evil and needing punishment and, in the worst case, tragically act before their families can stop them. This type of depression almost always responds to treatment, but while in its throes a mother may not realize what is wrong.

What places a woman at risk for developing postpartum depression? Fedele et al. noted that studies show a clear association between its occurrence and unsupportive environments. Put simply, women lacking emotional support, including that of their spouses, are at greater risk. Yet the authors also pointed to the complexity of factors contributing to postpartum crises, including socioeconomic status, previous psychiatric history, family history of depression, motivation for the pregnancy, and internal conflicts concerning motherhood. Carol's story, for example, reminds us that many postpartum depressions are not simply biological, but codetermined by a multiplicity of issues. Her story also reminds us how, for some women, a supportive spouse is not sufficient and may feel oppressive, even toxic.

For Carol, motherhood activated problems she had thought long solved, such as her need to be faultless and self-sufficient, as well as her dread of becoming depressed and dependent, as did her mother. Once she had an infant, she feared that her marriage would begin to resemble her parents'. Before childbirth these issues were minor side paths, not very significant as long as she stayed on the marked trail. Afterward, magnified by motherhood's lens, they became impasses.

Some women are fortunate that their internal compasses point reliably toward a good working model of parenting. For them, motherhood's enhanced vision allows increased access to their ideals. Others, however, find their needles swing widely, as they recognize troubled features of their own mothers and fear modeling them. Managing motherhood's disequilibrium is much easier with a good internal guide.

Fatherhood's Confusion

Similarly, fathers may become very anxious around the reworking that parenthood requires. Jarvis (1962) was one of the first clinicians to focus on the transition to fatherhood. Observing activation of unconscious conflicts in four men in psychoanalytic treatment during their wives' pregnancies, he found that resolution could lead to new psychological equilibrium, to flight, or even to psychosis. One of his patients, apparently happily married until his wife became pregnant, then realized he had "made a mistake" in marrying her, fell in love with another woman, and filed for divorce. Jarvis concluded:

> Pregnancy and the birth of a child tend to act as powerful stimuli to the father's psyche. His mental equilibrium must undergo a shift to a new psychological balance of forces which involves the psychic meaning of the child. There are many possible solutions; on the one hand, the happy father may experience a syntonic strengthening of his attachment to his newly augmented family, while he may in some instances react to pregnancy or childbirth with marked disturbances resembling post-partum psychoses in women. (p. 689)

Other clinicians pioneering the study of transition to fatherhood included Wainwright, LaCoursiere, and Jessner. Working with men for whom fatherhood appeared decisive in triggering mental illness—including severe depression, debilitating panic attacks, and psychosis—Wainwright (1966) was surprised to find that each of these new fathers attributed his breakdown to some other factor. Wainwright thought this denial represented a psychological defense against recognizing the origin of their anxieties about parenthood. LaCoursiere (1972), reviewing the phenomenon of couvade (the development of pregnancy-like symptoms in expectant fathers), noted that in some cultures fathers actually take to their beds following the birth of their children; he thought this ritual expressed both envy and imitation of the female role, as well as a need to protect newborns from their fathers' ambivalence. Jessner et al. (1970) drew on a number of cases to describe the type of crises new parents may develop; these researchers believed rebellion against fatherhood, in addition to being caused by activation of unconscious conflicts, could also be due to a type of developmental delay in which a man holds on to adolescent ideals, including that of slender feminine beauty.

Gurwitt (1982) described the case of a man in psychoanalysis when his wife became pregnant, who through the course of treatment reworked issues relating to his sense of self as well as his relationship with parents and siblings. Activated themes included competition with and yearning for his father, envy of and fear of entrapment by women, jealousy toward younger siblings, and loosening of boundaries between "male" and "female" aspects of himself, as he discovered new internal sources of creativity. His wife, he complained, seemed mysteriously different, and his marriage became significantly strained for the first time. Of importance, Gurwitt drew attention to the critical nature of prospective fatherhood as a developmental stage preparing men for child rearing.

More recently, by interviewing expectant husbands, Osofsky and Culp (1989) further documented how transition to fatherhood can become a crisis. Following initial excitement and pride upon learning of their wives' pregnancies, some husbands described feeling "strange": they spoke of their own needs and rivalry toward their babies, an overwhelming sense of responsibility, severe panic reactions, feeling trapped, wondering if they were ready to settle down or if they would make adequate fathers, envy of their wives' ability to bear children, and their own compensatory creativity. Ambivalent about their pregnant wives—at times seeing them as more beautiful, at other times as ugly and clumsy—some fathers fantasized about other women, and a few became involved in extramarital affairs. Most men in the study had sexual concerns, including in some cases impotence, surfacing for the first time.

Nor did this turmoil resolve after the baby was born. Rather, new problems arose in how husbands felt about their wives. Whereas sometimes their relationships felt closer and warmer, at other times men complained that they lacked time with their wives and were growing apart. They felt confused about their attraction toward their wives, who, on the one hand, seemed more beautiful than ever but, on the other hand, appeared disfigured by changes to their bodies. As they made psychological adjustments to being intimate with women who were formerly simply wives but now also mothers, many husbands, in their confusion, turned off sexually. They acknowledged that sometimes they felt angry and jealous toward their new babies.

Of note, the husbands in Osofsky and Culp's study were not selected on the basis of any preexisting marital difficulties. Their reactions to their wives' pregnancies, accordingly, may be read as indicative of the large range of normal responses. In a similar prospective study of over 100 married couples expecting their first child, the same authors found a high incidence of depression among husbands and concluded:

Not all men experience conscious severe upheavals. Yet it appears that all men, especially when they become fathers for the first time, undergo considerable shifts and internal disequilibrium, and few of them are the same as they were before their wives' pregnancy. (pp. 159-160)

Osofsky and Culp, along with other writers mentioned in this section, concluded that, similar to motherhood, fatherhood creates a state of normal internal crisis. Fathers, though not contending with pregnancy's physiologic upheaval, may still experience profound internal disequilibrium. Previously unconscious issues, like unexposed negatives, are reworked and redeveloped in the laboratory of the new family.

These writers represent only a few of the many therapists who have observed activation of unconscious issues in new parents. What exactly are these issues? Are they unique to each individual, or do universal patterns exist?

SARAH AND ZACH:
WHEN MATERNAL PREOCCUPATION FEELS TOXIC

Sarah separated twice, within a few months after each daughter was born, from her husband Zach. Although they reunited after their first separation, their second has been permanent. Our interview took place five years later.

After Sarah and Zach met in college, they quickly developed a deeply caring and trusting relationship. Not only were they in love, but Sarah felt they were also a team. Sharing many of the same dreams and ambitions, including a passion for classical dance, a love of travel, and a wish not to be too tied down to suburban life, they seemed perfect for each other. Their relationship was the envy of their friends.

Although after the birth of their first child, their marriage was stressed to the point that they separated briefly, within a few months they reunited and seemed to work through their problems. Gradually their tension resolved; enjoying parenting together, they got along well once again. A few years later, they moved to a larger house in a pleasant, suburban neighborhood outside Chicago that seemed perfect for raising children. Although Zach spoke about his conflict between wanting to settle down and his antipathy toward "bourgeois" life, he also told Sarah, convincingly, that he had worked out his ambivalence and would like to have another child. Eager for her to conceive, he affirmed that the joy of having children overcame the sacrifices in his personal freedom. Sarah became pregnant on their first try.

At twenty-six weeks Sarah's water broke and she was rushed to the hospital. Her doctors, at first trying to delay labor, later delivered her baby by emergency cesarean section. Sarah remembers how quick it was, how awe inspiring: someone put a needle in her spine, a sheet over her stomach; she saw a hand move; out came her daughter. Weighing only two pounds, covered with down and lacking body fat, Becky was so premature that she looked to her mother like a cute little monkey. Hardly able to believe the miracle, Sarah felt as if she were watching evolution in progress. Unfortunately, twenty-four hours later Becky's lungs collapsed, and for the next month she required a respirator. She was fed through a nasal tube, while her arms were placed in splints to prevent contractures. Sarah gave her a little air pillow so her head would not become deformed from resting against the hard mattress and pumped her own milk for her.

During this time, Zach was by Sarah's side. Although very concerned about Becky, he tended to focus on the scientific aspects of her survival, perhaps because this was his way of handling anxiety. As Becky fought for her life, Sarah gave her every ounce of her own physical and emotional strength. She admits she did not have much energy left over for her husband. Between the physical challenges of recovering from surgery and pumping her milk and the emotional challenge of caring for her extremely premature newborn, she was utterly exhausted.

After Becky came home from the hospital, Zach began staying out until 3 or 4 a.m. Then he began an affair with a woman whom he had met shortly before Becky's birth. Several months later, he moved out to live with his new girlfriend. He gave Sarah several reasons for leaving: (1) She did not have enough time for him (he complained that she doted too much on Becky). (2) They had lost their dream: to travel. (3) He was tired of the responsibility of being the breadwinner. (4) He felt that Sarah was taking too long after her C-section to get back on her feet. Meanwhile Sarah completed evolution, nurturing her fragile baby. Becky, she knew, was a miracle.

Five years later, although still developmentally delayed, Becky is physically healthy. Continuing to live with his girlfriend, Zach has remained an involved father; several days a week he spends time with his children after school. Sometimes he takes them one weekend day, and occasionally they stay overnight. These visits, however, are limited by one problem. Zach does not want his children to know he lives with another woman. Fearful his relationship with his daughters will suffer if they find out the truth, he has told them it was *Sarah's* fault the marriage broke up—that *she* kicked *him* out. Not wanting them to meet his girlfriend, he usually visits his daughters in their own house or takes them on the road. Though angry at Zach for not accepting responsibility for the breakup, Sarah is grateful that he has been generous with money, consistently giving her more than the minimum required under child support guidelines.

Sarah thinks there are a number of reasons Zach left, and they are not the ones he gave. His father, who was very intelligent and held several doctorate degrees, was disappointed not to have pursued a career commensurate with his abilities. Convinced he had been cheated of better opportunities due to the demands of child rearing, he often let his son know he resented having children. Sarah thinks Zach assimilated his father's belief that ordinary family life is antithetical to personal development.

In addition, Sarah notes that Zach had difficulty not being number one. After childbirth, he seemed unable to accept Sarah's natural maternal preoccupation, as, due to the extra demands of Becky's medical condition, she was unable to give him her usual attention. Perhaps never having felt he was special to his dad, he may have craved extra reassurance from Sarah.

Her recovery has not been easy. Describing her state when Zach left for the second time, after having a child they had both planned and desired, she said, "You lack sleep, you can't hold a conversation, nothing fits, you're still in maternity clothes, your body is still unhealed. It's emotional abuse to choose that moment to leave." Nevertheless, for a long time she blamed herself. Similar to an abuse victim, she questioned everything she had done, wondering where she had gone wrong. Maybe she had not given her husband enough attention; maybe she should have been more interesting, intellectual, or witty; maybe she had not listened to him enough; or was it that she had not been attractive? So ugly did she feel after he left, that for a long time she could not look in the mirror. Only gradually did she recognize that, whatever her faults, they did not justify his leaving at that particular time, without at least trying to work on their relationship. Nevertheless, five years later, she still feels wounded.

Sarah tries not to dwell on the past. She dreams of meeting another man who will bond with her children and not leave. Although this has not yet happened, for her to go forward, none of her dreams have to come true: she only needs to hope.

Although we can only speculate secondhand about what Zach was feeling, similar to Carol in the previous story, he appeared to have been happy in his marriage until having children, when he experienced activation of a number of issues concerning becoming a parent. Although he may have truly believed he desired a second child, once this was accomplished, even while fulfilling his duties as a nonresidential father, he fled from full-time involvement.

Both Sarah's story and Carol's suggest problems concerning identification with (and fear of repeating) problems in parenting. Carol feared repeating her mother's history of chronic depression and dependence; as her own depression deepened and she became increasingly angry at her husband for trying to help, she panicked and left. Zach, we may speculate, feared repeating his father's history. Resentful that the requirements of family life deprived him of better career opportunities, Zach's father had remained unhappily burdened by family responsibilities. Zach did not want to be like his father. Instead, he tried to leave open his options to fulfill both career and personal goals. Before his second daughter arrived, he could still reassure himself that such choices, including being able to travel, having time to explore hobbies, and being free to choose work not solely on the basis of salary, were still available. After Becky's birth, however, Zach may have felt these options narrowing. In addition, he may have experienced activation of other issues relating to his father, including a vulnerability to narcissistic injury. Sarah's natural maternal preoccupation may have felt toxic.

Carol's and Sarah's stories begin to elucidate a few of the issues that can be activated by childbirth. Gurwitt (1989) listed some others he believed to be common. Although these were not all directly observed in my interviews, they are worth reviewing, as they represent a wide range of clinical experience. Furthermore, although Gurwitt applied these issues specifically to new fathers, I believe they can be applied to new mothers as well.

ISSUES ACTIVATED BY CHILDBIRTH

Fear of Narcissistic and Self-Object Needs Being Unmet

Before becoming parents, husband and wife may have satisfied many of each other's relational needs. Romantic partner, best friend, confidant, and caretaker may have been among their roles; they may also have fulfilled each other's self-object needs, such as those to be understood, mirrored, and validated. Many couples have worked out a balance, a give-and-take, that in a dyadic context allowed a stable solution. Two-person relationships, as with two-variable equations, are usually solvable.

The infant's arrival abruptly reshapes this configuration. Suddenly a third person—a very needy third—requires a great deal of attention. This third, similar to adding a z variable to an xy equation, greatly increases the complexity of the situation. Especially during the first months, as parents fall in love with their newcomer, they may find they have little energy left over for each other.

Most adults require some ongoing mirroring and approval, but those who received insufficient validation early in life may suffer when the pipeline is later diverted, even temporarily. Unlike the satisfaction of other needs, which can often be delayed, frustration of self-object ones cannot always be tolerated. If unable to sustain a sense of worth without a stable source of attention (which may be subtle, as his wife's having just the right smile for him, or a reassuring tone in her "good morning") a new father, for example, may be vulnerable to a precipitous drop in self-respect. Following the birth of his child, he may exhibit rage, aggression, and a sense of entitlement. Although some husbands may acknowledge their vulnerability, others do not appreciate how profoundly their children's births will shift the balance of needs in their families.

Although new fathers are probably most vulnerable to narcissistic injury, mothers may also be affected. For example, a woman whose self-esteem was largely contingent on positive feedback at work, admiring glances at her slender figure, or validation of her sexual attractiveness from her mate may suffer if these sources of pride are unavailable postpartum. Particularly in a culture where an ideal of adolescent feminine beauty prevails, the physical changes brought about by motherhood may erode a woman's confidence in her attractiveness. When all goes well, her baby's love and smile reassure her she is still beautiful, perhaps even more so than before, but she may also need her husband's reassurance that, with her transformation into a mother, she has not lost her status as a romantic partner.

Envy of Women's Ability to Bear Children

Perhaps one of nature's greatest mysteries is found neither in the reaches of outer space nor in the intricacies of particle physics, but in the miracle of childbirth. The ability to create a new human being in one's body, outside of conscious control, to recapitulate millions of years of evolution without even trying, is one of life's most transcendent experiences. No wonder women think men envy it; probably some do. It is no surprise, then, that soon after Freud speculated that girls compensate for penis envy by desiring babies, other psychoanalysts proposed that boys compensate for womb envy by overinvesting in symbols of phallic power. Later clinicians synthesized these discussions, emphasizing that neither gender has a monopoly on envy. Each may desire something belonging to the other (Fast, 1993).

By underlining what women have that men do not, pregnancy and childbirth may powerfully remind fathers of what they are lacking. Leading to compensatory creativity, or less productively to feeling empty, marginal, or even useless, envy of their wives' capacity to bear children may motivate some to seek other women, particularly younger ones for whom motherhood is yet remote, to avoid reminders of their barrenness.

On the other hand, although women may take great pleasure in motherhood, they may envy men's ability to procreate efficiently, without the nuisance of hormonal changes, without the loss of autonomy that accompanies pregnancy, delivery, and breast-feeding. Noting their husbands' freedom to maintain the rest of their lives relatively intact, new mothers may resent fatherhood's seemingly lower price tag.

Fear of Merging Back into Mother

Mahler et al. (1975) believed that during the first few months of life, infants experience a state of psychological fusion with their mothers, whom they do not perceive as separate. According to this theory, children later both yearn to reestablish this symbiosis and dread its return, as they alternate strivings for autonomy with attempts at reconnection. Contemporary infant researchers question both the existence of a symbiotic phase as well as the need to separate, under normal conditions, aggressively from the mother. Nevertheless, some people who experienced overly engulfing or controlling mothers may find that pregnancy triggers a fear of being sucked back into a woman's orbit, never to escape. Expectant fathers may abruptly reassert their need for masculine independence by becoming hostile, or even leaving their wives, and these "merging" fears may be further compounded by a culture that judges a high degree of infant involvement as feminine.

Women, too, may fear being entrapped and enslaved in maternal roles that will require them to give up their identities and independence. For example, if a woman felt overly merged with her own mother, who may have written a "destiny prescription" ordering her daughter to be a bearer of grandchildren, she may rebel against such an override of her other personal needs.

Revival of Sibling Rivalry

As the baby opens up the couple's dyadic bond, either parent may experience the newcomer as a rival. This dynamic may operate off a number of preexisting templates, one of which involves the memory of a younger sibling's birth. Activating this template, the new baby may cause a parent to revisit feelings of rivalry toward a younger competitor. A new father, for example, may feel disgust at his wife's full pregnant figure, disgust that masks a rekindling of childhood jealousy toward an intruding sibling (Jessner et al., 1970).

Similarly, a new mother may unconsciously associate the birth of her baby with that of one of her younger siblings. She may fear that, similar to the childhood intruder, her newborn will drive a one-way wedge between her and her partner. Parents who as children suffered much jealousy toward younger siblings may be particularly vulnerable, as a younger sibling may have interrupted parental attentiveness toward the older one.

Oedipal Issues

Another template off of which the baby may be experienced as a rival is that of the oedipal scene. In one of its versions, a young child aggressively competes with the same-sex parent for the other's love and attention. This script usually becomes dormant during later childhood but may once again be activated during transition to parenthood.

A new father may revisit this drama in at least two ways, both of which involve the unconscious association "wife equals mother." In the first, he experiences the infant as rival for his wife's attention, as he once experienced his father as rival for his mother's love. This is an important battle that must now, as well as then, be neither won nor lost. If he fears defeat, if he believes his wife will love the baby more than him, he may become acutely depressed.

But he may also fear winning, for the second way a new father may revisit the oedipal scene involves the unconscious recognition that by having a baby with his wife-mother, he has symbolically committed incest. Subsequently he feels guilt and anxiety, compounded by a sense of having won a battle he never should have. Though he may not be able to name the source of his anxiety, he may feel repulsed by his wife, seek attention from less maternally oriented women, and be unable to enjoy his child.

Similarly, a new mother may revisit oedipal conflicts. The baby may remind her of an intruding mother who interfered with her happiness with her father. Alternatively, the child may represent oedipal victory. As with her husband, she may experience anxiety concerning enjoying parenthood and may turn away from both husband and child.

Because of their forbidden nature, oedipal issues tend to be unconscious. Most adults are not aware of ever having had strong competitive feelings, much less sexual ones, toward their parents. The incest taboo, universal to all human cultures and possibly involving a neurological, maturational component, places these feelings behind one-way turnstiles, which work particularly well between growing child and parent (less well in reverse, as indicated by the high incidence of sexual abuse). As a result, activation of oedipal issues is not a problem most new parents would consciously anticipate. But precisely because these issues are both unconscious and intensely activated by childbirth, they may cause unexpected difficulties.

Identification with an Impaired Parent

Adults whose parents did not provide adequate nurturing may lack a sense of their own internal, parental ideals. When they later take on the challenge of raising children, they may suffer from these deficits. Just as women who had distant or uninvolved mothers may fear they never learned the skills necessary for warm nurturing, so may men who experienced early father absence have difficulty accessing positive images of masculine caretaking (Gurwitt, 1989). Reactivation of hostility toward their own parents, and fears of becoming like them, may develop (Wainwright, 1966). Lacking an internal compass, they may lose their way above parenting's treeline.

Identification, however, is not a simple process. Children's experiences are filtered through multiple lenses, including not just their own sensitivities, but also those of their other caretakers.

Lansky (1989), for instance, working in therapy with men who initially recalled their fathers as weak, ineffective, or critical, found that, after further exploration, these "memories" were not necessarily of real interactions, but rather of dialogues with discontented mothers portraying their husbands in ways that were divisive, devaluing, and contemptuous. In other words, not only is the boy's direct experience of father important, but so is the mother's representation of him to her son. Highlighting the complexity of the identification process, as well as the difficulty of raising children in an acrimonious atmosphere such as often occurs after divorce, Lansky showed that a child's internal representations of one parent can strongly depend on how that one is viewed by the other. Identification with an impaired parent is a complex phenomenon, depending not only on "real" experiences, but also on how they were interpreted to the child by important others.

Recent researchers make a further distinction between verbal memory, which is often consciously available in a declarative, narrative form, and procedural memory, which involves nonverbal scripts for carrying out actions. An example of a verbal memory would be a parent's conscious recollection, in narrative form, of a childhood experience, while one of a procedural memory would be a tendency, possibly outside awareness, to play similar games with one's newborn as did one's own parents. Many identifications with impaired parents may remain outside conscious knowledge in the form of procedural memory.

We will return to a discussion of memory, but first let us compare Gurwitt's list of issues with those of another researcher.

INTERNAL SCHEMAS ACTIVATED BY CHILDBIRTH: STERN

Gurwitt used the traditional language and concepts of psychoanalysis to describe the types of issues, conscious and unconscious, that may be activated by childbirth. By contrast, Stern (1995, pp. 19-20) drew on direct observations of parent-infant pairs to develop, in a somewhat different language, his own ideas about this process. As discussed in the last chapter, he used the phrase "schemas-of-being-with" to refer to internal representations of interactive experiences, either real or fantasized. Some schemas are available verbally as conscious memories, offering the advantage that they may be reflected upon and deliberately modified, if appropriate. Others are not available consciously and may encode nonverbal, procedural knowledge. They remain potentials, ready to be actualized.

Childbirth activates verbal as well as procedural schemas (pp. 199-200), leading to unanticipated patterns of thought, behavior, and desire. Once activated, such schemas may be expressed through a number of channels. On the one hand, they may become conscious and available for reflection. Alternatively, they may remain unconscious and be expressed through enactments. Motherhood, as a unique remembering context, activates many schemas that were previously dormant.

For Stern, such memories are not simply waiting to be activated, but are always reworked and cocreated by the interaction between mother and infant. They are very specific to the context of new motherhood. I will briefly review those he believed most common (pp. 23-34), with some additional comments of my own.

Mother's Schemas About Her Infant

Before her infant is born, a mother has many predictions, conscious and unconscious, about how temperament, character, and development will unfold. Such fantasies have origins as far back as her own childhood; when as a young girl she played with dolls, she was already creating inner pictures, though subject to much later modification, of her future children. These pictures, many of which became dormant, are later activated during pregnancy. According to Stern (1995), researchers have found that around the time of quickening, mothers exhibit a proliferation of fantasies about their unborn children, fantasies that begin to subside toward the end of pregnancy to make room for the "real" baby (p. 23). Just as the infant brain develops by first proliferating synapses and then pruning them in response to environmental inputs, so, too, do maternal representations of infants undergo a similar process, but with one difference: many of a mother's schemas may not be completely erased but simply recede from consciousness.

We have seen that other clinicians, such as Lester and Notman (1986), explored pregnant mothers' positive as well as negative fantasies about their unborn children. Negative fantasies may include a sense of the fetus as a parasite, destroying the mother's body and independence, an interloper who will confine her to a life of submission to maternal duty. Stern (1995), in less drastic language, noted that one of the most difficult tasks for new mothers is learning to put the baby first, a task that may involve profound inner reorganization (p. 25).

As a result, even though a woman may greatly desire children, her pregnancy may activate previously dormant schemas about her infant, including some that are quite negative. Once activated, they may contribute to pregnancy's "crisis" and lead to unanticipated reactions, including sudden aversion to motherhood, anger at her spouse, or even flight.

Mother's Schemas About Herself

Stern (1995) noted that with childbirth a new mother undergoes a "sweeping reappraisal of the organization and priority of most of her self-representations," leading to a sudden, irrevocable change in her status and identity (p. 24). This reorganization includes how she views herself as a woman, wife, career person, friend, daughter, and granddaughter; her role in society; her place in her own family; her legal status; having responsibility for another human being; having a new body; and being part of the chain of evolution (p. 24). As just one example, Stern suggested that new mothers, as they shift from being daughters to mothers, must mourn the loss of that position in their own families (p. 25).

As a new mother reworks previous schemas about herself in this new context, much positive growth may occur. As Benedek noted, the baby holds up a mirror that helps consolidate the mother's sense of goodness. Motherhood, accordingly, is not only a unique remembering context, but also a unique transformer, a right-angle bend in the fiber optics of narcissism. When all goes well, the mother is able to mourn the loss of her independence because it has been replaced by a new relationship, enhancing her sense of being a loving, complete person. If this does not occur, if her reworking does not have a positive result, she may instead experience a distressing sense of inner disorganization.

Mother's Schemas About Her Husband

As she enters motherhood, a woman may find that, not only schemas about herself require reworking, but also those about her husband. Whereas formerly she may have thought of him primarily as a romantic and sexual partner, now he may at least temporarily represent more a protector of the family's frame that allows her to focus on nurturing her infant. Even though his role is vital, he may feel pushed to the side.

Furthermore, just as a new mother adjusts to her family becoming a triad, so, too, does she shift her ideas about how her husband fits in. Stern (1995) suggested that, for some mothers, previously latent negative representations of their husbands may become activated by the triadic context, outlining the fault lines of the marriage (p. 26). As an example, he cited the case of a mother who "settled" on marrying after she was rejected by a man she loved more passionately; after childbirth, her baby unconsciously represented her new "lover," who would compensate for what she missed in her marriage. Her husband became less interesting than ever to her, and she began to push him more actively away (p. 26).

I will add that as a new mother reworks schemas about her husband, old ones about her own father may become activated. Was he a good provider, a protector of his family's frame? Was he involved with his children? Was he able to balance marriage, children, and career? Sometimes a daughter has tried hard not to replicate her parents' marriage and, in the dyadic context, may have achieved this. Childbirth, however, may activate old representations about her father that may interact with her current perception of her husband to create sudden, new difficulties in her marriage. As she begins to fear that her husband may fail as a father, she becomes hyperalert for such signs, sometimes creating a self-fulfilling prophecy.

Schemas About Her Own Mother

Stern (1995) believed that some of the most important schemas activated in the new mother are those involving her own primary parent (p. 180). As noted in Chapter 1, to the extent this had been the mother, Stern referred to the grandmother-mother-baby axis as an important component of the "motherhood constellation."

Other clinicians have noted the importance of this axis as well. Lester and Notman (1986, p. 363) stated that "[t]he course of pregnancy is above all determined by factors pointing to the woman's earliest experiences with the maternal object." Women with representations of their own mothers as inadequate have difficulty navigating parenthood.

These statements, I believe, are similar to those of Gurwitt and Herzog (1989), who suggested that identification with an impaired parent may hinder development of one's own parental ideals. (Gurwitt and Herzog discussed fathers' difficulties; Stern focused on mothers'.) We have seen that identification is not a simple process but is influenced by how parents represent each other to their children (Lansky, 1989).

Yet Stern (1995) added an important point, which may come as a bit of a surprise. Whether a woman has positive or negative representations of her own mother does not, in itself, predict future difficulties raising her children. Drawing on extensive attachment research, he noted that it is not simply the degree of her positive or negative representations that predicts how well she will attach to her child. Rather, it is the *coherence* of her narrative about her childhood, good or bad, that matters. The sense she makes of it and the quality of her understanding of how it affected her predict how securely her own child will attach to her.

What is "coherence," and how is it measured? The Adult Attachment Interview (AAI) was developed by George et al. (1985) to measure the quality of adults' stories about their childhoods. Responses were found to cluster into three categories: dismissing, preoccupied, or secure. Adults who were "dismissing" seemed not to acknowledge the emotional impact of early childhood experiences and resorted to either idealizing or devaluing their parents and early years in an empty way, devoid of detail. Their stories lacked coherence; even though *trauma* some "remembered" happy childhoods and claimed to identify with *abuse ?* nearly perfect parents, as we listened to these accounts, we would have sensed something was wrong. "Preoccupied" adults, on the other hand, still seemed overinvolved with their parents, with much unresolved anger often out of proportion to remembered events. Finally, "secure" adults presented coherent, internally consistent narratives about their childhoods. Again, these classifications depended not so much on whether the memories were good or bad, but on the quality of the narratives. A mother with a very abusive childhood might be classified as "secure" if she told her story in a way that was internally congruent. Similarly, even if she related a very happy childhood, she might be classified as "dismissing" if her story seemed unconvincing.

What relation is there between a mother's AAI classification and her quality of attachment with her own child? Main and Goldwyn (1990) found a high correlation between a mother's secure AAI rating when her child is age six and having had a securely attached one-year-old infant, as measured by standard methods (these will be described in more detail in Chapter 7). In fact, high correlation between attachment styles within mother-infant pairs has been demonstrated by at least eighteen different studies (van IJzendoorn, 1995). Furthermore, in a prospective study, Fonagy, Steele, and Steele (1991) found that a one-year-old's attachment status to mother could be predicted by how she scored, *during pregnancy,* on the AAI. In other words, the coherence of a mother's narrative about her own childhood, told before she even sees her newborn, strongly predicts the quality of her infant's later attachment.

Fonagy, Steele, Steele, et al. (1991) became interested in further defining this important quality of coherence. Examining it more closely, they believed it is linked to a "reflective-self function," a capacity to understand one's own and others' mental states (p. 204). Caregivers who understand their children's mental states will be more sensitive to their needs and provide an environment more likely to make them feel secure, and this trait, Fonagy et al. thought, is the best predictor of secure attachment. By contrast, standard measures of personality, psychopathology, vocabulary, self-esteem, or marital satisfaction failed to predict security of attachment at one year.

To summarize our brief divergence into attachment theory: after childbirth, parents' internal representations of their own caretakers may be activated, and this will be most problematic when these schemas lack coherence. People with a high level of unresolved feelings about their childhoods, a dismissing attitude toward the importance of early attachments, or an inability to understand their own parents' mental states may have the most difficulty forming secure attachments with their infants.

Mother's Schemas About Her Own Father

Stern (1995) believed that as a woman enters pregnancy and childbirth, schemas about her father are generally less active than those about her mother. He suggested that this is because, for most women, their mothers were their primary parents; in cases where fathers assumed more prominent roles, representations involving them may be more salient.

I believe that, in making this statement, Stern was referring to a mother's immediate task of bonding to her newborn, as during these first months she is naturally oriented toward people who offer her good models of infant caretaking. Yet, as I suggested earlier, representations about her father may also be important. After all, infant bonding is not her only task; she must now include baby and husband in a new triad. Formerly only a romantic partner, he is now also a father and may be compared to the standard that her own set. To the extent this was an idealized one, she may set the bar impossibly high, but, conversely, if she viewed her own father as ineffective, she may fear her husband will similarly fail. Although her representations of her father may be of less direct importance to her immediate dyadic relationship to her newborn, they are of great relevance to how she relates in a triadic context.

Mother's Schemas About the Culture

Stern (1995) noted that our culture presents powerful messages to mothers about how they should feel and behave. Although I believe he is correct, I also believe that we actually have no coherent cultural ideal of motherhood and, as a result, are bombarded with a loose, often contradictory assortment of prescriptions. Women may find it difficult to integrate messages encouraging them to celebrate independence, career, slimness, and romance with those celebrating selfless dedication to motherhood. It is difficult to be all things at once, and fears of falling short of superwoman may be activated.

HOW ARE ISSUES AND INTERNAL REPRESENTATIONS ACTIVATED?

We have examined a number of issues, or in Stern's (1995) more relational language "schemas-of-being-with," which may be activated by childbirth. What is the mechanism of this activation? Although this is a complex topic, I will review two contemporary researchers' notions.

First, we have seen how Stern believed childbirth, as a specific remembering context, activates multiple schemas that may or may not have been previously conscious. These may include ones about the baby, the mother herself, her parents, her partner, or her relationship to the culture. They may be dyadic, involving a relationship with just one other individual, or triadic, involving rivalry and competition. They may be remembered in conscious narrative form or become activated while still remaining unconscious. In this second form they may be "remembered" through reenactments.

What determines whether a memory, once activated, reaches awareness? Westen and Gabbard (in press), reviewing the ideas of classical psychoanalysis, clarified two categories of unconscious memory. One type—the type I believe Stern (1995) referred to predominantly—involves preconscious material that may be fairly easily activated by current environmental cues or "primers." These memories are not repressed in the sense of needing to be kept out of awareness to protect the self; they are simply not active but may easily be brought online. By contrast, memories belonging to the dynamic unconscious must be defended against to avoid unpleasant effects; the defense, furthermore, occurs outside conscious awareness.

These are the well-known tenets of classical psychoanalysis. For many years researchers outside this field, particular those in academic psychology, did not necessarily endorse them because they could not be directly observed or inferred from the type of experiments being performed. Westen and Gabbard (in press) noted that, until the 1980s, cognitive science was dominated by the "modal model" of the mind, according to which sensory information is initially registered, sent to short-term memory, and then sent to long-term memory in a linear process. Retrieving a memory was thought to occur by reversing this process, the ease of which depended on how recently the memory was stored, as well as on the strength of current environmental cues. For example, people remember an event more readily if they are in a state of mind similar to that when the event occurred; in the same way, when first unconsciously primed with a certain word, they recognize and remember similar ones more quickly (pp. 6-8). This model of memory involved linear processing, with no distinction between the preconscious and dynamic unconscious.

Westen and Gabbard update us on the "second cognitive revolution," which over the past ten years has recognized that when presented with a large number of stimuli, we must select from an equally large number of memories which ones to activate—and this selection process is itself unconscious. Unlike the earlier serial processing model, this one involves simultaneous parallel processing of multiple lines of information. The serial model, representing consciousness, may be actually neurologically superimposed on a parallel processing system that is unconscious.

Westen and Gabbard also discussed modern neuroscience's finding that there are two types of memory, implicit versus explicit. Basically, these correspond to classical notions of preconscious versus conscious, but although cognitive researchers initially believed that explicit memory was encoded verbally in conscious narrative form and implicit memory was encoded nonverbally in unconscious procedural form, Westen and Gabbard clarified that this distinction does not always hold. Verbal memories may remain unconscious, and we may be aware of procedural knowledge that defies being put into language, such as how to play the piano. Most important, either type of memory may be actively kept unconscious.

Until recently, cognitive researchers thought that implicit memories encoded procedures, such as certain social customs, that had simply become automated outside of awareness to increase efficiency. But in the last few years, according to Westen and Gabbard, a large body of more sophisticated cognitive research has revealed that some memories may be actively kept out of awareness by unconscious defenses, to protect the self from emotionally disturbing material. Furthermore, these recent studies have demonstrated that simply defending against a thought or feeling may place it in a state of heightened activation; instructing a person not to think about a topic leads to successful "forgetting" but also a heightened unconscious watchfulness for associated thoughts, memories, or feelings. Precisely those representations which are actively warded off, which we try to forget or defend against, become most highly activated. In other words, coming from a completely different tradition, one frankly biased against the existence of a dynamic unconscious, many cognitive psychologists have reached similar conclusions to those of classical psychoanalysis.

Memories, accordingly, may be activated either consciously or unconsciously, either verbally or procedurally, by current environmental "primers" as well as, paradoxically, by the need to protect the self from certain feelings or truths. Some, even while activated, may remain outside of awareness but still affect behavior profoundly. Let us now apply these ideas to the context of transition to parenthood.

After childbirth, memories may be activated in several ways. First, those of which a person has always been aware may simply become more prominent. These are probably not too disturbing, as they have, after all, been at least vaguely conscious; even if they invoke unhappiness, they come as no surprise. Second, memories that were unconscious, but not dynamically repressed, may now enter awareness. Although they may take a person by surprise, they are still relatively easy to assimilate, as they tend to be compatible with self-esteem and worldview; although they may include forgotten aspects of childhood, they do not conflict in a major way with a sense of self. Third, memories that were dynamically repressed may become conscious. These may be extremely upsetting, but once available for reflection, they can be reworked before action is taken. Fourth, dynamically repressed memories may be activated but remain unconscious. If too upsetting to be allowed into awareness, they may lead to panic and flight, and they may be directly acted upon without contemplation.

WHAT GOES WRONG?
FROM PERSONAL CRISIS TO MELTDOWN

Transition to parenthood activates a wide variety of issues, internal representations, and memories that were previously dormant, often unconscious. Like negatives awaiting development, they remain in potential space until "exposed" by the particular events of one's life—including, most potently, having a child. Just as the particular chemistry of a darkroom determines the final form of a developed photograph, so, too, do current life events interact with our unconscious blueprints to influence their expression. Whether taking the form of explicit, verbal memories or enactments of implicit, procedural knowledge, these animated representations may create sudden internal shifts as well as changes in behavior. Some may have been dynamically repressed—that is, kept out of awareness due to the extremely disturbing or traumatic effects they would unleash if made conscious—and the more they were defended against, the more they may now influence behavior. Parenthood may powerfully activate not only the unknown self but also the self one does not wish to know.

We have seen, so far, some of the possible outcomes. For Carol, stimulation of fears she might follow in her mother's unhappy footsteps led to panic. For Zach, activation of narcissistic vulnerability as well as identification with an unhappy father led him to flee both marriage and full-time commitment to his children. Yet, despite separating from their spouses, both Carol and Zach remained involved parents; neither abandoned their children. Even more problematic are situations in which a parent abandons both partner *and* children. Relevant to these may be reactivation of old trauma. Let us turn to Martha's story.

Martha and Peter: Whose Tears?

Martha, a twenty-eight-year-old nurse currently eight months pregnant, was married five years before separating several weeks before our interview. Even though there were multiple stresses on her marriage, she was surprised at the suddenness with which Peter, who had wanted to be a father, left.

Martha had long known that her husband had a problem with his temper. Soon after they met, when they were both just out of college, she noticed he became very irritable over small things, such as a restaurant no longer serving his favorite dish. She also noticed that he drank more than he should. But in spite of these problems, she fell in love with him; she wanted to take care of him and help him become happy. Peter seemed to love her, and to be willing to work on his problems.

After marrying, at Martha's suggestion, Peter made an appointment with a psychiatrist in order to address both his irritability and his drinking. Unfortunately, he did not tell his doctor about the second problem; consequently, the medications prescribed for his mood swings were not helpful and sometimes mixed poorly with alcohol. Depressed and irascible, he became physically abusive, one night throwing a vase at Martha and significantly injuring her.

Peter was not always abusive; he had an affectionate side as well. Over the next two years, he doted on her at times, as during the vacation trip they took one fall, when he could hardly do enough for her. During good intervals they loved each other and were still planning a life together. Because he really seemed to enjoy children, Martha was hopeful that, in spite of his problems, he would make a good father. She also felt utterly secure of one thing: he loved her and would never leave. Martha really wanted to be a mother, and her biological clock was ticking; there was always time for Peter to stop drinking, but the time for her to have a child would run out. He agreed, and with his encouragement, she began trying to conceive.

Although he had repeatedly told her he wanted children, when he learned she was pregnant, Peter reacted poorly. At first denying the possibility, later he became enraged. Drinking more than ever, he now completely shut Martha out. Clearly he was not interested in her pregnancy. Friday nights he would return home, refuse to eat, open the beer cans, put on earphones, and zone out. Becoming violent again, he grabbed her by the throat and threw her to the floor; for the first time, she became truly frightened. Concerned as she was, she felt she had no alternative but to complete her pregnancy and hope that Peter would calm down.

As Martha neared term, Peter stopped hitting her; instead he ignored her, leaving her alone while he went out drinking. He accused her of getting pregnant in order to try to keep him. She was now crying all the time, but he seemed unmoved. He announced he wanted a divorce and moved out when she was eight months pregnant.

When Martha asked him why he was leaving, he gave three reasons. First of all, he told her, he needed independence; he wanted to do things on his own, without anyone relying on him. Second, he said, they had never been friends. (Martha disagreed; they had actually been good friends, especially in the earlier days when he was not drinking so much.) Third, he said, he must leave because, although he "loved" her, he was not "in love." His reasons for marital breakdown did not include drinking, mood swings, or physical abuse.

Martha felt belittled. After quickly serving her with divorce papers, he did little to help. "You're lucky I pay child support," he informed her. "I could just take off." Although he discarded Martha, he demanded to see their future baby on weekends and spoke vociferously about his father's rights. "It comes from me; it's mine. I have a right to see it," he initially proclaimed. Later he changed his tack, making it clear he will not be involved as a father.

Trying to understand what happened, Martha realizes that her marriage may have been doomed from the beginning. Peter's alcoholism, resistant to treatment, relentlessly eroded the foundation of their trust. Yet she thinks other factors contributed to his sudden departure, too. After all, he had been drinking for years but had made no earlier move toward divorce. On the contrary, he had seemed quite needy and dependent before her pregnancy.

Martha reflected a bit on his background. He once told her that after his eighteen-year-old mother had conceived him, she had been unable to obtain a legal abortion in her small town in Italy, so had felt forced to marry his father. Three years later, Peter's parents had divorced. Raised by his mother, Peter became estranged from his father, who allegedly was a crazy, violent man prone to throwing his son against a wall for crying. The way Peter used to talk to Martha about his father indicated he had obviously been traumatized, yet he had been unable to show any feelings. Sometimes Martha had cried for him.

Martha remembered other conversations with Peter in which he told her that, when he was ten, his mother had remarried. Never close to his stepfather, he then developed discipline problems, stealing both money and medications from his mother. As a teenager he began to suffer severe depressions, at one point attempting suicide. He also began drinking, as did his mother, who used this method to cope with her unhappy second marriage. She died in Italy while he was in college in the United States.

Despite all these problems, Martha cannot believe that Peter did not stay with her. She had thought she could count on his loyalty and commitment. Now he wants a divorce so quickly, he cannot seem to wait. In shock, she is crying much of the time and has difficulty feeling excited about her pregnancy; she no longer talks lovingly to the baby inside her, as she did before her husband left. Rather, she fears her unborn hears her sobbing. Maybe, she thinks, her tears are the ones Peter never shed.

When asked why he left his pregnant wife, Peter stated he did not want anyone to depend on him. Although it would be easy to attribute his attitude to drinking and depression, there may have been another factor: a dread that if his own young and vulnerable child depended on him, he would fail his son as his father had failed him. Engraved in Peter's mind was an image of a father who violently threw him against a wall for crying. Although aware of this memory, he had been unable either to express feelings about it or to incorporate it into a coherent narrative. When it was activated by pregnancy, Peter unconsciously "knew" he might reenact this script. Better to flee than face this ghost.

The Role of Previous Trauma: Ghosts in the Nursery

Although reworking the past can be difficult for many, those who suffered unusually traumatic childhoods, such as those characterized by repeated emotional, physical, or sexual abuse, may have especially severe reactions. These may be the new parents most likely to take complete flight, to "melt down."

Fraiberg et al. (1975) addressed this problem in their now classic lines:

> In every nursery there are ghosts. They are the visitors from the unremembered past of the parents: the uninvited guests at the christening. Under all favorable circumstances the unfriendly and

unbidden spirits are banished from the nursery and return to their subterranean dwelling place. The baby makes his own imperative claim upon parental love and, in strict analogy with the fairy tales, the bonds of love protect the child and his parents against the intruders, the malevolent ghosts.

    This is not to say that ghosts cannot invent mischief from their burial places. Even among families where the love bonds are stable and strong, the intruders from the parental past may break through the magic circle in an unguarded moment, and a parent and his child may find themselves reenacting a moment or a scene from another time with another set of characters. (p. 387)

Although the authors did not specifically address abuse, they did refer to a tendency to repeat old traumas: when maladaptive patterns are repeated rather than reworked, past ghosts become present. As did Peter, some parents flee rather than risk reenacting such scripts. Yet repetition is not inevitable:

Then, too, we must reflect that, if history predicted with fidelity, the human family itself would have long ago been drowned in its own oppressive past. The race improves. And this may be because the largest number of men and women who have known suffering find renewal and the healing of childhood pain in the experience of bringing a child into the world. In the simplest terms—we have heard it often from parents—the parent says, "I want something better for my child than I have had." (p. 389)

    The key to not repeating our own childhood traumas with our children, according to Fraiberg et al., is the ability to both remember past traumatic events and bear their associated painful feelings. When this can be done, we can avoid repeating old patterns. On the other hand, if such feelings remain isolated and unintegrated, we may be at risk for unwittingly repeating what we would rather not.

    This, then, is the critical work of becoming a parent: reliving with one's child one's own childhood, while having full emotional access to those memories necessary not to repeat the bad. As a mother rocks her newborn, she touches his or her face as her mother touched hers. The positive body language of love is transmitted subterraneanly, unknowingly, unreflectingly, connecting generation to generation by its thread. Here there is no need to remember consciously because the unconscious remembering is good. But where the mother reenacts with her newborn the traumas of her own childhood, remembering must take place in order to change.

Referring to the repetition compulsion as the "scar tissue of the capacity to feel," Paul Russell (1998) also wrote about the importance of remembering and working through past trauma. We repeat what we cannot mourn. "Affective competence," according to Russell, involves feeling what we must in order to avoid repeating what we must not.

All of us have some unpleasant remembering to do. It is usually manageable. But for parents such as Peter, terribly scarred by early experience, it may not be bearable. Not up to the full demands of this task, parents desperately trying to avoid remembering or repeating earlier trauma may find an escape hatch through divorce. Some, by avoiding physical custody, may continue to see and enjoy their children, but from enough distance that they do not reignite old nightmares. Others, such as Peter, may abandon their children, fearing old demons will once again reign.

Fraiberg et al. (1975) implied that, to heal, those who suffered early trauma need to link verbal, "factual" accounts of such memories to their associated feelings. This notion of therapeutic change is concordant with that of attachment researchers cited previously. Fonagy et al. (1993, p. 971), referring to their finding that the security of an infant's attachment to his or her mother is foreshadowed prenatally by the quality of her narrative about her own childhood, stated, "The ghost haunting the nursery, as predicted by Fraiberg, is more likely to appear when the parents' defensive stance is apparently formidable." Parents who are in denial about the meaning or impact of early events or who, similar to Peter, defend against integrating memories with painful emotions carry the ghost within.

Although achieving a coherent narrative about one's life may be one useful therapeutic goal, many therapists believe that positive change may sometimes occur without such conscious, verbal insight. Westen and Gabbard (in press, b), for example, stated that explicit recall of painful past events may or may not be beneficial, depending on a number of conditions, such as the context in which the memory is recalled, the degree of control one has over the memory, the awareness of emotions associated with it, and whether one is able to rework or change its intensity or meaning. At times, recall may be less important than altering implicit associative networks. A growing number of therapists and researchers (see also Fonagy, 1999) argue that change in unconscious structures, rather than recovery of explicit memories, is an important ingredient of therapeutic change. If modification of such structures occurs by other means, such as by experiencing a new type of relationship, this may also help new parents exorcise their "ghosts." One such modifier, when all goes well, is the baby.

In Peter's case, all did not go well. His story illustrates one factor that may lead to flight from parenthood: activation of a particularly strong fear of reenacting old trauma. Compared to the issues we reviewed in the last section, this one may engender a particularly high degree of anxiety, as it may imply a possibility of direct harm to the infant. It would be misleading, however, to suggest that simply a history of trauma predicts panic to the point of flight. Other factors are at work as well, making such behavior multidetermined.

Additional Factors

Insufficient Ego or Superego Strengths

The id-ego-superego model of the mind, known as the structural model, is one older but still useful paradigm through which to view this problem. For instance, as strong as a new father's fear may be of repeating old trauma, he may be able to call upon ego strengths to help manage his anxiety. These strengths include coping skills, such as the ability to delay impulsive action, tolerate strong feelings, ask for help when needed, and weigh the true risks and benefits of leaving. Similarly, he may be able to call upon his superego, or conscience, to remind him that abandoning his wife at childbirth is against his moral code. Under usual circumstances ego and superego strengths reinforce each other to provide an internal holding environment, until the consequences of such a decision can be adequately assessed in all their complexity.

Sometimes under the extreme stress of reactivation of childhood trauma, the balance between mental structures breaks down. Flooded with anxiety, a person may lose ego functioning first, so that he may feel torn between what he "wants" to do—flee—and what he feels he "ought" to do—stay. In this situation, the superego can become quite punitive, as realistic assessment of the pros and cons of the marriage may take a backseat to a tug-of-war between want and ought.

Alcohol or Drug Abuse

Although previous trauma probably played a significant role in Peter's flight from fatherhood, we cannot ignore the effect of his drinking. Chronic alcoholism relentlessly erodes the foundation of marriage, the confidence one can become a good parent, and one's accurate judgment. It erodes, moreover, many biological functions of the brain, including those skills just listed, to the point that severe alcoholics may be unable to either delay impulsive action or adequately weigh the risks of leaving their marriages. Perhaps without his drinking, Peter could have overcome his fear of reliving his trauma, and perhaps he would have let his baby gradually show him how to be a good father. Yet alcoholism and trauma go hand in hand; Peter, similar to many others, may have developed his addiction as he attempted to deal with overwhelming early trauma.

Other Factors

Not only did Peter suffer from childhood trauma and current alcoholism, but he also lacked a sufficiently broad base of support from friends or family. Although his wife had been very supportive during their marriage, he had begun to see her as the "enemy." Unfortunately, he had no one else. Perhaps, as Herzog (1982) found in his study of expectant fathers, if Peter had had a reliable male figure to whom he could turn for advice or as a role model for successful parenting, he could have slowed his impulsive flight sufficiently to have obtained help. Friends, family, and adequate same-sex mentors may help "contain" a new parent's panic, but when these are not readily available, parents such as Peter may find themselves lacking either an internal map or a visitor's guide to parenthood's new territory.

SUMMARY

Why can transition to parenthood be so difficult? In the last chapter, we learned that sociological studies, overturning the traditional notion that childbirth makes marriages happier, focused on external stresses such as lack of downtime and affordable child care. Psychoanalytic studies, focusing on how childbirth can trigger profound psychological changes, attempted to trace the development of nurturing parental attitudes over the course of childhood and adolescence.

While disagreeing about any "normal" prescription for this course, psychoanalysts did agree that the foundation for future nurturing begins early in life. They also stressed the importance of parenthood as a developmental phase—not in the sense that everyone needs to experience this particular stage, but that, once entered, there is no turning back. Parenthood involves reliving one's own childhood, sometimes consciously, sometimes unconsciously, and finding better solutions the second time around.

In this chapter, we reviewed ways in which parenthood may become a personal crisis. Some new parents experience activation of profoundly anxiety-provoking issues, memories, or internal representations. Carol, for instance, initially fled her marriage out of fear she would reenact her mother's misery, and Zach, we speculated, may have fled out of fear he would repeat his father's chronic dissatisfaction. Eventually, both Carol and Zach reworked their fears to find new solutions. Childbirth provided them with a unique context within which to reorganize their inner worlds. Not all parents, however, are able to make use of their second chances. For some, second chances are recurrent nightmares.

Often multiple factors are involved when a new parent takes total flight, abandoning children as well as spouse. Peter, for instance, suffered not only a history of trauma but also a severe current drinking problem; furthermore, he lacked a network of family or friends who could help. The ghosts from his past overtook him.

Parenthood, accordingly, may trigger extreme personal crises. When previously unconscious but troubling memories are activated, or when the emotional components of such memories cannot be coherently integrated, severe anxiety may develop. Even with a supportive partner, some people cannot overcome their fear, and they flee. For some spouses, divorce at childbirth reflects the culmination of an ongoing, dysfunctional dynamic coming to a boiling point over a baby, but for others, troubled by such issues as we have discussed, childbirth triggers profound internal turmoil, which may result in their fleeing marriages previously cherished. When this happens, the departing partner may appear suddenly, unexpectedly transformed.

In the next chapter we will compare and contrast these two paradigms of divorce at childbirth: *transition* versus *transformation*.

Chapter 3

Transition versus Transformation: Comparing Two Models

When new parents are suddenly confronted by major changes in themselves or their partners, the passage to parenthood becomes less a transition than a transformation. Before childbirth, husband and wife may have "known" themselves, but in the tunnel of turbulence at the boundary of birth and parenthood, they may no longer be able to predict their moods or behavior. For those not unduly stressed, a new equilibrium will likely be reached. Others, however, experience a different result; after a period of turmoil, they seem to have changed radically. Altered values or morality, new and uncontrollable addictions, or construction of novel professional or social identities may occur.

Furthermore, such developments may have been difficult to foresee. Becoming a parent not only is a sudden *event* but, like ice melting into a river, involves a change in *state*. With a transition to parenthood comes a transformation into a somewhat new person. As in any state change, at the boundary lies turbulence, even chaos. Small alterations in initial parameters, such as a person's unconscious representations, make large differences over time (the butterfly effect). It is impossible to predict exactly how parenthood, as a state change, will move us.

I do believe that parenthood is a transforming event. We are not quite who we were before having children. A woman previously entirely devoted to her work, with little capacity for nurturing, may be transformed into a loving, playful mother delighted to spend hours gazing at her newborn. Looking back, she may feel she was previously only half alive. Such changes in a direction toward parenthood are so common that they are almost taken for granted. But what accounts for the extreme difficulties some people have?

We have seen how childbirth, by triggering previously covert psychological issues, can cause apparent personality changes. We have also seen how activation of such issues can lead to unexpected difficulty incorporating the baby into a triad. Yet not all marital difficulties at this time are due to internal transformations. Divorce at childbirth may also result from overt, long-standing stresses on the couple. Substance abuse, medical illness, and financial hardship are just a few of the many conditions, on top of which may arrive a baby. In this second model, divorce at childbirth is explained by persistence of stresses already active. These marriages were already riddled with problems; the baby simply added one more, pushing the couple beyond its coping capacity.

Let us now elaborate on these two models, transformation versus transition, with further interviews as well as clinical material. In practice, these models are not always separate, as many divorces at childbirth involve both.

MODEL ONE: TRANSFORMATION

In the last chapter, we reviewed how new parents may enter sudden states of crisis. Triggered by activation of previously dormant issues or representations, such states, if they engender panic, may result in flight; short of this, unanticipated patterns of destructive behavior may emerge that quickly erode the marriage. Transformation is not always a negative event, however. Childbirth may activate hidden strengths that guide a person toward, not away from, parenthood. In either case, activation of unconscious material is the hallmark of transformation. We have seen that the nature of this material varies, and includes, not only issues and fears such as those listed by Gurwitt (1989), but also representations of interactions, real or fantasized, referred to as "schemas-of-being-with" by Stern (1995).

Childbirth may also activate aspects of a person's character structure. Informed by both issues and schemas, character structure refers to stable, ingrained ways of approaching situations. It is a broader category than the first two and includes traits such as a general resilience versus vulnerability in the face of hardship, perception of others as helpful versus hurtful, or kindness versus cruelty toward those with less power.

Many clinicians have attempted to further define character structure. Steiner (1996) referred to one of its building blocks—attempts, sometimes maladaptive, to defend against unwanted thoughts and feelings. Such defenses then become "installed" as permanent features of the personality (p. 1074). Steiner noted that character defenses may operate not just internally but also between people, through a process known as projective identification, in which one person disavows troubling aspects of himself or herself and then projects these onto another whom he or she tries to control. Abusiveness, one such character defense, was a frequent theme in the stories of the women I interviewed.

Thus, at least three overlapping aspects of personality may be activated by childbirth: issues, internal representations, or character defenses. While all of these may be either conscious or unconscious prior to childbirth, it is the unconscious ones, particularly those which have remained so due to their disturbing nature, that may cause the most profound disruptions. When such "programs" are opened, new parents must deal not only with the external stresses, difficult enough, of childbirth but also, in many cases, with a sense of internal chaos. No wonder some turn to extramarital affairs; these parents are not wishing to complicate their lives but are instead trying to prevent their emotional systems from crashing. Often they seek an outsider to soothe inner turmoil and anxiety, to restore a comfortable sense of self. Paradoxically, such affairs may further contribute to radical personality shifts.

All of these factors—activation of previously unconscious material, exposure of hidden character vulnerabilities, and attempts to restore emotional equilibrium by turning to extramarital affairs—may contribute to apparent sudden transformations.

Activation of Issues and Representations

In the last chapter we reviewed issues Gurwitt (1989) believed are frequently activated by childbirth. In my own clinical work, I have observed similar ones, in particular, the following four: fear of repeating the past, fear of losing self-object support, fear of being defective and unlovable, and a sense of guilt precluding the ability to enjoy parenthood. Whether or not conscious prior to childbirth, all involve fears—either of failing to be a good-enough parent or of failing to sustain a vital internal equilibrium. They are usually, but not always, accompanied by activation of a corresponding representation of the person's own impaired parent.

Here I will give some examples (disguised to ensure confidentiality) drawn from my own practice. Although not pertaining directly to the immediate postpartum period, these vignettes do illustrate some of the issues that may be triggered by having children, or even contemplating having them.

First, many of my patients expressing aversion to parenthood dread repeating their own childhood trauma. Some adult victims of childhood abuse worry that, despite of their best efforts, they will subject their own children to the same, as though propelled by some demonic force. Thankfully, as Fraiberg (1975) and Fonagy et al. (1993) pointed out, by remembering and reflecting on the past, this is unlikely to occur. Those who desire children can be reassured that they can become not the feared parent of their childhood but, in many ways, the parent for whom they themselves yearned.

Martha grew up with an alcoholic mother who was extremely verbally abusive and who told her from an early age that she was fat, ugly, and worthless. Martha had virtually no memories of her mother saying anything positive to her. By contrast, she recalled her mother idealizing an older brother, who was athletic, handsome, and could do no wrong. Martha felt so bad about herself that as a child she frequently thought she just "shouldn't be here." Nevertheless, she did not give up trying to please her mother. She continued to do many things for her, often putting her own life on hold, without ever receiving recognition.

Due to her considerable strengths, Martha was able to develop a rewarding career and marry happily. She and her husband greatly desired children. Yet as the time approached, she discovered she was dreading repeating her own miserable past. Rather than give into her fears, she gave birth to two healthy children. However, she found that when her older daughter reached age four (about the time she remembers her mother turning on her), she began to yell at her, repeating some of her mother's horrible phrases almost verbatim. In addition, she found herself splitting her affection for her children, as had her own mother. Increasingly concerned she might abuse them, she sought counseling.

After entering therapy, Martha was able to grieve that she had never had a good relationship with her mother. Through this grief work she realized that her mother, not herself, had been the problem. Although she had always been aware of the "facts" about her childhood, until she was in therapy, she had not been able to link her anger, which had been free-floating, with memories of her mother's treatment of her. After doing so, Martha stopped yelling at her children and began to bond with them more equally. By developing an emotionally coherent narrative of her childhood and gaining compassion for her own experience, she was able to become the mother she wished to be.

Martha's story illustrates how people who experienced quite abusive childhoods may fear, sometimes correctly, that they may repeat history. Yet Martha, similar to many others, took a leap of faith into parenthood; when later she encountered difficulties, she was able to avoid repeating the past by reworking it.

Some of my patients who fear repeating the past, however, do not seem to have experienced severe childhood trauma. Rather than re-calling a particularly abusive parent, they describe growing up in a family where, for any number of reasons, there just was not much joy associated with having children. Perhaps their parents were over-worked, ill, or depressed; perhaps they were burned out and yearned for freedom from child-rearing's constant cares. Identifying with their impaired parents, this group does not associate parenthood with happiness. Dreading to repeat a life of dreary toil and fatigue, they do not want to risk such emotional bankruptcy. They may also be con-summating, unknown to them, their parents' desire for liberation.

Bill grew up in a religious, working-class family. Well-off compared to many of his neighbors, he attended a private school and had a stable home life. He denied any history of abuse. Yet, in spite of his mother's devoting her life to child rearing, he never wanted to have children. Witnessing his father's life as a plumber, work-ing long hours and coming home exhausted with little energy or interest left for his children, led Bill to only one conclusion: he would not repeat the seeming meaninglessness of his father's existence. In order not to be trapped into such a life, Bill adamantly resolved not to have children.

Both Martha's and Bill's fears of parenthood were conscious. Al-though these were activated by having children, or in Bill's case by just thinking of having them, neither person experienced sudden transformations—because each had been struggling with these issues for years. Martha, long aware of her mother's temper, was prepared when children triggered her own angry streak; Bill dreaded father-hood enough to avoid it altogether. For other new parents, however, such fears may have remained unconscious until considering child-birth. They may be unready for the panic that ensues.

If, for example, a man unconsciously believes that he is not deserv-ing of happiness, he may deprive himself of accomplishments. Until his sense of guilt is ameliorated, he may wish, in theory, to have chil-dren but not allow himself any pleasure in fatherhood. Similarly, a woman may be deeply convinced she does not deserve to be a mother. She may fear she is so defective that she cannot become pregnant, or even that her offspring will be physically deformed. While adverse early childhood experiences may have contributed to these concerns, they may also reflect guilt concerning separation and autonomy.

Karen grew up in an upper-class household with numerous material advantages. Although her mother suffered from depression, her father had many strengths. Very intelligent, Karen later obtained advanced degrees and made notable contributions to her field. However, when she met the man of her dreams and moved away from home, her mother was brokenhearted that her daughter would be leaving her. As mother's depression deepened, it became clear that she would never recover from Karen's "desertion."

After marrying, as Karen began to consider having children, she developed strong fears that she would either be infertile or, if she did succeed in conceiving, would grow a "monster" child impossible to nurture. These fears were of almost delusional proportions. Although aware of her guilt over leaving her mother, she did not consciously link it with her fears of pregnancy, yet, unconsciously, these fears were the price she would have to pay for trying to be happy at her mother's expense. As her husband spoke more about having children, she experienced activation of the monster-child fantasy. Previously well put together, Karen now entered a state of panic bordering on psychosis.

Karen entered therapy, where she began to explore her fears and work through her guilt about separating from her mother. After she took a job babysitting a young child, Karen began to consider that perhaps she could be loved by her own. For the first time she dared discuss her fears with a gynecologist and, to her amazement, was told that nothing was medically wrong. She realized that she did want children and began trying to conceive.

Whereas both Martha and Bill dreaded repeating something undesirable about their pasts, Karen's story illustrates that fear of parenthood does not always operate directly from a template of severe childhood deprivation. Even people remembering relatively happy childhoods may panic if they unconsciously feel undeserving of parenthood's rewards.

Whereas Karen's main burden was guilt over her mother no longer being number one to her, other prospective parents may worry that if they have children, they themselves would have to give up being number one. For example, a woman may enjoy being her husband's "baby" and not wish to relinquish that position. Having a real child of her own would place her in the caretaking role and require reorganization of her relationship with her husband.

Sarah, the oldest of eight, had been required from an early age to look after her younger siblings. Her mother, suffering from a medical illness confining her to bed much of the time, rewarded her by frequently exclaiming she could never manage without her. Sarah's father, a hardworking man, was too exhausted when he returned home in the evening to play much with his children.

Although as a young girl Sarah took pride in her precocious role, by the time she was in her early twenties and married, she was glad to be liberated. Never having experienced much attention from either parent, she now enjoyed that of her husband. It felt so good to have someone focus just on her for a change.

By her midthirties, Sarah felt ready to have children. Yet even though she had anticipated this with great pleasure, after childbirth, as her husband doted on their beautiful new daughter, Sarah began to worry he was more in love with their newborn than with her. Sarah became increasingly jealous and needy, as she felt the leading edge of her husband's interest shift temporarily to their daughter. Even though he reassured her he loved her just as much as ever, she felt intensely rejected and feared her marriage would never be the same. As previously unconscious anger about her childhood broke through, she became furious at both her husband and her infant and finally sought counseling for a precipitous fall in self-esteem.

All four of these people, in addition to experiencing activation of anxiety-provoking issues, also suffered from lack of good-enough role models in their same-sex parents. Not only were they feeling overwhelmed by their individual issues, but they also lacked internal guides to whom they could turn.

Activation of such issues and representations, particularly if unanticipated, may result in parenthood being experienced less as a transition than as a transformation. A new mother, for instance, may feel she is a different person—that she has found her true self, her soul, even God. She may not connect her old self with her new. Unable to recall why she loved her spouse or wanted children, she may be at risk for leaving. Acting on current feelings without reference to the past, she may think, "That was then, this is now"; losing track of the coordinates of her desire, she may consummate her immediate needs.

Enter the Transforming Other

In emotional turmoil and chaos, a new parent may seek a transforming other. Bollas (1987) used this term to refer to a person, originally the mother, who is able to alter, soothe, and reintegrate painful self-experience. As Bollas pointed out, not only children, but adults too, may seek transforming others to regulate inner turbulence. Possession of the other as a romantic partner is not the main goal. Rather, the person is sought in order to surrender to a medium that alters the self. Bollas stated, "The intensity with which the transforming other is pursued is not due simply to its being an object of desire, but to it being identified with powerful metamorphoses of being" (p. 17).

Bollas's notion of the transforming other may help explain the peculiar vulnerability of new parents to having affairs. Such extramarital liaisons may be sought, not so much for the experience of a new romantic attachment between equals, as from a desire to transmute emotional turmoil into calm. This demand may be so urgent that these relationships are pursued with great intensity:

> This anticipation of being transformed by an object . . . inspires the subject with a reverential attitude towards it, so that even though the transformation of the self will not take place on the scale it reached during early life, the adult subject tends to nominate such objects as sacred. (pp. 16-17)

While in reality the new partners may not be any more "sacred" than the old, the illusion that they will soothe painful reactivation of old wounds may be irresistible. Bollas's concept explains the desperation with which some new parents throw themselves into extramarital liaisons, even when they had previously felt romantically fulfilled.

Lauren and Pierre: Three Strands of Transformation

Lauren, a thirty-one-year-old computer consultant, separated from her husband Pierre when their daughter was just under twelve months old. They had been married a little over two years.

Lauren met Pierre when she was in her early twenties. In his late twenties at the time, he had already been divorced. Initially troubled by this, Lauren was able to accept it after he explained that his separation had been amicable. After dating for ten months, they were faced with a decision: stay in this country or return to Pierre's homeland, Canada, to complete his education. As there were considerable financial advantages to the latter plan, he urged Lauren to accompany him, and she agreed.

After moving to Canada, their relationship deepened. Loving and considerate, Pierre showed his affection in many ways. Devoted as they were to each other, when the subject of marriage first came up, neither wanted to rush. He hesitated because he had already experienced one failed marriage, while she wanted to make sure they did not repeat his earlier unhappy history. As a result, they continued just to live together for several more years, but as they both wanted children and were in love, eventually they overcame their hesitations and married.

After the wedding, Pierre was eager to become a father. Lauren, however, wished to wait a few months before trying to conceive, as it felt good to have this time for just the two of them. Then about six months later, she felt ready. After succeeding, they both were very pleased.

Within eight weeks, however, Pierre suddenly began taking more business trips. Other changes occurred in his behavior, too. When they ate out at restaurants, Lauren noticed he paid attention to other women in a strange, new way. Although he told friends how thrilled he was about fatherhood, as Lauren's pregnancy progressed, he was less attentive to her—a marked change from his previous manner. Appearing tired and strained, he became irritable and depressed and seemed in emotional turmoil. He admitted he was afraid he might not make a good father.

When Lauren was eight and a half months pregnant, Pierre began to stay out routinely until 2 a.m. She suspected that he had started an affair and thought she knew the other woman who was younger, very pretty, but less educated. Lauren confronted him. He denied it. But she was quite certain it was true.

As over the years Pierre had repeatedly told her how much he loved her, Lauren had felt secure in her marriage. She had thought she could safely entrust him with the ultimate commitment of having a child, binding their genes and lives irreversibly. Discovering that he had changed his mind, that he no longer cared for her but for another woman, was like being punched in the stomach. Lauren's self-esteem collapsed. Near term, she became increasingly depressed. For the first time in her life, she felt suicidal. Praying to God for both her and the baby to die, she was physically unable to sustain labor and delivered by emergency cesarean section.

After their daughter was born, Pierre sent flowers to his girlfriend rather than to his wife. Then he told Lauren the truth: indeed, he had started an affair during the last month of her pregnancy. Unable to function, she wept for days. Due to her doctors' concern, her hospital stay was extended. Confronted with the damage he had wreaked, Pierre seemed genuinely sorrowful. Apologetic, he bought her an expensive Tiffany necklace and swore he would end the affair.

Life was not easy after they returned home. For the first few months, their baby screamed inconsolably; Lauren wondered if her daughter was picking up on her depression. Trying to resolve what had happened, she and Pierre entered couples counseling. In these sessions, he reassured her that his affair had been a passing fling, a reaction to the responsibility of fatherhood, and reiterated that he was committed to their marriage. His girlfriend, he admitted, had helped divert him from anxieties about fatherhood, which had emerged quite unexpectedly after Lauren had become pregnant. Now bonding well with his daughter, he seemed happy again, like his old self. Lauren began to relax. They seemed back on track.

Lauren's story, so far, illustrates two points. First, some expectant fathers, even after greatly desiring children, enter a time of emotional duress. Although I did not interview Pierre so cannot directly report his experience, Lauren believed that he became depressed once she was expecting. In addition, she noticed he seemed very anxious about whether he would make a good father, and this anxiety was out of proportion to his previous doubts.

Second, some fathers, finding themselves in unexpected turmoil after conceiving a child, are vulnerable to having an affair. The new partner may provide a regulatory function by helping to restore emotional equilibrium, which may allow enough healing that the marriage can continue after the affair ends. With Lauren and Pierre, things were not so simple. Let us continue.

Later that year, Lauren and her husband decided to return to the United States, where opportunities for both of them would be greater. Before leaving Canada, they each lined up a job in the Denver area. The flight over was uneventful, as the stewardess doted on their smiling, playful baby. As they were stepping off the plane, however, Pierre announced, "I don't want to be a husband or a father." Lauren looked at him uncomprehendingly.

Over the next weeks it was clear he was serious. Reminding him that it was too late to decide he "didn't want" marriage or parenthood, Lauren promised she would work with him in every conceivable way to help him find happiness in the life and responsibilities he had already chosen.

Although she had tried to be supportive, he did not hear her words in that way. Instead, he bristled at being told what to do. Then he got nasty: Lauren says he turned on her like an animal. Telling her she was ugly and hateful, and furthermore that he disliked their daughter, he threatened to sue her for all her assets (due to an inheritance she had entered the marriage considerably wealthier than he). Trying to stay calm, she urged him to honor his commitments. Instead, he caught a flight to Montreal, explaining that he needed both distance and the opportunity to date other women before deciding if Lauren was the right partner for him.

At the time of our interview four months after separation, Lauren still could not comprehend how, after loving her for so many years, Pierre could have turned on her so cruelly. In fact, much of his personality seems to have changed. He had seemed a considerate, thoughtful man—with a quick temper perhaps, but never nasty. His friends are equally disturbed by the "new Pierre."

For many months after his turning on her, Lauren questioned whether she could have been at fault. Examining and reexamining her marriage, she thought of all the little things she could have done better. So painful was this process that she wished he had actually hit her instead. That, she mused, by contrast, would have been a piece of cake. Knowing that hitting was abuse, she would not have blamed herself. What Pierre did was much worse than physical hurt; she felt he had destroyed her soul.

Lauren related some details of her husband's history. Most notably, when he was in elementary school, his father had died; growing up poor in Nova Scotia and considering himself a misfit, he suffered from depression during adolescence. Later he came to America, where his first marriage ended after three years. Searching for more information, Lauren recently contacted his former wife, who confided that, throughout their relationship, he had been quite emotionally abusive. This was a revelation to Lauren. His first marriage had ended not on the harmonious note he had portrayed but, rather, due to his bullying streak.

Separated only four months, Lauren is feeling single motherhood's stress. Even though Pierre pays the court-ordered amount of child support, to support herself and her baby, she must still work full-time. Child care has been unreliable; she has gone through three nannies already. With little time to herself, she finds it difficult to see her friends.

Nevertheless, Lauren knows she is strong. Long before she ever met Pierre, she survived a difficult childhood. Her mother, suffering from psychiatric illness as well as alcoholism, attempted suicide many times. To preserve her own sanity, Lauren left home when still a teenager. Later her mother succeeded in killing herself.

As traumatic as these events were, Lauren learned she had the power to recover from the loss of any relationship she could mourn. Unfortunately, she is finding it hard to mourn the loss of her husband because he is not really gone: he remains intimately welded to her through their daughter Nicole. Although such reminders are extremely painful to her, not only does Lauren keep pictures of Pierre visible so Nicole will not forget him between visits, but when he does fly in to Denver, she allows him to stay at her apartment, so Nicole does not have to spend nights in a motel room missing her mom. Furthermore, Lauren feels limited in what she can say to Pierre. Although very angry, she needs child support to pay basic expenses. Be honest about her feelings, and he might cut back on the money, she worries. Neither her ongoing connection to Pierre nor this self-imposed muffler on her true feelings help her heal.

But Lauren is determined to survive. Having examined her own role from every conceivable angle, she has concluded that Pierre's personality change was not her fault. Rather, her pregnancy unleashed a dormant abusive character streak, previously witnessed by his first wife. Such discussions with Pierre's former wife have been helpful; in addition, Lauren has received support from numerous friends as well as her father, who has lost some of his former reserve. Above all, what pulls her through is her love for her healthy daughter, opening her fresh eyes upon the world, and now the joy of her life.

Lauren's story illustrates all three strands of transformation: first, the suddenness with which a person can enter emotional turmoil upon expecting a child; second, the power of a transforming other to soothe such turmoil; and, third, the activation of not just issues and representations about parenthood but also previously dormant character defenses, such as emotional abusiveness. The viciousness with which Pierre suddenly turned on Lauren, his suing her for all her assets, his hateful name-calling, his entitlement and lack of responsibility for the great pain he was causing—all were far from the kind, considerate husband she had known. Although Pierre certainly had issues concerning fatherhood, which may have included a fear of failure, as well as painful memories of losing his own father in child-hood, neither of these accounted for the extremely hostile way in which he left his marriage.

Childbirth, accordingly, can activate not just issues or internal rep-resentations but also some old, discarded character defenses for han-dling anxiety, including ones for becoming abusive. To some extent these scripts may be based on actual past interactions, but not always.

Activation of Problems in Character Structure: The Role of Emotional Abuse

Not all transformations at childbirth result from activation of spe-cific fears, issues, or representations. They can also result from a crack along a fault line, revealing long-standing, though previously hidden, problems in character structure. Discarding one's spouse at this time may represent a cruel, sadistic act. Why, we wonder, could the departing spouse not have worked on the marriage, or at least waited for a less vulnerable moment? As suggested in the last chap-ter, not just specific issues but also structural problems—such as in-ability to delay gratification, impulsivity, lacunae in moral structure, or difficulty assessing the best interests of oneself and one's chil-dren—may be involved. In addition, certain character defenses may be revived, which in extreme cases may contribute to sexual, physi-cal, or emotional abuse.

Abuse of all types has made headlines in recent years, but the widespread marital breakdown characteristic of our time has gener-ally been considered more of a reciprocal problem between husband and wife than an enactment of emotional abuse (consider the label "no-fault" divorce). On the one hand, most divorces probably *do* rep-resent a reciprocal problem, a mutual dance in which it took two to tango to an unworkable end—but not all. Some men and women abandoned by their partners actually had little to do with the dissolu-tion of their marriages. Particularly when the departing one's behav-ior was at great odds with previous conduct, when it was triggered by a major life upheaval such as childbirth, or when it occurred at a vul-nerable time when prudence and compassion would ordinarily dic-tate a conservative option may the rejected partner feel more like an unwilling bystander thrown into a boxing ring, rather than part of a poorly dancing duo. Yet because the latter metaphor has dominated both popular and clinical narratives of divorce, some men and women have been entreated to look at what they did wrong rather than recognize, when appropriate, that they were victims of forces beyond their control. Let us make no mistake; unexpected divorce at childbirth is extremely destructive to its recipients. Given a choice, many, such as Lauren, would have even preferred physical mistreatment.

Why do some spouses become more abusive toward their partners at childbirth?

The reasons are complex. Some new parents, perhaps violent for the first time, are later horrified at having reenacted old scripts. Others, unable to feel guilt, express entitlement that their families must adapt. For still others, abuse is about power. Members of the last group are likely to pick their targets, often those who appear weak and unlikely to fight back. Just as needy, neglected children may be at greater risk for sexual abuse, so may a woman's pregnancy place her at increased peril for physical or emotional maltreatment.

This last statement cuts against the grain of what we wish to believe about our culture. A pregnant woman's full figure and vulnerability trigger male protection, we think. Yet these qualities may also increase sadistic tendencies in a few men who, perceiving their wives' dependency and perhaps also jealous of their special status, may now vent their anger unchecked. Whereas earlier in their marriages they might not have dared to unleash their rage, now, as they perceive their wives' increasing vulnerability, this restraint is loosened.

Some such men, fortunately a small number, become more violent during their wives' pregnancies. Others become emotionally abusive and resort to the ultimate hurt: leaving in a rejecting, critical way at a time many women consider the most vulnerable in their lives. Far from taking responsibility for the breakup, such leavers may create a litany of complaints designed to shift blame onto their wounded partners. Perhaps, as we discussed earlier, they are attempting to disavow their own problems by projecting them onto their wives, who are then subjected to the same brutal treatment that these men secretly feel they themselves deserve. It becomes irrelevant that they are destroying the mothers of their children.

Such character problems are not always latent; in fact, they are often quite apparent long before children arrive. Whereas the first year of fatherhood triggered a previously *dormant* abusiveness in Lauren's husband, for other new parents, childbirth simply stresses a troubled character structure already *manifest*. These new parents do not so much experience activation of dormant problems, as encounter new challenges to which they have difficulty accommodating.

The following story portrays a marriage with a long-standing, overt pattern of abuse. This is an example of "model two" divorce at childbirth, in which parenthood is perceived as a stressful transition, not transformation.

MODEL TWO: TRANSITION

Kathy and Jerry: Divorce As One More Hurt

Kathy, a thoughtful, articulate woman in her midthirties, separated from Jerry after three years of marriage, when their daughter was six months old. Our interview took place three and a half years later.

After growing up in a small town in Texas, Kathy and Jerry had dated for two years before deciding to marry. Although Jerry sporadically abused alcohol, they had gotten along well before the wedding, and Kathy had hoped that marriage would give him the stability he needed to stop drinking. Shortly after the wedding, however, more problems developed. For the first time, he became physically abusive. In rages he began to raise his fists and throw things at his wife. At first she thought his behavior would improve, but finally realizing she could not help him, she decided to leave.

Kathy's plans were interrupted when she became unexpectedly pregnant. An abortion was against her religious principles, and now frightened of being a single mother, she began to question her decision to leave. Family assistance was not available, nor was she sufficiently financially secure to support herself and a baby. Desperate, she decided to stay with her husband, hoping that fatherhood might motivate him to change.

Unfortunately, during her pregnancy his abuse markedly escalated. Telling her she was fat and ugly, four nights out of seven he came home loud and drunk, awakening her and demanding she stay up with him, depriving her of sleep while she listened to his problems. Nor did he return the favor. When she woke up in the middle of the night with labor pains, he called her a "bitch" for bothering him, rolled over, and went back to sleep. Their daughter's birth did not soften his behavior either. Shortly thereafter he allegedly put his fist through a door; another time he threw a bottle at her while she was holding the baby; when the baby cried, he shook her. Finally, telling Kathy she was impossible to live with, he moved out, having already begun an affair.

After separating, Kathy complied with the court-ordered recommendations for Jerry's visits and made every effort to make sure they occurred. Soon after the divorce papers were signed, however, her daughter started showing signs of distress. She returned from visits crying, saying she did not want to go back to her father's. Seeking the advice of a neutral party, Kathy agreed to have a *guardian ad lidum* (GAL) appointed, who, after hearing all sides of the story, ordered more, not less, visitation—presumably to help the young girl acclimate to separations from her mother. After this occurred, Kathy's daughter became even more distressed. Appearing dissociated, she allegedly began to relate episodes of her father's inappropriate sexual contact.

With these concerns, Kathy and her lawyer went back to court in Texas. Arguing that his ex-wife was putting false ideas in their daughter's head in order to block visitation, Jerry denied the allegations. Siding with him, the judge awarded him temporary sole physical custody. Greatly distraught, Kathy was forced to hand over her daughter. After the order was reversed a few days later, she regained physical custody, but only on the condition that she both allow visitation and terminate her daughter's current counseling sessions. In fact, she was ordered not to take her daughter to any abuse-related evaluation, counseling, or medical checkup. Her lawyer's request for an independent evaluation was also denied.

Months passed. According to Kathy, her daughter returned from visits hitting herself, biting herself, and trying to put her hands up her vagina. Sometimes in the middle of the night she would scream, "I'm not safe." A new GAL was enlisted. While awaiting the report, Kathy returned to court numerous times, but to no avail.

Finally, a different judge hearing the case ordered an independent sexual abuse evaluation, which eventually substantiated abuse had quite likely occurred. As a result, Jerry was allowed only supervised visitation. By then their daughter was over three.

Since then, Kathy has continued to support Jerry's visitation as long as it is supervised. Even though she believes he was guilty of sexual abuse, she knows her daughter misses him. As long as it can be done safely, Kathy feels her daughter needs to see him, both to sustain a relationship with him and to avoid receiving the message that if she tells the truth, she will lose someone she loves.

Within a few months of her husband's leaving, Kathy was fortunate to meet a new man; several years later, she is now remarried. Trying to understand Jerry's behavior, she wonders if her new happiness might have triggered his rage. She also wonders if it might have triggered his fears that her new partner would outshine him as a father. Perhaps that is why he sexually abused her daughter, she thinks—to create something "special" in their relationship that could not be shared.

Kathy's strengths include not only her ability to take an intellectual interest in her trauma (subsequently, she read widely on the subject) but also her being an attractive, intelligent woman who was able to quickly find a new, loving relationship. Her current husband is very supportive and, unlike Jerry, neither alcoholic nor violent. She credits him with a large part of her psychological survival.

At this point, happy in her second marriage, she is hoping for another child and is looking forward to the next chapter of her life. Although she can neither forget nor forgive the harm she believes Jerry caused her and her daughter, for the divorce itself she no longer bears bitterness—only relief.

Kathy's story illustrates a frequent occurrence in divorces involving young children: accusations of sexual abuse. Because we heard only her side, we cannot judge whether the abuse actually did occur. In fact, many people with much more information had different assessments of the truth. The point of her story, for us, is that Kathy, while greatly concerned for her daughter, could not easily prove or disprove her fears. Caught in the no-man's-land of unamicable separation, the trust between parents becomes tangled barbed wire.

Kathy and her husband did not experience sudden activation of dormant issues or character traits. Rather, their marital problems, already severe, simply escalated. Unlike Pierre, who in the previous story seemed to undergo a sudden negative transformation, Jerry clearly exhibited abusive tendencies before his wife conceived. Afterward, he showed more of the same, only worse; the changes were quantitative, not qualitative. Model two, difficult transition to parenthood as a paradigm of additive stress, applies here.

In contrast to model one, model two involves an escalating continuum of stress, not sudden quantum leaps. As a result, such divorces are more predictable. They evolve out of marriages for which we would have had a sense, ahead of time, that a baby would overstrain the relationship. They obey the laws of statistics, the laws of linear addition of probability. They are divorce as we usually know it.

Kathy's story reveals one frequent theme in model two divorces— a continuation of a pattern of abuse—but many other factors may contribute. Long-standing marital conflict, poor communication, and lack of spousal intimacy are just a few of the relevant parent variables; premature delivery, perinatal medical problems, or colicky temperament represent some infant ones that can add up to overwhelm coping capacity. Parents' overall support systems, including spouse, family, friends, work, and community, are important too, since how difficult a transition new parents make may partly depend on how they are psychologically "held" by their partners, family, and friends. Other factors include economic pressures as well as difficulty giving up a pursuit, such as drug addiction or excessive gambling, or even choice of a career, that mixes poorly with family life.

Gradual escalation of any of these dysfunctions, including ones that had been previously tolerated, may propel the other partner to leave once a child is born. Although Kathy did not feel empowered to leave her marriage, some women in her frightening situation do find the courage to separate. If a mother perceives her child to be physically at risk as a result of the father's behavior, and if it appears unlikely he can change, her only reasonable course may be to depart. At this point, she has responded not just to an additive continuum of stress but to her own internal transformation. What was tolerable for her is not so for her baby.

Now let us turn to a story that reminds us that, in practice, many divorces at childbirth are explained by a combined model: not only is a pattern of escalating stress present, but one partner also internally transforms.

COMBINED MODEL:
ADDITIVE STRESS PLUS TRANSFORMATION

Mary: Transformation Toward Parenthood

Mary, a thirty-year-old professional photographer, separated after two and a half years of marriage, while pregnant with her second child. Our interview took place one year later.

After graduating from college, Mary lived in a small suburb of Cincinnati, where she was introduced to Dan by her neighbors. She was attracted to him through their mutual interest in country music, as well as by how nicely he related to a son he had conceived out of wedlock. Dan seemed like such a kind, generous father, and the little boy just sparkled with fun. Although Dan's relationship with his former girlfriend had lasted only a few weeks (the boy's mother had allegedly been addicted to drugs and had a very difficult temperament), Mary heard horror stories of countless court involvements, culminating in a sad paucity of visitation for Dan. Mary felt sorry for him. He seemed like a decent person, potentially a great father for her own children.

Early in the relationship, however, Mary became aware that Dan himself had a drug problem. Initially she noticed he drank heavily and smoked pot. As alcohol had been a part of her own college culture, she was not immediately alarmed; she thought he would grow out of it. He did not. In fact, she herself began to drink more to keep up with him. Mary also learned that Dan used cocaine, about which, in contrast to alcohol, she knew very little. Having been sheltered from the realities of hard drugs, and with little idea of the devastation cocaine could bring to her life, she did not worry about these issues when he proposed marriage. In spite of his problems, they had a special emotional connection, and she felt she had truly met her soul mate. Engaged a few months after meeting, they married a year later.

A few weeks after her wedding, Mary became pregnant. At that point, she stopped drinking to protect her baby. Dan, on the other hand, began escalating his use of both cocaine and alcohol. Unable to face the devastating reality that he was addicted and impaired, instead she denied the seriousness of their situation, as she could not bear the catastrophic consequences for her life. By now the stakes were too high.

Mary gave birth and, after three months maternity leave, returned to full-time work. Dan, on the other hand, began to work more sporadically. For the first time, he pressured her to do cocaine with him. She had two choices: either confront him and face the possible end of her marriage or tolerate his use. Increasingly socially isolated and feeling under enormous pressure, she acquiesced. Hoping that by sharing his lifestyle she could avoid losing him, initially she found that cocaine seemed to improve their relationship, for when they were both high they were in good moods and made conversation easily.

This improvement was short-lived. Dan, now intoxicated most of the time, began to spend his entire paycheck on cocaine. He also began using while his six-year-old son visited. "He's just a kid," he told Mary. "He doesn't know the difference."

As Dan's use spiraled out of control, Mary confronted him. "Don't give me an ultimatum," he barked. "I don't do cocaine that much." Sensing his anger, she backed down. Even though in her heart she knew it was wrong, she was too afraid of losing Dan to stand her ground. She continued to use with him, and although her habit was much less, she too began to experience cocaine highs and lows. Panicked that she was becoming addicted, Mary once again attempted to talk to Dan. Attempting to stay calm, she told him they had a serious problem. "No, we don't," he responded, refusing to talk further.

About this time Mary's family intervened. Advising her either to insist Dan get treatment or to leave him, her brother offered to help support her during the transition. Her parents also offered her refuge in their home. Mary was not sure that she wanted to take them up on this, but one weekend when Dan left unannounced for the Caribbean for a few days, she decided to spend the weekend with her parents, bringing her son, Sam, along. When Dan returned, not only was he unreceptive to getting treatment, but he was enraged she had dared leave. Fearing he might become violent, Mary stayed with her parents, thankful for their support and shelter. As Sam missed his father, Mary urged him to visit. After all, she still was not planning on this being a permanent separation; as soon as Dan got over his anger, she hoped to be able to return home.

A few weeks after moving out, Mary was surprised to discover she was pregnant. Remembering she had been intimate with Dan during the weeks before she left, she was also frightened; still using cocaine and alcohol at that time, she had exposed her baby. Immediately, she saw her obstetrician, who suggested she have drug tests at every visit. These all came back negative, as she devoted herself to staying off drugs and alcohol, and to getting her life back in order.

When she initially took refuge at her parents, Mary had not definitely decided to leave Dan. In fact, she was still hoping, slim as the chance seemed, their marriage could be saved. When she discovered she was pregnant, however, she changed her mind. Until then she had been willing to tolerate his drug abuse to avoid the trauma of divorce, but now something in her shifted: she just could not tolerate raising yet another child under these conditions. Indeed, Dan posed a real danger, for at this point he was constantly intoxicated. In one last attempt to keep her family intact, Mary composed a list of things he needed to do, including starting treatment for drug addiction, establishing a savings account, and having some long-term goals. He never responded.

Instead, he just took down all her pictures and told his son, "Mary's gone." Although Dan continued to have both of his children visit, he never explained to Alex why his stepmother and half brother had moved out. Perhaps as a result, Alex began to develop behavior problems at school, but because Dan never told

Alex's teachers or mother about his own change in marital status, they did not have a clue what was wrong. Devastatingly, when Alex began to complain that he missed Mary, Dan became irritated by such questions and abruptly cut off contact with his son. After Mary gave birth a second time, she reflected on her husband's inability to quit drugs as well as his destructive treatment of Alex. Certain she could not continue her marriage, she filed for divorce.

Mary revealed a bit about her background. Growing up in a stable, middle-class family outside of Cincinnati, she had had a happy childhood. Her parents, while very supportive, had also been somewhat strict and sheltering.

Mary also revealed her impression of her husband's family. Dan, she believed, had always clashed with his father. In addition, Dan had grown up poorly supervised. When he was only fourteen, his parents gave him a basement room that functioned as an independent apartment where, unnoticed, he began to smoke pot heavily. Mary thinks that his lack of a paternal role model, as well as his premature independence, contributed to his later difficulties.

By contrast, Mary feels fortunate with her parents. Supportive emotionally, they are also providing her with a place to stay, and her mother quit her own job to baby-sit full-time, so that Mary can continue to work. With less than $400 a month in child support, without her parents' help, she does not believe she could remain off welfare.

Determined to stay sober, Mary realizes in retrospect that her judgment about Dan was seriously impaired, partly because of her naïveté, partly because she wanted to believe everything was fine when it was not, but mostly because she herself was drinking during much of their relationship. If she could have addressed this earlier, she could have avoided marrying Dan. Nevertheless, she takes responsibility for her choices and holds no bitterness toward him. She hopes he can eventually recover and, if so, play an important role in their children's lives.

Dan was a partner for her in her early twenties when they were both still partying, but her second pregnancy signified a fork in this road. While for Dan it triggered increasing anger and even more alcohol and drugs, for her it transformed her vision, which, as it cleared, revealed she could not safely raise a child with him. In spite of its hardships, she feels she "grew up" during her second pregnancy and made the right decision for herself and her children.

Mary's case illustrates the problems that couples with long-standing patterns of alcoholism and drug abuse have when confronted with the challenges of parenthood. As Mary and Dan were already dealing with chronic addiction, loss of judgment, social isolation, frequent job changes, and financial problems, is it any wonder they could not raise children together? Such marriages, already suffering much erosion, are not strong enough to withstand the further upheavals of childbirth.

Before we attribute her divorce entirely to the additive stress model, however, let us note that Mary actually transformed, quite dramatically, during her second pregnancy. Previously partying along with her husband, now she responded to the life within her with a new sense of responsibility. With the support of her family, she was able to give Dan an ultimatum, long overdue, but not previously in her repertoire. What had been good enough for her was no longer good enough for her child.

Mary, similar to several other women in this book, transformed in a direction toward parenthood. Had she not been pregnant, she might have returned, as she had originally intended, to live with her husband, continuing a destructive lifestyle. Under the influence of her second pregnancy, however, as she contemplated raising yet another child with Dan, her fuse for tolerating his behavior blew. With a growing life inside, she was able to reaccess older, healthier parts of her personality, including happier memories of her own, more protected childhood. For the first time, she was able to envision her maternal ideal. For people such as Mary, childbirth transforms in a positive direction. Divorce, under these conditions, is not so much an end of hope, as its beginning.

SUMMARY

Becoming a parent is a state change. One moment we are responsible primarily for ourselves; the next we are bound inextricably to another human being, whose presence we can hardly imagine was once lacking. As with every state change, at the boundary lies turbulence or even chaos until a new equilibrium is reached. When the alchemy is finished, we are no longer quite the same. Usually our old and new selves are sufficiently similar to ensure a sense of continuity, but sometimes radical changes occur.

In the first model of divorce at childbirth, parents exhibit major psychological transformations. On the one hand, these may be caused by sudden activation of troubling issues or representations that, no longer dormant, now raise anxiety to escape velocity, or, as we saw in Pierre's case, old character defenses may be revitalized, quickly deteriorating a marriage. On the other hand, parents may transform in a direction toward taking good care of their children and, in the process, come to a painful realization that their marriages must end. In either case, such divorces may have been difficult to foresee.

In the second model, stresses on parents add linearly to overwhelm coping capacity. Already marred by alcoholism and a chronic pattern of physical and emotional abuse, Kathy and Jerry's marriage, for example, was unable to accommodate a baby—not because either parent dramatically changed, but because a baby could not fit into their already damaged relationship. This is divorce at childbirth as we usually think of it.

In practice, many divorces at childbirth, such as Mary and Dan's, involve both models. Not only is there a pattern of escalating stress and dysfunction, but one partner also transforms, abruptly leaving the marriage.

I would like to make two further points.

First, few of the couples in my study arrived mutually at the decision to separate. More often, one of the partners quite suddenly, unilaterally, wanted out. Divorce at childbirth, in my sample, was seldom a two-person choice.

Second, unlike Mary, many exiting partners did not give credible explanations for their departures. A certain degree of self-deception seemed to occur, with some "leavers" rewriting the history of their marriages to give their actions a slant useful in supporting internal defenses. For example, several husbands suffering from severe alcoholism neglected to mention their drinking as one reason their marriages ended. In denial about the severity of their addictions, perhaps they resorted to pseudoexplanations to give their exits an illusion of coherence.

Because of these two factors, divorce at childbirth is an unusually traumatic type of divorce. Mothers, coping with postpartum physiological changes as well as the demands of infant care, may feel particularly betrayed at this time; fathers so left may appropriately feel terror that they have lost not only their wives but also, in many cases, the opportunity to live with their children. As a result, divorce at childbirth may unleash powerful animosity between former partners, one of whom feels terribly betrayed, the other entitled to wave freedom's banner. In the middle, of course, is the baby.

So let us turn, in the next section, to the effects of such divorces. How do newly separated parents cope with the demands of infant care, and under what conditions might divorce at this time represent a positive decision—hope's beginning?

PART II:
EFFECTS OF DIVORCE
AT CHILDBIRTH

We began the last section with Amy's story. Only eleven months had passed since she had separated from her husband. She was still in emotional shock, trying to understand why Bill, with whom she had thought she had a good marriage, suddenly left. Although she had made much progress dealing with the practicalities of her untimely divorce, and although she had begun to understand that Bill had kept many aspects of himself hidden, she continued to struggle with a profound loss of self-esteem as well as rage. How, we wonder, do mothers such as Amy and their children fare over time? How do fathers such as Bill, no longer living at home, form attachments with infants from whose mothers they are severely estranged?

Perhaps Amy will be able to forgive Bill enough to coparent with him, and perhaps Bill will work through his problems sufficiently to make an adequate father. Given the initial circumstances of their divorce, however, we wonder what emotional alchemy will be necessary to turn their animosity into such gold.

To address this question, in Chapter 4, I will review the psychological effects of divorce on adults, examining how spouses cope with its initial turmoil as well as its aftershocks. To highlight differences that I believe are critical to the quality of recovery, I will compare reactions of grief to those of trauma.

Although the focus of Part II is on psychological effects of divorce, because they are so intimately linked with financial ones, in Chapter 5, I will review the latter. Although affecting all family members, economic sequelae are particularly devastating to women and children, for whom divorce often makes real gold vanish—an event particularly poignant when occurring at childbirth.

Finally, in Chapters 6 and 7, I turn to the effect of divorce on children. How do older children recover from divorce, and how might we extrapolate these findings to infants? Although little research has considered the last question, I believe that the field of infant development provides some clues.

Chapter 4

Psychological Effects of Divorce at Childbirth: How Do Parents Cope Emotionally?

Rupturing the bonds of biology as well as social custom, divorce at childbirth has profound effects on parents, children, and society. In this chapter, we will focus on how parents emotionally traverse this event. Examining both short-term and long-term effects, we will attempt to answer the question, How do parents psychologically recover—or not—from divorce under such extreme conditions? Because research on the effects of divorce, particularly those at childbirth, has not caught up in scale to the social reality, we will also review older data on how people mourn and heal from a partner's death. This synopsis will not only inform our understanding of recovery from divorce but also provide a contrast, for although death and divorce have similarities, they also have differences—differences in their processes of mourning.

INITIAL EFFECTS OF DIVORCE: ACTIVATION OF THE ATTACHMENT SYSTEM

Many couples in my study exhibited heightened attachment behavior during the divorce process. Thomas, as we saw in Chapter 2, continued to entreat his wife to return, even though she gave him little cause for hope. His pleading, which annoyed her and pushed her even further away, seemed counterproductive. Advising him to "let her go," his friends may have speculated that he was too needy, even masochistic, yet many people similar to Thomas find that divorce activates intense yearning for the other partner. Just when such feelings should logically be fading, they may suddenly bloom, paradoxically, out of season.

Although after a lengthy separation Thomas was able to reunite with his wife, others in my study who experienced intense yearning were not so fortunate. Some, in fact, remained emotionally stuck for years, longing for their spouses' returns. Why do some people have difficulty letting go, even when it is clear their marriages are over? There are many possible explanations—some practical or economic, others reflecting a partner's unique psychological history—but one prism through which to view this behavior is that of attachment theory, which helps organize these multiple factors. Thomas's reaction, typical of those confronted with sudden, unexpected rejection by a loved partner, was quite understandable from this perspective.

Attachment theory, developed in the 1950s and 1960s by Bowlby (1969, 1973) and his followers, described from an evolutionary viewpoint the way humans form lasting interpersonal bonds. All children, according to this theory, are thought to be endowed with universal, inherited, and biologically mediated mechanisms, both for forming close attachments and for dealing with their disruption. Children separated from their primary caretakers, accordingly, show three phases of adjustment: an initial one of protest, characterized by hyperarousal, searching, and agitation; a second one of withdrawal and relative immobility; and a third one, if child and caretaker are not reunited, of hopelessness, depression, and despair. These reactions serve at least two purposes. First and foremost, they function as an attempt to secure the caregiver's return. Second, they help the child conserve energy if such return is not forthcoming, saving valuable resources until the arrival of a substitute figure. Although initially exploring the bond between parent and child, attachment theorists later extended their findings to adult relationships, including marriage.

One of the most pronounced immediate emotional effects of divorce involves the psychological and physiological sequelae of breaking an attachment bond. In his classic book *Marital Separation,* Weiss (1975) described his interviews with numerous men and women in the process of divorce. His discovery: far from fading as childhood is left behind, the attachment system remains active in adulthood, particularly between marriage partners. Even after becoming disillusioned with a spouse and deciding to divorce, a person may find that actually taking this step is extremely difficult because dissolving this union leads to the same initial symptoms that children exhibit if separated from their caretakers for too long—severe physiological hyperarousal, agitation, and intense longing for the lost one. Weiss discovered a similar reaction between adults who lost a spouse through divorce and children who lost a parent to death.

Fortunately, for most adults in secure marriages, their attachment systems function quietly in the background. Just as children who count on a parent's presence feel safe to explore their worlds, so may adults in healthy love relationships feel free to pursue their separate interests. Although initially while falling in love, they may experience a type of obsession with each other, characterized by intense yearning, neediness, and an inability to attend to the rest of their lives, if their relationships become secure, these feelings will likely recede. Brief absences, whether physical or emotional, can then be easily tolerated. On the other hand, just as the child whose parent is preoccupied may become more attention-seeking, so may the adult whose partner is perceived unreliable yearn, increasingly demandingly, for a closeness that always eludes. Even slight absences may become difficult to tolerate, fueling anger and frustration until the relationship is strained.

When a couple decides to divorce, each of their attachment systems, which may have operated quietly in the past during more secure periods of the relationship, is activated. Both partners may feel panicked and experience separation anxiety in all its force. A departing husband, for example, may be surprised by his anxious yearning for his wife, even though when married he dreaded coming home and went out of his way to avoid her. Conversely, if his wife is the one leaving, he may desperately plead her to return, even though she may be treating him quite cruelly. If his friends ask, "Why do you want her if she doesn't love you anymore?" he can answer that millions of years of evolution are at work, for according to attachment theory, it is entirely normal to cling, even desperately, to a departing spouse. Far from a sign of weakness, it is the reponse of a normal brain. Rather than labeling such behavior as aberrant, we need to recognize that during separation and divorce, both spouses, but particularly one left unexpectedly or under vulnerable circumstances, may experience marked separation distress.

These remarks, which apply to divorce in general, apply even more strongly to divorce at childbirth. When could the bond designed by nature to hold partners together be tighter, or the results of breaking it more devastating? Modern evolutionary biology, while allowing for dual mating strategies for both sexes, also acknowledges the advantage to children if they profit from both parents' full investments. Consequently, even adults favoring promiscuous mating strategies may be acting against their own genetic interests if they abandon offspring too early. New parents have a strong biological tie to each other, a tie designed by nature to prevent abrupt departures during this sensitive period of infant development. During the latter part of the twentieth century, when we are seeing that tie unknotted on an unprecedented scale, many parents are in a state of emotional crisis. What happens when their partners do not return?

We know that if a child's primary caretaker does not return, the results are usually devastating. Should not healthy adults have more resiliency and be able to grieve the loss of their loved ones, eventually moving on to enjoy life and fully engage in new, satisfying relationships?

BELLA: HOPE'S CAPTIVE

Bella, an intelligent, well-educated, but currently unemployed mother in her midforties, separated from her husband at the time their son Aaron, now four years old, was born.

When Bella first met Jacques, she was impressed by his intellect (he held several higher degrees) and sophistication. They fell in love and were married the same year. Initially their marriage was happy but volatile, as his frequent travel, both for business and for visiting family abroad, was hard at times on Bella. Overall, however, she thought they had a good marriage. Although she missed him during his trips, she adjusted to them well, knowing he always returned glad to see her.

Although Jacques had never wanted children, after several years of marriage Bella accidentally became pregnant. Not wanting to upset him, she made the decision on her own to have an abortion. When he later found out, he was angry he had not been included in the decision process but relieved not to have fatherhood's responsibility.

Bella's abortion was emotionally traumatic, so she was careful not to become pregnant again. Once in her forties, however, she thought she was no longer fertile, as she believed she was in early menopause. When she unexpectedly became pregnant a second time, Jacques reacted just as before: he really did not want children. Nevertheless, he did not advise her to get an abortion. In fact, knowing how traumatic the last one had been for her, he told her he would support whatever decision she made. This time Bella knew she very much wanted to keep her baby—so much so that she thought she could tolerate her husband's ambivalence. After all, he had assured her he would remain committed to their marriage.

Unfortunately, Bella developed serious medical problems during her pregnancy. Starting at eight months, she was confined to bed rest. Jacques, who until then had been more supportive and even anticipating fatherhood with some excitement, then abruptly went abroad, ostensibly on a business trip. As her two months of bed rest dragged on, Bella craved her husband's presence. If only he were there to hold her hand, she felt, everything would be okay. But he stayed away.

Aaron, born after a difficult delivery, was a beautiful, wide-eyed baby. One day later, however, he was rushed to emergency surgery with a life-threatening congenital condition. After weeks of intensive care, he was sufficiently well to return home. His father was still absent.

With no other available help, Bella was forced to move in with her parents. As she did not enjoy a good relationship with them, she hoped this solution would be only temporary; after all, she just could not believe that Jacques was not returning. Gradually this reality dawned on her, and, increasingly distraught, sometimes she was not sure who was in more distress, she or her baby. Barely able to eat or sleep, she spent her days pacing the floors, awaiting some word from Jacques. Even when she was able to fall asleep, she would often be awakened with a sensation of an alarm going off inside her body. Then Aaron needed more surgery. Living at the hospital, trying to breast-feed, Bella became overwhelmed.

Months later, Jacques had neither returned nor given any hint he would do so. Bella took the advice of friends and family and reluctantly filed for divorce, requesting sole physical and legal custody. One week later Jacques showed up, wanting to return and be a father. Any woman can bring up a child, he said, but fathering is more special.

Once home it became clear he was not going to stay; in fact, he already had planned an extensive foreign itinerary. After he left again, the case went to trial, as he now, surprisingly, wanted sole custody of his son. According to Bella, the trial was brutal. Jacques' lawyer brought up Bella's history of childhood sexual abuse, arguing that this previous trauma would impair her mothering skills, which actually were being tested, as not only did she have to contend with the jury trial, but she also had an ill, one-year-old son she was trying to nurture on her own. Her husband, furthermore, had sent no child support. A welfare check of $405 a month was her total income.

The judge awarded Bella sole legal and physical custody, with Jacques' visitation to be supervised, out of concern that he might try to kidnap his son.

After the trial, Jacques disappeared. He surfaced several years later, with a sudden desire to take his son to Disney World. Bella refused. When Jacques took his request to court, he had an unpleasant surprise: the judge incarcerated him for not paying child support. Even this had little effect. Since his release, Bella has received only sporadic payments, rarely even the meager $200 a month he owes.

Four years later, Bella is trying to reorganize her life, but this is not easy. Although she would like to return to work (previously she worked in a research field that provided a moderate income), now she cannot afford a baby-sitter even to look for a job. She doubts she could find much at her income level that would allow her to pay for child care, anyway. Her parents are helping as much as they can, but they do not have much money to spare. One solution would be for her to meet another man; with this in mind, she joined a singles' group. So far she has had no luck. In her midforties, she is tired, poor, and feels older than her age; she can neither afford to color her graying hair nor pay a dentist to replace a missing tooth. Having lost her youthfulness, on welfare with a young child, she does not feel very competitive in the singles scene. Even friends are hard to keep. Before the divorce, she had a wide circle of married friends, but since she and Jacques separated, social invitations have dwindled. As she struggles to make new connections, hardest for her is hearing Aaron ask for a new daddy, whom she knows she may not be able to find.

She tries to draw on her strengths, which she identifies as religion and her relationship with her son. A practicing Christian, she says she could never get through this without her faith; perhaps, she thinks, her life is all part of a plan. Her other strength is that she loves motherhood. Aaron, now healthy, full of personality, and very bright, is a great gift.

Nonetheless, even four years after separating, Bella still craves reuniting with her husband. She knows he did not treat her well; not only did he abandon her at a most vulnerable moment, but he behaved cruelly during the divorce. She certainly tries to forget about him, yet often a minor event, such as seeing an intact family taking a Sunday walk together, triggers her missing him, and, of course, the major reminder is her son, Aaron. Such reminders, large and small, sewn into the fabric of her daily life, give her little peace. Remembering the good, she feels reuniting with Jacques might be better for both her and her son. Many years after divorce seemed to close the book on her marriage, Bella continues to yearn for her husband's return—not simply because life would be easier, but because her attachment bond, superficially severed by legal decree, cannot so easily be severed in her heart.

Bella's story illustrates how one's attachment system may become activated during divorce. Earlier in her marriage Bella had felt relatively secure with Jacques; knowing he always returned from his travels, she had been able to tolerate his frequent absences. Once she became aware he might not return, however, she developed symptoms similar to those explicated by Bowlby (1963) and Weiss (1975)—intense yearning, physiologic hyperarousal, and agitation. Nor were her symptoms short-lived. Long after it was clear Jacques was not interested in renewing the marriage, she had difficulty letting go. She remained her hope's captive, frozen in time.

Besides illustrating activation of her attachment system, Bella's story also reveals a painful fact: time does not necessarily heal divorce's wounds. Years after the final decree, many people, similar to Bella, still yearn for their former partners. Sometimes their reasons are more practical than not, as harsh economic and social realities set in for those less than fortunate in finances or opportunities for youthful second chances. Yet practical considerations are not the only factors. Many people have trouble healing due to internal difficulty processing their divorces. Bella, for example, never finished grieving the loss of her husband. Perhaps because his disappearance at childbirth was so hurtful, she could not forgive him enough to grieve; perhaps because his ongoing presence in the form of persistent legal struggles prevented her from acquiring enough distance, she could not proceed with mourning; whatever the cause, the result was that she could not climb down, even years later, the ladder of her hope. Emotionally, she remained trapped in the burning building of her divorce. How can we better understand the difficulties people such as Bella have grieving their losses? A review of some literature is in order, but with one caveat: it is largely based on loss due to death, not divorce.

GRIEFS TERMINABLE AND INTERMINABLE

Because divorce has only recently become widespread, our understanding of how people grieve and recover from it is still incomplete. We do understand somewhat more fully how people grieve a death. Discerning the ancient roots of this knowledge, Brahms, in writing his *German Requiem,* chose a biblical text ("Blessed are they that mourn, for they shall be comforted") to express not only religion's comfort but also the restoring function of mourning itself. Yet mourning does not always freely proceed. There are sorrows that do not melt into the new day's enterprise, griefs that cannot be relinquished.

The Deep Structure of Grief: Freud and Klein

In "Mourning and Melancholia," Freud (1915), making a link between pathological mourning and subsequent depression, was one of the first to address the deep structure of grief. According to his view, when we lose people we love, we withdraw energy we had invested in those relationships, liberating it for new attachments. To prevent the shock of too rapid a divestment, as an intermediary step we may internalize aspects of the deceased in an effort not to "lose" them. After experiencing death of our loved ones, for example, we commonly assume some of their characteristics. A mother who lost a daughter may begin to wear her daughter's clothes or jewelry, change her hairstyle to a similar one, or develop congruent interests. Such identifications are considered part of normal grief.

The problem, according to Freud, arises if the relationship has been marked by considerable ambivalence. In this case, the bereaved has two choices: either avoid mourning or internalize aspects of a person partially loved, partially hated—thereby identifying not just with the good but also with the bad. In the most extreme case, angry recriminations formerly directed toward the deceased are now directed internally. On the one hand, proceeding with this process may eventually lead to severe depression, but on the other, avoiding it may mean bypassing its potential to heal; such, for Freud, was the Sophie's choice of mourning a highly ambivalent love.

Similar to Freud, Melanie Klein also directed her attention to the role of mourning, but unlike Freud, she focused on its role in childhood. Basing her theory on what she believed to be the prototypic loss, that of the mother's breast during weaning, she developed the concept of the "depressive position," in which the infant both mourns the loss of the breast but also feels guilty that his own greedy, destructive impulses caused his mother to withdraw (Klein, 1935). Far from considering this guilt pathological, Klein considered it to represent a healthy developmental achievement, the recognition that one's inevitable aggression, coming from within, has consequences for others. When all goes well, the infant's relationship with his mother remains sufficiently good to reassure him he has not destroyed her, and his guilt is assuaged. Because the child's first major loss is linked to the development of aggressive biting impulses, Klein thought that the vicissitudes of weaning create a template for later associations between loss and guilt.

Klein did not limit her study to children. She also observed that, throughout life, guilt is an inextricable part of mourning. When an adult loses a loved one, Klein (1940) believed, fears may be activated that previously unconscious hostile or "triumph" fantasies, which may have been present before the loss even if the relationship had been quite loving, have magically prevailed. Although these feelings usually remain largely unconscious, survivors may also be aware of disturbing, discordant thoughts, such as, "I'm glad it was him and not I who was killed in the accident," or "Now I don't have to deal with her nagging," along with more usual expressions of acute grief. To assuage guilt accompanying such hostile thoughts, which Klein believed are almost universally present, the bereaved must have sufficiently good memories to maintain a sense of the departed as benevolent, not retaliatory. Just as they originally needed to have had good-enough relationships with their mothers to survive the development of the biting instinct, so do they need to have had good-enough relationships with their lost adult partners for hostile fantasies not to engender enormous guilt and depression. They must know that they would have been forgiven.

Klein (1940) knew how important it is to be able to idealize our lost ones, as these feelings bring much relief and reassurance. Although she was well aware of the difficulties in grieving an ambivalent love, she nevertheless believed that in successful mourning, "hatred has receded and love is freed" (1940, p. 140). If hatred gets the upper hand, however, pathological mourning ensues; threatened by the fantasy of a menacing, retaliatory inner object, the survivor feels overwhelmed by guilt. Neither does avoiding mourning offer a way out. For those who fail to grieve, Klein believed the result will be emotional constriction and impoverishment.

Both Freud (1915) and Klein (1935, 1940) developed models of the deep structure of mourning. While Freud emphasized the role of internalizing the lost object, Klein emphasized that of unconscious guilt. While Freud recognized the dangers of anger turned inward, Klein recognized those of destructive fantasy. Both clinicians addressed problems in grieving an ambivalent love, and throughout their writings ran one clear theme: the difficulty mourning a person toward whom one harbored considerable hostility.

Freud's (1915) and Klein's (1940) most important insight, for our purposes, was that it is especially the loss of troubled relationships that leads to difficulty with mourning. This is, of course, exactly the problem in extreme-condition divorce. When one spouse leaves suddenly, at a vulnerable time, forcing divorce unilaterally or in a demeaning, cruel way, then the rejected spouse has a Herculean task indeed: he or she must contend with mourning the loss of a partner, previously loved, who has inflicted not just loss but trauma. The usual manner of grieving—to recollect positive aspects of the deceased, internalize them, and then gradually emotionally divest—seems blocked for survivors of such traumatic divorce, as it may be just too difficult to reconcile loving memories with the exiting spouse's present behavior.

Divorcing partners may have difficulty with any part of this process. Bella, for example, was able to recall many loving moments from her marriage but then was unable to let go, perhaps because in doing so she might have had to recognize the full force of her husband's cruelty. Unlike Bella, many of those I interviewed could no longer access any positive feelings toward their former mates. Although intellectually they knew they had once loved their husbands, such memories were no longer availabale to them. It was often unbearable to remember a partner's previous love, after it viciously turned; mourning in the traditional sense could not precede.

Behavioral Descriptions: Lindemann and Bowlby

While Freud (1915) and Klein (1935, 1940) elaborated the deep structure of grief, Lindemann (1944) turned toward a behavioral understanding of reactions to acute loss. Interviewing over 100 subjects (including bereaved disaster victims of the Coconut Grove Fire, relatives of armed forces killed during World War II, and relatives of patients who had died in the hospital from medical illnesses), he vividly described the survivor's initial torment. Although Lindemann wrote over a half century ago, his lines are worth repeating, as few since have matched his detail:

> common to all is the following syndrome: sensations of somatic distress occurring in waves lasting from twenty minutes to an hour at a time, a feeling of tightness in the throat, choking with shortness of breath, need for sighing, and an empty feeling in the abdomen, lack of muscular power, and an intense subjective distress described as tension or mental pain. . . . The sensorium is generally somewhat altered. There is commonly a slight sense of unreality, a feeling of increased emotional distance from other people (sometimes they appear shadowy or small), and there is intense preoccupation with the image of the deceased. (p. 141)

Lindemann described the bereaved's push of speech, inability to sit still, searching for the lost partner, disorganization, and conflict between wanting to talk about the loss and wishing to avoid its recollection. He also noted, as had Freud, a tendency to assume traits similar to those of the deceased.

Similar to Lindemann, Bowlby elaborated the behavioral aspects of acute grief, but he went further. Observing three phases of mourning—protest, despair, and reorganization—Bowlby (1963) hypothesized that evolution has equipped adults with a biological response to loss, modeled on the young child's normal reaction to separation. Just as the child's reaction was designed to procure the return of the caretaker and discourage further absences, so did the adult's represent to Bowlby a psychological searching for the departed. According to his theory, open protest and demand for return is an important initial stage not only for children but also for adults. In fact, Bowlby believed that without allowing these feelings, a person may not be able to proceed with the work of mourning. Anger directed toward the deceased may then be deflected onto others, including friends, family, and even the bereaved, who may remain preoccupied with the lost one, organizing his or her life as though the latter would return.

Lindemann (1944) and Bowlby (1963) remind us of the extreme turmoil and dysfunction caused by acute bereavement. Physiologic hyperarousal, searching for the deceased, inability to sit still, and difficulty engaging in organized activity are well articulated by these writers. Nor, we note, are these dysfunctions limited to loss due to death, as many of the women I interviewed experienced similar states during the initial stages of their divorces. One young mother, similar to Bella when unexpectedly left, was so agitated that she was unable to rest. For weeks she paced her house or took long walks, repeatedly reviewing the events leading to the separation. Similar to Bella, she described an inner alarm system that interrupted any temporary state of relaxation. Another mother in my study was unable to understand the meaning of her husband's departure; continuing to write love letters to him, and unable to grasp that he would not be returning, she remained so preoccupied that her bonding with her infant suffered.

Even though, according to Lindemann (1944) and Bowlby (1963), such temporary dysfunction is normal and possibly adaptive for a parent, it becomes problematic if, such as in Bella's case, it is prolonged. Many, like Bella, are unable to move through subsequent stages of mourning. Particularly if children are involved, we wonder how quickly can recovery take place.

Research on Recovery from Loss

As a pioneer in the field, Lindemann (1944) attempted to answer this question. Trying to help people through the mourning process as quickly as possible, he devised a type of short-term psychotherapy called "grief work," which focused on gradually relinquishing emotional ties to the deceased, liberating energy for new attachments, and readjusting to the environment. Such concentrated grief work, Lindemann maintained, could help his patients heal in about three months. He was optimistic that they could then resume relatively normal lives.

His projection, however, was a gross underestimate. Although Lindemann made a number of other contributions to our understanding of mourning, he greatly misjudged the time it takes to recover from a partner's death. We now know that it takes four to five years—sometimes longer. As outdated as is his time course, our culture nevertheless subscribes to the notion that healing from a spouse's death can occur relatively rapidly. We do not seem to have assimilated more recent research, or perhaps we do not want to face its consequences.

Robert Weiss (personal communication, 1997), for example, interviewed people after the death of a spouse and found that it took an average of four years for the survivor to recover. Recovery, moreover, was defined quite conservatively: returning to usual function in the world; having adequate energy; being able to plan for the future; not being excessively bothered by intrusive thoughts about the deceased; and being able to respond to the question "How's your husband (or wife)?" without bursting into tears. Even with this conservative definition, not everyone met the four-year mark. Those forty-five years or older at time of bereavement had less chance, as did those whose spouses died without warning. Those unable to make new romantic attachments also did less well (interestingly, none whose partners had died suddenly had been able to make new attachments). Similar to earlier researchers Weiss also found that a history of significant ambivalence toward the deceased interfered with recovery.

These findings, sobering enough, applied to a mixed sample in which partners had died from a broad spectrum of causes. Other researchers have emphasized the even greater difficulty people may have healing from specific types of loss. Lehman et al. (1987), for instance, found that most who lose a spouse or child suddenly in a motor vehicle crash fail to recover fully. Similarly, Finkbeiner (1996), interviewing parents who had lost a child, found that even many years later they are not healed. Her results were typical of other researchers; although ten or twenty years after losing a child, parents can once again adequately function in their roles at home and work, enjoy events, and participate in life in a way that might appear "recovered" to outsiders, nevertheless, their inner worlds remain seriously impaired. Speaking of "having a greater distance from people . . . other people unable to understand the loss . . . a one way street . . . eventually going on but never regaining the same sense of joy and purpose in life," many develop a peculiar jumpiness, desire for distraction, and need to stay unnaturally busy that do not fade with time (p. 195).

In summary, contrary to earlier views that after the death of a close family member, most people can fully recover within a few years, it now appears tht this is not the case. On the one hand, if recovery is defined simply as return to adequate functioning, then this may be possible after several years, but particularly if the loss was traumatic, such as occurring unexpectedly or involving a young child, then recovery in the sense of having the same emotional capacity for participation in life as before may remain a distant mirage.

Turning to the emotional sequelae of divorce, we ask, Are they any less devastating than those for death?

SANDRA: UNABLE TO GRIEVE

Sandra, an intelligent, articulate woman in her late thirties, was married to Jerry four years before separating a few months after childbirth. Their triplets are now age five.

Sandra was born in Ireland. After her biological father died during her early childhood, her mother remarried and immigrated to the United States, hoping to give her children better educational opportunities. Both Sandra's stepfather, a quiet, hard-working man, and her more nurturing mother expected a lot from her, including baby-sitting younger siblings as well as assisting after school in a family business. She did not have much time for play or parties. Work and education came first.

When Sandra met Jerry during her first year at New York University, she liked him because he seemed open about his thoughts and feelings. In contrast to her family, he encouraged her to talk about anything. They were also attracted to each other by their common Irish heritage. Although they were planning to finish school and then marry, during his senior year, Jerry was presented with a unique business opportunity in Las Vegas. Feeling it would be a mistake to pass this up, he suggested that he move first, and then after Sandra graduated, she could join him.

After getting her master's in business adminstration (MBA), Sandra found a lucrative job near Jerry and joined him as planned. Very happy, they married two years later and, over the next few years began to consider having children. Jerry was eager to start a family, and Sandra thought he would make a great father.

They were not able to conceive quickly, but after trying for several years, Sandra became pregnant. Elated, she took excellent care of herself. Nevertheless, she went into labor extremely prematurely and, after giving birth to triplets, wondered if they would survive, as they appeared so fragile. She had her own health problems, too, as following her cesarean section, insurance limitations forced her to return home while still in considerable pain, making walking difficult and driving impossible. Formerly quite independent, for the first time she felt physically and emotionally dependent on Jerry. Waiting each afternoon for him to return home to drive her to the hospital, she pumped her milk for her triplets, trying to give them what she could while she watched the clock for Jerry's return. His thoughts were elsewhere, however, as he began to have sex with another woman.

Sandra did not know that yet, but she had started to suspect. Something about him seemed different; he was less attentive, going out at night without revealing his destination. One day while doing his laundry, she found a note with a woman's name and phone number. Sandra kept the paper. At first she just thought it was odd and puzzled over it, but later, her curiosity growing, she asked him about it. She remembers the scene, crystal clear: they were driving down a main street and stopped at a light. Foot on the brake, she showed him the note. He looked straight at her and said, "I won't betray you." The light turned green; relieved and embarrassed, at dinner later that night, she apologized for having questioned him.

A month passed. The triplets' condition remained critical. Not certain they would survive, Sandra was under great strain, added to which was that Jerry's habits continued to be odd. In spite of his reassurances, something still seemed wrong. When she questioned him again, this time he was less convincing, as he stormed out of the house, refusing to answer. A few hours later he returned. "There's something I have to tell you," he announced. "I've met somebody." She went into shock. Sorrowfully he explained that the affair was a mistake, that it had been trivial, that it was over, but it was not. He continued to see his girlfriend.

Understanding that no one is perfect, Sandra tried to forgive him. She realized they had both been greatly stressed, trying to cope with their own busy lives as well as their premature triplets' life-threatening condition. Moreover, an additional stress was becoming increasingly apparent: Jerry was on the verge of bankruptcy. His gambling had finally caught up with him.

Jerry's gambling addiction had developed gradually. Earlier in their marriage, he and Sandra had enjoyed going to casinos for occasional recreation, but slowly Sandra realized there was a crucial difference between the two of them. She was able to decide in advance how much money she could lose and at that point walk away. Gambling for her was recreational; she never thought of it as a way to make money. Jerry, on the other hand, could not walk away. Sometimes he won large amounts—thousands—so much that they hardly knew what to do with it. More often he lost—thousands and thousands. When this happened, he became unable to pay his taxes to the Internal Revenue Service (IRS) and was forced to borrow money from increasingly shady characters. To make matters worse, several years previously, Sandra's family had trusted him sufficiently to lend him a large amount of money for his business.

Given this situation, Jerry should have been anxious. Yet in spite of his alarming financial situation, he did not seem concerned. He continued to gamble, reassuring himself that he would eventually win back the huge lost sums. By the time the triplets were born, Jerry was just beginning to grasp how deeply in trouble he was. It was just beginning to dawn on him—and Sandra—that he might not be able to repay his loans.

Rather than address these problems, Jerry began spending more nights out. Sometimes he returned wearing expensive new clothes bought by his girlfriend. In a daze, Sandra put up with his behavior. At this point, she did not feel particularly angry. Instead, although she had done nothing wrong, she irrationally blamed herself for both the triplets' premature births and for Jerry's untimely departure. Recognizing the huge stress he had been under, she kept trying to make things better for him, to forgive him. Still loving him and thinking he must still love her, she wanted to keep her family together. Surely, she thought, Jerry would return to being the person she knew after he adjusted to fatherhood, and maybe with parenthood's greater responsibility, he would give up gambling too. Sandra was hopeful for herself and her triplets. They had already been through so much and had had such a traumatic start, the least they deserved, she felt, was an intact family.

The triplets would not get the family Sandra had in mind, however. Traveling back and forth between households, Jerry continued to see his girlfriend, who was also married. Sandra actually got to know her and was surprised to learn that she had no knowledge that Jerry was married or a father. When Sandra gave her the heads-up, it did not change her pursuit of him, however. "Don't blame me if you can't hold on to your husband," she informed Sandra. Over the next months, Jerry moved out completely.

Although Sandra had always been a strong person and able to cope with almost anything, now she began to worry she might be having a nervous breakdown. Unable to sleep, she stayed awake at night crying. Her mother, living in a distant city, realized her distress and moved in to care for the triplets. Sandra was thankful, as by now she was too distraught to be a good mother herself. In spite of her anguish, however, she kept her husband's affair a secret. Isolated by fear and shame, she did not tell anyone, not even her own mother, the reasons for her separation.

Sandra struggled to get back on her feet. With huge debts from Jerry's gambling and no child support, she knew she had to return to work, so her mother watched the triplets while Sandra jump-started her career, trying to make enough money to placate the creditors. She thought she was making progress until about a year later, around the time the IRS put a lien on her condo, when she lost her job. Her company, responding to shareholders' pressures, was downsizing middle-management positions such as hers.

Fortunately, Sandra found another job, and although she had to take time off for the triplets' numerous medical appointments, she was able to support herself. Continuing to address Jerry's financial predicament (he had now disappeared, embarking on a long trip cross-country), she found herself dealing with the IRS as well as with a number of less savory characters. Sometimes, with good reason, she was frightened. Caring for her children would have been impossible without her mother's live-in presence over the next two years.

By the time the triplets were three, Sandra's mother could no longer override a desire to return to her own husband and home. In a painful decision, Sandra let her mother take the triplets with her, where they could be cared for by her large, extended family; Sandra planned to join them as soon as she could pay off enough of

Jerry's creditors to avoid bankruptcy and loss of her family's fortune. Her mother departed with the triplets, and Sandra began to commute frequently back and forth.

A year later Jerry made a surprise return. Accompanied by his girlfriend, he arrived at the doorstep with divorce papers, pressuring Sandra to sign them right then and there. Instead, she suggested that, first, they both get lawyers. Eventually he filed for divorce in the usual manner.

Although by now Sandra had no illusions about saving her marriage, Jerry's timing was nevertheless poor; she had lost her job again and was about to lose her battle against bankruptcy. Exhausted as she was, the divorce proceeded relentlessly. Trying to be resourceful, she decided to apply for a job as a math tutor but failed a qualifying test three times. Jerry's behavior, the divorce, and separation from her children had all taken an emotional toll. Her friends kidded her about having an MBA but being unable to pass a simple math test. Persevering, she did finally pass the test, and, thankfully, another consulting job opened up, enabling her once again to support herself.

In spite of these accomplishments, by the time of our interview one year later, she still was not able to join her family. This might seem strange, but it is understandable in light of the substantial sum her parents lent Jerry—a sum that, if not reclaimed, would wipe out their life savings. In adddition, I suspect an element of fear is involved: not all of his creditors may take no for an answer. As Sandra struggles to solve these problems, she receives no help from Jerry, who, working sporadically, says he cannot spare any money. Neither can he spare any time for his children, even though she has brought them to his doorstep on at least one occasion.

Five years after separating, Sandra still agonizes over what happened to her marriage. Until the births of their triplets, she had thought her husband loved her and wanted to be a father. Although she knew he had a gambling problem, she never imagined he would leave. Jerry, unable to give her a reason, at this point justifies his choice by explaining that his girlfriend threatens to harm herself if he leaves her. So his moral obligation is to stay with his girlfriend, he tells Sandra, who does not tell him how often she, during the early months of their divorce, struggled with depression perhaps much more serious.

Sandra has many strengths, including intelligence, an open personality, advanced degrees in marketable fields, and love for her triplets, but at the five-year mark, she has not yet been able to heal. She still feels numb, neither engaged fully in life nor with herself. Large areas of her inner world remain walled off, with access to many memories, thoughts, and feelings markedly constricted. She and the triplets have lost immeasurably. Nevertheless, she still hopes to straighten out her life. She is determined not to disappoint herself, her family, or her children.

Sandra, similar to Bella in the previous story, had difficulty healing from divorce. Unlike Bella, Sandra enjoyed many advantages, such as a marketable profession, youth, and a supportive family with the flexibility to offer full-time child care; unlike Bella, Sandra did not yearn indefinitely for her ex-husband's return. Nevertheless, similar to Bella, five years after separation, Sandra has not been able to put her emotional life back on track. She is not the strong, confident person she used to be. Something in her still feels numb, once removed from life, in shock. She has not been able to mourn.

Why do some people recover quickly from divorce, and others remain stuck in no-man's land, a shell of their former selves? Sandra's story provides some clues. First, we note she may have circumvented the initial "protest" phase that Bowlby (1963) thought helpful, as she seemed unusually accommodating toward her husband and kept the reasons for her separation, along with her anger, hidden from even her mother. Second, she experienced her divorce more as a trauma than a loss and, as with many trauma survivors, became emotionally numb and constricted. Is her case typical? Let us turn to some studies on recovery.

LONG-TERM IMPACT OF DIVORCE: WHAT HELPS; WHAT DOES NOT

Researchers initially made two assumptions about recovery from divorce: first, it was expected to take place within one to two years, given reasonable psychological health, and, second, losing a partner to divorce was expected to be less devastating than losing one to death. Unfortunately, both assumptions have been found to be false. Despite the prevalent belief that divorce should be easier to adjust to than death of a spouse, it is often even more traumatic. This is not to underestimate the devastation that death can bring, particularly when untimely or when children are affected. Nor do we wish to obscure the unique complexity of each situation with blanket conclusions. Granted that many factors contribute to an individual's response, the research on divorce, however, is not sanguine.

Take the figures on divorce's long-term health consequences. Although it is widely known that widows and widowers are at increased risk of medical illness, a number of studies show that, generally, even more physical and mental health problems affect the divorced. Data collected by Verbrugge (1979), for instance, found separated and divorced individuals have the worst health status; the bereaved come next, followed by singles, and finally the married, who are the healthiest. Although cause and effect could be debated here, several subsequent studies (Segraves, 1980; Fenwick and Barresi, 1981) demonstrated that it is the *change* in marital status that coincides with the critical point in time of deterioration of health. Similarly, although some selection effect may exist through which less healthy people are more prone to divorce, this effect is overshadowed by the direct one of divorce itself, particularly for women (Cheung, 1998; Hope et al., 1999). Especially hard hit are those divorcing mothers experiencing downward socioeconomic mobility at the same time they are raising young children (Hope et al., 1999). In contrast to childless women, who tend to experience a more temporary malaise after divorce, these mothers develop long-term psychological and medical problems.

Long-term health consequences serve as one marker for the enormous stresses experienced by the divorced. What factors mediate this stress? If these could be identified, perhaps some of their negative sequelae could be attenuated. Interviewing people during the immediate separation as well as years afterward, researchers have tried to pinpoint these factors. Although it is beyond the scope of this chapter to provide a complete review, I will mention several studies.

Divorcing Mothers

L'Hommedieu (1984), in her small but in-depth study relying on lengthy interviews rather than questionnaires, noted the shock, disorientation, and rage felt by women left against their wishes. The unilateral, unforeseen, and unwelcome nature of their husbands' decisions to divorce appeared most causal in these wives' distress, which was severe enough in some cases for them to lose interest in their children or even to deteriorate their usual benign forms of discipline to the point of physical abuse, as their coping mechanisms crumbled. Asking what had helped these women heal, L'Hommedieu compared the coping mechanisms of working-class mothers with those of the middle class: the former group became stronger by solving one practical problem after another, gaining confidence as they regained hope they could manage their lives, while the latter gained strength by developing new identities through careers. In spite of both groups showing considerable improvement in their coping skills, however, one and a half to two years following divorce, many mothers continued to have angry, conflicted relationships with their former husbands.

Similarly, Grossman (1986) studied forty mothers and children (latency age to preadolescence) between five to eighteen months after the final divorce decree. Her single most powerful finding was that it was which parent *initiated* divorce proceedings that had the largest impact on how both mother and children subsequently fared. Only six of her forty couples divorced by mutual consent, and of the mothers whose husbands initiated separation, fully one-third were taken by surprise; they had thought either that they were in happy marriages or that their problems were solvable. They did not fare nearly as well as those who had taken a more active role in the decision, a difference Grossman attributed to the advantage of better psychological and practical preparation.

Not surprisingly, Grossman found that in addition to having had a role in the decision to separate, mothers able to form a serious new romantic relationship recovered more easily, but—and here was the surprise—none of the women "left" by their husbands fell into this group; those on the receiving end of the suggestion to divorce were not able to form significant new love relationships within the study's time frame. The importance of this factor superseded that of others commonly thought to influence adjustment (p. 30).

Recovery from divorce, accordingly, may depend on who did the leaving, as well as on *how* it took place—was it prepared for? For a mother, the worst prognosis might follow her husband's sudden, unexpected departure, amputating a marriage that she had thought was healthy.

Leaver versus Leavee: Spanier's Study

Spanier and Thompson (1987) also studied couples who were separated or divorced at least two years. Similar to Grossman (1986), they noted many of their subjects had been surprised by the suddenness with which their marriages collapsed. For about 40 percent, in fact, the first open discussion about divorce coincided with one partner's certainty about the marriage's end (Spanier and Thompson, 1987, p. 48), with no forewarning or openness to working on problems. Although slightly more than half of the couples did discuss the possibility of divorce before making a final decision, Spanier and Thompson's data highlighted the significant number of partners who are suddenly, unexpectedly, confronted by the other's departure. Although divorce is typically considered a mutual and voluntary decision, the authors concluded that accounts of failed marriages consistently reveal otherwise (p. 53).

Yet Spanier and Thompson pointed out that specifying "leaver" and "left" does not always accurately portray the complexity of control over the process. It is common, for example, for a dissatisfied spouse to deliberately maneuver the other to suggest a divorce. Taking responsibility for the initial suggestion to separate and taking blame for the breakup are two different things: very few partners in their study assumed fault for even a one-sided breakup. The vast majority of those unilaterally ending marriages blamed their divorce on their spouses.

Data on extramarital affairs confirmed this point (p. 65). Looking at couples in which at least one partner had had an affair, Spanier and Thompson found that about one-half (52 percent of men and 46 percent of women) said their *spouses'* extramarital affairs contributed to marital breakdown, whereas only 6 percent thought that their *own* did so. Spanier and Thompson stated:

> This one bit of data provides a powerful indication, it seems, to us, that there is little objective reality to the circumstances of marital separation and its evaluation. Respondents construct their own views of marriage and accounts of its dissolution, and these views may have little relationship to each other. (p. 69)

These remarks are a reminder that "his" and "her" divorce stories often bear little resemblance. Details may vary enormously, as may assignment of blame. While recognizing the complexity of both the divorce process and its chronicle, Spanier and Thompson nevertheless confirmed that many people *are* surprised by their partners' sudden divorce announcements—announcements neither anticipated nor desired. Quick exits may follow, with little discussion of other options, as departing spouses construct accounts most advantageous to themselves.

Most significantly, similar to L'Hommedieu (1984) and Grossman (1986), Spanier and Thompson (1987) found that feeling rejected generally has more severe consequences than feeling guilty. For both sexes, the former state is associated with more difficulty accepting the breakup, greater loneliness, and more intense longing. One-fifth of the women in Spanier's study, unable to accept the end of their marriages, seriously considered suicide. Some made attempts (p. 110), and actual contact with former partners contributed to their despair (p. 228).

A number of researchers, accordingly, have found that who initiates divorce does matter. Even though the process is complex, even though the one suggesting divorce may not be the only one desiring it, nevertheless, the initiator tends to fare better. In cases in which both spouses do, on some level, want to separate, helping them "own" their feelings may help equalize the leaver-leavee power gap, but in other cases, one partner is truly surprised by a completely unwanted separation. Such partners may have little to "own" but emotional shock and a recognition that recovery may be more problematic than it might have been with adequate time to prepare.

Fathers' Adjustment to Divorce

Much literature has focused on the hardships of divorced mothers. Perhaps because traditionally they performed a larger share of child rearing as well as bore the brunt of divorce's economic stress, their difficulties caught the attention of earlier researchers. To some extent, the study of divorced fathers was neglected. Research on this subject, however, is catching up rapidly.

Jacobs (1986), in review, noted that many divorced fathers experience great loneliness. Overwhelmed with the pain of separation from their children, some distance themselves rather than face the anguish of repeated separations. Jacobs also described an "involuntary child absence" syndrome (pp. 38-51), in which fathers react with great anxiety if they are prevented, or fear they may be prevented, from seeing their children. Even if the threat is imaginary, they may panic.

Huntington (1986) noted the rage and helplessness fathers may feel if custody and visitation seem out of their control. She also found that, compared to women, men tend to have less clarity about what caused the breakup of their marriages. As a result, when divorce is not of their choosing, they may experience the event as a crushing blow and, feeling acutely violated and humiliated, may engage in protracted legal battles over money and custody as they attempt to reestablish justice. For such men, the added loss of daily contact with their children may lead to further despair. Yet even fathers who instigate divorce may experience much pain, particularly if their children turn on them angrily for having "caused" the breakup. Leaving their wives for what they felt were justifiable reasons, they are taken off guard by their children's resentment.

Thompson (1994) noted that fathers are often considered the villains in contemporary divorce. He pointed out that while the custodial parent, usually the mother, is concerned with economic survival and supporting her children, the nonresident one may be equally concerned with maintaining a meaningful parenting role. A visiting father may feel unneeded, cut off from the day-to-day issues in the child's life, like a kite without a reel. Sadly, he may feel that his most important contribution is his paycheck.

One focus of research has been the unfortunate tendency of divorced fathers to drift away, emotionally and physically, from their children; estimates of such father absence ranged from 50 percent in the mid-1980s to 30 percent in more recent studies (Arendell, 1995, p. 142). This process, known to be harmful for many children, is also associated with a less publicized trend: whether cause or effect, fathers who lose contact with their children make poorer adaptations themselves (Atkins, 1989). Although it might be conjectured that such findings are more a function of previous parenting patterns than of divorce itself, this may not always be the case. Surprisingly, little continuity may exist between a father's pre- and postdivorce parenting styles.

Atkins (1989), for example, cited studies showing that fathers' prior patterns do not predict their postdivorce involvement with their children (Hetherington et al., 1976; Wallerstein and Kelly, 1980), and in his own work, he also found no clear evidence that a previously involved father will remain consistently so. Although Atkins (1989) recognized the contribution of fathers' past traumas to their current reactions, he also showed how their perception of being at either end of divorce's perpetrator-victim spectrum factors significantly in their postdivorce adjustment, including, most critically, the quality of contact with their children. He cited the case of one father who after a painful divorce avoided memories of his ex-wife by severing contact with their children, whom he referred to as "hers." Fathers' healing after divorce, similar to that of mothers, is significantly impaired if one party has inflicted great hurt on the other. Most tragically, if memories of the marriage are too painful, a father may abandon his children because of their close connection with his former wife.

Based on a study she conducted in the early 1990s, Arendell (1995) came to similar conclusions. She interviewed seventy-five divorced fathers, predominantly Caucasian and middle income, with an average age of thirty-eight and a median time since divorce of almost five years, and noticed two patterns.

The first group of fathers (representing the majority, sixty-six of the seventy-five) felt victimized by the divorce process. Their rights, they felt, had been trampled upon (p. 153). As their children were a constant reminder of such unresolved, intense feelings, these fathers disengaged (p. 157). Furthermore, when they perceived their children's anger, they withdrew even further (p. 149). Of these sixty-six fathers, thirty-five had very limited contact, while the other thirty-one vacillated between being involved and not (p. 17). For all sixty-six, the perception of having been victimized by the divorce interfered significantly with maintaining ties with their children (p. 102).

The second, much smaller group (nine of the seventy-five fathers) became very nurturing of their children after divorce. These men maintained respectful, sometimes friendly relationships with their former wives, toward whom they felt sufficiently benign to develop active parenting partnerships (p. 203). What distinguished this group from the former were not financial arrangements or type of custody per se, but the ability to sustain respectful, cooperative relationships with their former wives. Perhaps as a result, these men were less worried about their rights and more concerned about being good, involved fathers.

Similar to other researchers, Arendell found that fathers' predivorce parenting patterns do not always predict their postdivorce ones. Of her nine very involved fathers, only two had been so during marriage. For the other seven, divorce triggered major internal changes that actually enhanced their commitment to fatherhood (p. 220). Yet Arendell pointed out that, for most men in her study, achieving such a facilitating level of communication with their former spouses was difficult (p. 209). As the marriage crumbled, so did their bonds with their children.

Overall, Arendell's study highlighted the considerable number of fathers who feel extremely bitter about their divorces. Their anger, ongoing and intense, is reflected by the fact that almost a quarter of her respondents frequently fantasized about murdering their former wives (p. 121). Feeling intensely powerless, up to a quarter also contemplated suicide (p. 137). Perhaps it was no coincidence that two-thirds felt divorce was not their own fault. Feeling victimized and marginalized, they were most concerned with asserting their rights and obtaining revenge, and some forgot their pain by avoiding their families.

In the process, they lost more than their children. Parenthood, as we discussed earlier, is a one-way challenge. Once a person has had children, circumventing this developmental phase often leads to psychological impoverishment. Unable to grieve, remaining riveted on how to defend themselves against traumatic memories rather than join their children's creative play, many of Arendell's fathers lost their way.

Long-Term Studies: Wallerstein

While Arendell (1995) portrayed the difficulty divorced fathers have healing, Wallerstein and Blakeslee (1989) concluded that, for both sexes, time does not heal as swiftly as we might wish. Interviewing mothers eighteen months after separation, Wallerstein was not too surprised to find that about one-half were clinically depressed, many severely, but she was astonished to find ten and even twenty years later that many divorced parents had not recovered. Moreover, she noted a tendency for each divorcing couple to have a "winner" and a "loser." Many years later, one member's physical, psychological, and economic health seemed quite robust, while the other was doing poorly. Although her study has been criticized for using a nonrandom sample, one possibly biased toward couples with more problems, the length of follow-up and depth of her interviews provided a more complete psychological picture than had most previous studies.

TRAUMA VERSUS GRIEF

Overall, these researchers pointed to an important general theme: a spouse who feels victimized by divorce, powerless over the decision, or treated unfairly during the legal process, may have more difficulty with long-term recovery. Although these researchers did not specifically discuss the difference between trauma and grief responses, it may be useful to view their findings through this lens.

Grief responses, as explicated by Freud (1915), Klein (1935, 1940), Lindemann (1944), and Bowlby (1963), are characterized by sadness and a sense of loss, and involve a gradual emotional detachment from the departed. While the bereaved may feel anger as well as guilt, both feelings are tempered by love. The memory of the good relationship, the internalized positive interaction, keeps at bay destructive reactions. Mourning may go awry if the deceased was loved too ambivalently, if hate played too large a role; guilt is then difficult to overcome, and depression may ensue.

Trauma responses, on the other hand, are characterized by a sense of helplessness and often victimization. Instead of sadness and loss of love, rage and loss of self occur. "How could this person turn on me so suddenly?" the traumatized partner asks. In contrast to grief reactions, which often invoke a heightened sense of the lost one's presence, trauma responses are characterized by the need to avoid memories of the departed, as well as of any situations that might trigger these.

Let us consider the reaction of a mother I interviewed (she did not participate directly in my divorce study but had heard about it and wished to tell her story by way of contrast) who, while pregnant, had experienced the untimely death of her husband.

Marcia had felt blessed by a wonderful marriage until her thirty-three-year-old husband, previously in perfect health, died suddenly while jogging. Devastated, Marcia nonetheless took comfort in experiencing a heightened sense of her husband's presence, sometimes thinking she had heard his voice, other times dreaming about him so realistically that it took her several minutes upon awakening to remember he was dead. After several months, she felt sad when these experiences became less frequent. Worried she might lose a sense of connection with him, she spent much time looking at old photos and began to write down her memories of the special times they had enjoyed together. Every night before she went to sleep, she wrote in her journal and engaged in an imaginary conversation with her husband about their infant son, who to her delight looked much like his dad.

Unlike the divorced women in my study, Marcia found great comfort in memories of her husband, even though these must have also been painful reminders of what she had lost. Why, we might ask, did the divorced women not derive similar comfort from memories of previous good times in their marriages? This is a complicated topic, but at least one reason occurs to me. A number of the women I interviewed were traumatized by their divorces. Trauma involves a loss of self-esteem, a loss even of one's entire sense of self, that death of a loved one does not always precipitate. After traumatic abuse, assault, or divorce, another person has turned, often viciously, on oneself. Trying to understand why this has happened leads to alternating states of blaming the other and blaming oneself. A sense of internal chaos, of rage alternating with self-loathing, ensues that is so unstable that the mind must protect itself. As firefighters burn a border to contain a blaze, so does the mind wall off traumatic memories. Only if these can be understood in terms of a cause outside the perpetrator's control can trauma be readily converted to grief. In this sense, the insanity defense protects the victim.

Of course, not all divorces are traumatic; some can be grieved as losses. Many deaths, on the other hand, are traumatic—particularly those involving violent crimes, or those which are sudden, untimely, or affecting young children. Not only the event, but its meaning, influence its metabolism. Nevertheless, studies consistently reveal that many divorces do not engender grief but, rather, for at least one partner, trauma. For mothers, this state may profoundly deteriorate their parenting skills, while fathers may drift away.

These findings are particularly germane to divorces at childbirth, as many of those described in this book evoked more of a trauma than a grief response. Whereas women such as Bella became stuck in the grieving process, unable to move beyond pining for husbands remembered as good, others such as Sandra did not even begin to grieve in the traditional sense; they were simply unable to recall specific memories from the good years they and their husbands had enjoyed together. Instead, after an initial phase of disbelief, they walled off their trauma behind soundproof barriers, and with it large sectors of their feeling, memory, and self-esteem, resulting in muted inner worlds.

SUMMARY

In summary, immediate emotional effects of divorce at childbirth can be devastating. As after death of a loved one, activation of the attachment system may occur, initially causing extreme physiological disregulation. Increase in physical and mental illness, impaired ability to parent, child abuse, and suicide attempts have been frequently reported.

Turning from immediate effects to long-term recovery, it appears this process is neither simple nor speedy. Trying to understand how people heal, we note some similarities between recovery from di-

vorce and recovery from bereavement. Both involve initial physiological and psychological turmoil followed by social withdrawal and
sadness; both involve a gradual slide back into adequate functioning,
sometimes masking that it may take years to be able to mention the
departed one without tears, grief, or anger; and both are somewhat
ameliorated by adequate preparation for the loss, as well as by eventual engagement in new romantic relationships. Both may be traumatic, and both can engender grief and guilt.

There are, however, fundamental differences. Divorce is a choice
made by at least one person; death, unless by murder or suicide, is not.
Divorce involves human rejection; death involves an act of nature.
Klein (1940) noted that idealization of and love for the lost partner pro-
mote mourning by protecting the bereaved from being overwhelmed
by anger. Those mourning a divorce characterized by intense hostility,
however, have no such sanctuary. Freud (1915) wrote about loss of
ambivalent loves as problematic, leading to clinical depression. Following many divorces, however, spouses are not just ambivalent; they
very often hate each other. At the farthest end of that spectrum, where
the hate is white-hot, lie many divorces at childbirth.

Divorce at childbirth causes extremes of affect-emotion because it
is an extreme condition. Just as severely negative conditions in childhood lead to so-called borderline personality disorder, a condition of
rapidly oscillating mood and self-states, so does traumatic divorce
cause the breakdown of normal integration of emotions in many people, who may subject themselves, as well as their departed partners,
to wide swings of love and hate. Mourning may not be possible.

For many divorcing at this vulnerable time, healing may be elu-
sive. Although recovery may be superficially defined as resumption
of adequate functioning, this may occur without adequate well-being.
Free access to one's inner world, including memories, thoughts, feelings, and desires; free access to the roads of one's mind, to being able
to wander without too many stop signs—these are the costs of divorce's upheaval. Similar to other trauma, extreme-condition divorce
may block fully reconnecting one's landscape.

These remarks diverge from those of many popular books, which
tend to view divorce as a grieving opportunity. Although such a
model may be adequate for marital breakdown under ordinary conditions, it does not suffice for divorces in which one party is left unexpectedly, unilaterally, at a vulnerable time.

Given the dire psychological effects of traumatic divorce on parents, how can we expect their children to fare? Before turning to this topic, let us not forget that the psychological sequelae of divorce represent only one of its negative consequences. Parents must also deal with economic pressures sufficiently intense that no account of divorce at childbirth would be complete without considering them.

Chapter 5

Economic Impact of Divorce at Childbirth

In the previous chapter we explored the emotional consequences, often devastating, of divorce at childbirth. Equally harmful can be the economic ones. Many studies tracking families after divorce, in fact, have found financial and emotional adjustment to be highly intertwined. Although the primary focus of this book is on the psychological aspects of divorce at childbirth, after listening to the women in my study, I realized no work on this subject would be complete without addressing divorce's economic impact on families.

Turning to this topic, we confront one basic dilemma: for all but the most affluent couples, raising their children as they wish often requires both parents' full economic contributions. Consider the pressure on parents, even if married, to work full-time. This strain reflects the economic reality that, in many parts of our country, two full incomes are needed to provide children with certain advantages that their parents may have enjoyed during their own upbringings. Foremost in many couples' minds, for example, is the quality of their children's education. Many set their sights on moving to communities with good public schools. Unfortunately, real estate values fluctuate so widely according to this variable (outside certain cities, for example, the same house could double or triple in value if relocated from a suburb with mediocre to one with exceptional public schools) that affording even a modest home in such a highly desired neighborhood is beyond the reach of many, unless both spouses work full-time.

Of course, education is not the only opportunity parents wish to provide. Some forgo a second income, choosing instead to spend more time with their young. It might appear that these families are successfully managing on one salary.

This is not really true, however. Even those married parents who appear to be raising their children on "one income" present an illusion. Hidden in such arrangements is the wife's (or, in less traditional families, the husband's) financial contribution as homemaker. Organizing and running the household not only saves thousands, sometimes tens of thousands, of dollars per year in child care expenses (calculate fifty hours a week times ten dollars an hour for in-home care, or five dollars an hour for outside settings), but it also frees the other partner to pursue greater career development and earning potential; also, the children benefit from having a parent readily available to ensure, early in life, they receive a critical amount of nurturing. Such arrangements not only provide a rich reservoir of resources for children; they save families enormous sums of money. They represent, essentially, a second income—and in many cases, much more.

When middle-income parents divorce, accordingly, often funds are insufficient to provide for two households. Even under the best circumstances, in which full child support is paid, a significant decline in children's economic well-being is almost inevitable.

This comes as an unpleasant surprise. On the surface, it might appear that if luxury items were cut, divorced mothers and children could survive without significant economic decline. Such "frills," however, would have to include quality of neighborhood, schools, extracurricular activities, and time spent with parents—to name just a few. To illustrate this point, Arendell (1986, p. 38), in review, pointed out that although one researcher concluded that the custodial parent needs 80 percent of a family's predivorce income to maintain the children's standard of living, and although in other countries such as Sweden it has been determined that single-parent families actually need more income than others, by contrast, in the United States, the average total income, including child support, of women and children dropped by 50 percent after divorce. Although Arendell's research reflected conditions in the 1980s, more recent data show that fathers' child support payments continue to remain low compared to what would have been provided had their marriages not ended (Garfinkle et al., 1998). Only in situations in which one or both partners are quite affluent may divorce not create significant economic downslide.

DIVORCE ECONOMICS

Christine: From Wealth to Welfare

Christine, a stock broker in her midthirties, separated after five years of marriage. Her daughter, Susie, eight months at the time, is now one and a half years old. Soft-spoken and thoughtful, Christine tells me her story.

When she was in her late twenties and had just graduated from a prestigious business school, Christine landed an exceptionally good first job at a major San Francisco investment firm. As excited as she was by her new position, she was still single and wished to meet someone special, so she placed an ad in the personal section of a local paper, and after receiving many responses liked Tom's best; not only did he sound down-to-earth, but they seemed to have much in common. Remarkably, it turned out that they not only shared the same religion but also had family in the same small town in Ohio.

As soon as they met, Christine knew Tom was special. After dating for six months they moved in together, and two years later, they became engaged. By the time of her wedding, Christine thought she knew Tom well. In love, they were best friends and partners, sharing similar dreams. Christine felt very lucky.

Life had not always been so rosy for Christine: when she was six years old, her mother developed breast cancer. As Christine struggled to cope with her mother's illness and reaction to chemotherapy, her father had an affair. After their parents separated, Christine and her younger brother continued to live with their dying mother, until one year later she succumbed. Christine's life then became a blur. At times she lived with her father, but he did not seem emotionally invested in her. Neither could he manage finances. Pleading with him not to spend money frivolously so that they could pay their electric bills, not only did Christine have to take care of her dysfunctional father, but she also worried about her younger brother. Periodically her father felt overburdened and sent his children to relatives or friends so he could have some rest. Because of the chaotic quality of these frequent moves, she is now unable to remember their sequence.

Feeling so helpless as a child, Christine developed a strong capacity to take charge. Although this quality had earlier been one of her strengths, later it began to cause some problems in her marriage. After moving in with Tom, she had difficulty sharing personal space in their small, Bay-area apartment. Indeed, her need for self-sufficiency bothered him to the point that she sought individual therapy, and when they also began couples counseling, her need for control was identified as one of their major problems. Over time, by working through issues relating to her difficult childhood, she was able to relax. Therapy seemed very helpful.

Tom's problems, as with Christine's, did not seem insurmountable. Although very intelligent, as a child he had been diagnosed with both attention deficit hyperactivity disorder and a learning disability. Even with treatment, he had been unable to study effectively and, after dropping out of high school, developed an erratic job history. Nevertheless, he always worked hard, made a good income, and paid his share of the bills. He also completed his general equivalency diploma (GED) and hoped to attend a local college.

Before marrying, Tom revealed to Christine that, many years ago, as part of youthful experimentation, he had tried drugs. By the time they met, although he continued to smoke pot occasionally, he seldom drank; there was no indication he was continuing to use hard drugs. Christine herself had tried marijuana in college but had not liked its effects. She had not given Tom's drug use much thought since—never suspecting he might have a drug problem.

Since both Christine and Tom wanted children, after marrying they considered starting a family. Concerned that raising children might bring out their differences, Tom hesitated at first, but after thinking it over, he decided to go ahead. When Christine conceived, they were both happy. She, having worked through her control issues, and he, having found a career that suited him, both felt ready to be parents.

By the end of her pregnancy, however, some new problems were developing at home. Tom became increasingly lax about answering letters and paying bills, to the point that bags of his unopened mail began accumulating. When questioned about it, he became angry and, rather than address the problem, leveled accusations against her. He also became inexplicably exhausted, sleeping hours more than usual. On several occasions, Christine found him recumbent on the living room floor in broad daylight. Frankly, his behavior was so odd that she urged him to get a medical checkup.

After Christine gave birth, she quit her sixty-hour-a-week job to spend time with their baby. She had planned to stay home for several months and then work part-time out of their condo. Not worried about money, as in addition to sharing Tom's income she had saved a considerable sum for maternity leave, she had prepared financially so she could work less after childbirth. She knew the value of bonding closely with her daughter during the first year and was looking forward to this opportunity. She wanted to be a good mother.

Over the next few months, however, Christine began receiving daily messages from a new breed of callers—Tom's creditors. At first unaware of the magnitude of his spending, she simply paid the bills. After all, she thought, they had had large expenses before but had always caught up. But this time, as her savings dwindled, so did her husband's paycheck deposits. Suddenly they had little money left. Meanwhile, Tom began to behave even more erratically, once leaving her and the baby stranded for hours in the August heat with no bottles or diapers. He always had an excuse. Pointing the finger at her as the unreasonable one, he would exclaim, "What do you want me to do, Christine? I got caught in the traffic. How was I to get here any faster? You're just too controlling."

One night when Tom was still out at 2 a.m., Christine finally panicked. Maybe he had died, she thought, as she dialed 911. The officer's first question was whether Tom might be using drugs. Still thinking she knew her husband, she answered no, but when he returned at dawn, he finally broke down sobbing, as he confessed he was addicted to cocaine. Too exhausted to respond, Christine simply asked him to let him get some sleep.

The next day she tried to help him, as in a supportive tone, she suggested he go to a detox facility. He agreed. She also assssed his debts. Buying electronics that he had pawned to support his drug habit, he had charged over $50,000 to his credit cards.

Christine and Tom were in a difficult position. They had a huge mortgage and two car payments, a baby, and no income. Her carefully planned savings were gone. Nonetheless, as Christine knew how, she took charge. Convincing her old company to hire her back full-time, she returned to work at a high-stress, ten-hour-a-day job. She placed Susie in nearby day care and urged Tom to declare bankruptcy. After losing the cars and condo, she rented an apartment for her family within walking distance of work and day care. What she did not do was give up on her marriage, as she hoped that, with treatment, Tom would recover and be a good father.

After being discharged from the hospital, Tom did seem eager to stay off cocaine. Agreeing to attend daily recovery meetings, he also made weekly appointments with a counselor. Sadly, he was unable to fulfill his intentions. The day before they were to move to their new apartment, only two weeks after he was discharged from detox, he relapsed.

Christine awakened to the fact that Tom's addiction would not be easily treated. Not wanting to expose Susie to the dangers of living with a father addicted to crack cocaine, and feeling overwhelmed by the stresses of working full-time, caring for her daughter, and worrying about her husband's increasingly erratic behavior, she spoke to her own relatives in Ohio. Sympathetic to her situation, they invited her to live with them, rent free, until Tom recovered. Thankful for a safe, affordable haven, she procured a separation agreement and moved in with her aunt. Christine thought this arrangement would be temporary, as she still hoped she and Tom could reconcile.

He, however, quickly relapsed two more times. No longer appearing even slightly motivated to get treatment, he was not honest about his drug use, either. Supposedly agreeing to periodic drug tests, he dropped out of the monitoring program after testing positive. Skipping from job to job, he paid no child support, even though according to his income he owed $305 a month.

By the time of our interview ten months after separating, Christine is still living with her relatives and facing the fact that Tom's addiction is so severe, he may not recover. To make matters worse, she has been unable to find another job; even though she is well qualified, the job market in her current location is poor. Also, she has felt so distraught by the breakup of her marriage that she has not been able to pull herself together to face the very competitive job application process. Several times a day she breaks down and cries—so unpredictably that she has no confidence she could manage a job interview. As a temporary measure, she has accepted public assistance, and since it is clear that Tom is still using cocaine, she plans to file for divorce.

Tom recently revealed he had been using cocaine throughout their marriage, a confession that confronted Christine with both his deception and her own blindness. All those years she was in couples counseling trying to work on her "baggage," all those years he pointed the finger at her as the one who, due to her control issues, was causing their marital problems—he never bothered to tell her one detail: he was using cocaine. Not only Christine, but her friends and counselors, missed it. She will never trust his word again about anything.

When asked what is hardest about her divorce, Christine quickly answered that it is her financial situation. Accustomed to supporting herself, she never imagined her life could spin so out of control that she would be dependent on relatives, much less welfare.

Christine's strengths include her commitment to her daughter, enjoyment of motherhood, intelligence, high level of education, and career potential. She has a long history of taking care of herself, and has had much practice coping with adversity. Sometimes she feels quite hopeful, knows her next step, but other times, she feels numb, lost in a fog. Even though she is managing, she is not sure how long she will stay in shock, dull to ordinary life.

Christine's story reveals how even quite affluent mothers may experience severe economic decline after divorce. Although her difficulties were compounded by her husband's cocaine use, nevertheless, sudden, unanticipated divorce plunged this previously successful woman into poverty. The necessity of moving, the difficulty in finding a new job compatible with mothering an infant, lack of child support, and, perhaps most saliently, the emotional shock of unexpected, traumatic divorce unwound years of financial security. Christine may eventually reenter her profession and adequately support herself and her daughter. Other mothers, holding fewer educational cards, may not be so fortunate.

After divorce custodial parents, usually mothers, feel pressure to increase their income to offset what has been lost. Hoping to preserve their children's middle-class lifestyle, many work long hours, sacrificing health and parenting time. For Christine, it was impossible to remain where she was, but even if it had been feasible, similar to many custodial mothers, she might have discovered that as she tried to work sufficient hours to hold on to the same house, neighborhood, or schools for her child, she would have worn herself ragged while spending inadequate time with her daughter.

Unfortunately, child support does not sufficiently reverse this situation. Perhaps because his cocaine habit consumed his income, Tom paid none. Would the amount he owed have made a large difference to Christine, however? I think not. The $305 a month might have covered groceries, but it would have made little dent in rent, car, child care, or health insurance—expenses that escalated for Christine once she had a child. Shockingly, at the time of her divorce, this figure was just about the national average, $311 per month in 1995.

Tom's financial health was blighted by his cocaine addiction, but many fathers without excessive spending habits may still feel they cannot afford the support they are required to pay. Particularly if they did not want divorce, they may feel that a significant fraction of their incomes is going to raise children taken away from them. Although they may not spend money frivolously, they may feel socially compromised by not being able to offer new romantic partners the full economic benefits of their professional positions. After divorce, accordingly, both parents feel under increased pressure to make up the lost income. Both may become stressed from overwork, and find the quality of their lives and their children's substantially diminished.

Studies on the Economics of Divorce

In the 1980s, a number of researchers explored the economic effects of divorce. Nichols-Casebolt (1986), Weitzman (1981), Teachman and Paasch (1994), and Arendell (1986) were among the many who brought to public attention three now well-known, but nevertheless striking, findings. First, a large proportion of divorced mothers and children live in poverty. Second, this slide into poverty appears to be the effect, not the cause, of divorce. Third, and most controversially, unlike their former wives and children, divorced fathers, taken as a group, seem actually to make considerable gains in their standard of living. Although this last statement contradicts my own sense that these fathers suffer economically, too, it is a sufficiently consistent finding that I have included it. Let us look at some numbers.

Nichols-Casebolt (1986) found that between 1966 and 1981, 9.9 percent of married white women with minor children had incomes below the poverty line. Following divorce, that figure jumped to 28.7 percent. Among nonwhite married women with children, 33.4 percent lived below the poverty line when married, 44.3 percent after divorce. Although these figures were drawn from cross-sectional studies and may have represented the vulnerability of already economically stressed families to dissolution, they raised a flag that divorce may cause previously middle-income women and children to descend into poverty.

By contrast, multiple studies have shown that the percentage of men living in poverty decreases following divorce. Nichols-Casebolt (1986) found that among white men, 9.2 percent lived below the poverty line when married; following divorce this figure dropped to 4.8 percent. Among nonwhite men, 35.7 percent lived below the poverty line when married; 26.1 percent did so following divorce. Even more dramatically, Weitzman (1981) computed that, following divorce, women experienced a 73 percent drop in standard of living, men a 42 percent rise. Because of the large disparity between mothers' and fathers' economic situations after divorce, it appeared that these changes in living standards reflected relative economic health after— not before—the breakups.

Turning from cross-sectional to longitudinal studies, Teachman and Paasch (1994) reviewed an analysis of the Survey of Income and Program Participation (SIPP) study, in which over 20,000 households were interviewed every four months between 1983 and 1986, to report only slightly more benign conclusions: for married women and their children during those three years, mean family income rose an average of 8 percent, whereas for those whose fathers left, it declined by 22.6 percent. By 1986, 31 percent of divorced mothers and children in this study lived below the poverty line, compared to only 9.7 percent of those staying married. The former group, without remarriage, showed no trend toward improved economic well-being. According to Teachman and Paasch, other researchers have similarly found that the economic depression caused by divorce can last at least five years, sometimes longer.

Arendell (1986) also looked at long-term economic changes for women with children following divorce. Between 1983 and 1984, she studied sixty mothers at least two years after their final divorce decrees. Unlike the previous researchers, who pooled numbers representing a broad income spectrum, she specifically studied women who had been in middle-class marriages. Her sample was nonclinical (in other words, not subject to the bias of one drawn from people sufficiently distressed to be in psychological counseling). Her findings: for fifty-six of the sixty women interviewed, divorce pushed them immediately below the poverty line. Neither were her long-term results much more sanguine. At a median of four years postdivorce (in most cases several more years postseparation), only nine of the sixty mothers had managed to halt their economic slide. The other fifty-one experienced no recovery.

The large number of women and children falling below the poverty line after divorce does not simply reflect those previously on the brink. As Arendell and other researchers discovered, it is not only economically stressed families whose financial rope subsequently breaks; divorce also unravels the economic well-being of mothers and children of the middle class.

However, we might ask, Were not such findings the unfortunate by-product of the early years of the divorce revolution, before child support payments were sufficiently enforced? After all, these are now routinely deducted from divorced fathers' paychecks, and a growing number of such fathers consider themselves, not their children, poor. Should not we reconsider the notion of the postdivorce gender gap?

Surprisingly, more recent studies remained consistent with earlier ones. In spite of greater efforts to enforce child support payments, by 1991 the statistics looked almost as bleak as those of a decade earlier.

One large study found that 54.7 percent of separated or divorced mothers with children under the age of six lived below the poverty line; for those with children under the age of eighteen, 39.4 percent did so (data from the U.S. Bureau of the Census, as reported by Teachman and Paasch, 1994). Nor did the gender gap appear to be narrowing. In a longitudinal study comparing mothers' and fathers' pre- and postdivorce incomes, the average economic well-being of mothers and children one year after separation was found to be only 56 percent that of fathers. Put another way, fathers' average postdivorce income was three times the poverty level, custodial mothers' only 1.5 times (Bianchi et al., 1999). These figures took into account child support and alimony awards, which were added to mothers' income and subtracted from fathers'.

Even though nonresidential fathers do feel child support's pinch, which may run as high as 30 percent of their salaries, since they do not have to provide housing, schools, or day care for their children, and since they do not have to take time off from work to care for sick children, they do not suffer the same degree of economic strain as their former wives. While some studies have suggested that fathers released from such contingencies may actually enjoy an increased living standard, other studies have concluded that fathers do suffer economically after divorce, just not as severely as mothers.

Of course, these remarks are only generalizations. Some men feel that child support, which costs them dearly, does not sufficiently benefit their offspring; rather, it is spent on their ex-wives' wasteful lifestyles. Shielded from the immediacy of the bills, such men may fail to appreciate the enormous cost of raising children, as well as the fact that the building blocks of the custodial parents' lifestyles, including a safe home, neighborhood, and car, are exactly those most critical to their children. Other fathers, however, do report being "taken to the cleaners" by vindictive former wives using money as a weapon in a war that does not always remain cold. Most important, divorced fathers' relatively privileged economic position does not mitigate the pain they may feel by not living with their children—pain that they might gladly trade for less financial freedom. Particularly when divorce was not their choice, payment of child support may feel onerous.

I believe that both parents feel divorces' economic stress, but since it is generally so much more severe for custodial mothers, I will concentrate on their situation. This decision should not be read as any callousness on my part toward fathers, but only reflecting, to the best of my knowledge, that our children's national economic crisis is due to their custodial mothers', not their fathers', poverty. Nor should my focus be read as a single-minded endorsement of the value of money for parents' postdivorce recovery, as many other factors are clearly important, including internal psychological processing, extended family support, and individual resilience. Money, however, does mitigate much of divorce's tragic aftermath. Without the leisure to date and find new partners, without the ability to pay for child care while working, without being able to hire an occasional baby-sitter for a night off, and to the extent that they are mired in poverty after divorce, mothers may find their recovery options, for them and their children, severely curtailed.

Ameliorating Factors

What factors ameliorate divorced mothers' financial landslide? Several have been considered, including remarriage, receiving the full child support awarded, and entering the workplace. It is often assumed that if women actively pursue these goals, they will climb back up the economic ladder. Let us look at these factors more closely.

Remarriage

Remarriage has consistently been found to be one of the most robust variables affecting mothers' economic recovery. A new husband brings to the table income, health insurance, retirement savings, borrowing capacity, help with child care, and a significant array of other financial and time assets. Provided he is not himself paying out significant amounts of support for children from previous marriages, many of his new wife's financial problems may be solved. So important is remarriage, in fact, that Teachman and Paasch (1994), in review, concluded that without it divorced mothers may experience no financial recovery for at least five years.

Although it is widely assumed that mothers' difficulties will be only temporary until this happy event, young, childless divorcées may achieve this goal with considerably more facility than middle-aged mothers struggling with deficits in time, money, and energy. Furthermore, even if they eventually remarry, the time it may take to do so—although not a large fraction of their adult life spans—may represent a significant part of their children's lives spent in poverty.

Arendell (1986), for example, concluded that although divorced mothers' economic difficulties may lessen when they remarry, this event is achieved neither quickly nor easily. At a median of four years after divorce, only six of the sixty women in her study were in a steady relationship with a new partner, and only eighteen had been involved at any time since separation in a consistent romantic relationship. Age, Arendell pointed out, accounts for some striking gender differences; whereas men tend to remarry regardless of age, women are less likely to do so as they become older. One study she cited found that fewer than 28 percent of divorced women over age forty remarry (Weitzman, 1985). Because they did not feel, as single mothers nearing middle age, they were particularly eligible to compete with younger, childless women for the attention of the few available men they knew, most women in Arendell's study were not optimistic about their chances. In addition, they had little energy or time to put into dating, given the demands of their lives. It is a misassumption, Arendell stated, that remarriage will solve most divorced mothers' economic problems (pp. 156-157).

More recent data (*Monthly Vital Statistics Report,* 1995) continue to support this point. While in 1990 the remarriage rate for divorced women and men between ages twenty-five and twenty-nine was roughly equal, that for divorced women between ages forty-five and forty-nine was only 54 percent that of same-age divorced men, and less than 25 percent of the remarriage rate for women ages twenty-five to twenty-nine. Even women in their thirties, the average age of those in my sample, had significantly less chance of remarrying than their male counterparts. We can conclude, then, that although remarriage is a viable solution to younger divorced mothers' economic difficulties, older women may become discouraged and look to other options.

Collection of Child Support

Collection of child support is widely assumed to ameliorate mothers' postdivorce economic plight. Of the sixty women in Arendell's (1986) study, however, twenty-four received none. Another thirteen received it only irregularly and in amounts less than ordered, and for the twenty-three who did receive it in its entirety, few awards met even half of a child's living expenses (p. 15). Most awards, in fact, were far lower. Arendell noted that her findings, which pertained to families that were financially comfortable prior to divorce, were similar to those of other researchers.

This trend did not appear to improve much in later studies. Teachman and Paasch (1994, p. 73), reviewing a much broader range of data from the U.S. Bureau of the Census, found that, by 1989, only 48 percent of divorced mothers received child support, and for those who did, it was usually much lower than the cost of raising a child.

Furthermore, even if child support were fully collected, Teachman and Paasch believed the problem might only shift, as some researchers noted that many fathers, if forced to pay, would then fall below the poverty line themselves, as they remarried and attempted to support new children or stepchildren. On the one hand, Teachman and Paasch noted that poor fathers tend nearly to double their incomes by seven years after divorce, so that the burden of child support would be largest on them and their new families at first, but they also noted that by the time fathers are able to pay, they may have drifted away from their children.

By 1991 the average amount of child support among those women who received it was $3,011 a year, hardly enough to support a child, and this was the average among only the lucky 37 percent of divorced and single mothers who collected it (U.S. Bureau of the Census, 1995). By 1995, this amount showed considerable improvement, to $3,732 a year (U.S. Bureau of the Census, 1999a). Yet even this gain of about $700 a year added up to less than the amount many intact families spend on a pet dog's food and veterinarian bills. Subsequent studies continued to underline the distressing fact that although fathers who pay child support do help lower the postdivorce gender gap, their children's standard of living still falls far short of their own (Bianchi et al., 1999). Perhaps mixed with bitter feelings about unwanted divorce, further indignation about paying a "divorce tax" may explain why so many fathers still do not pay sufficient support. Perhaps, too, the cost of raising children in our competitive economy is higher than the courts recognize.

Mothers' Return to Work

Since many divorced mothers do not easily achieve remarriage, and since child support does not reliably provide them with sufficient income to raise a family, many decide either to return to work or to enter the marketplace for the first time. Indeed, many researches believed that by taking such steps, mothers could avoid significant economic affliction. This ameliorating effect, as with others previously discussed, was overestimated. The wage gender gap, the tendency of many mothers while still married to forgo high-paying careers for lower-paying ones with more flexible hours, and the high cost of child care all sufficiently reduce the benefits of returning to work that many divorced mothers find it a losing proposition. Only nine of Arendell's sixty reversed their economic decline by working, and of these, two asserted they had done so at the expense of good parenting. Most of the others returned to "pink-color" clerical jobs, offering mothers' hours along with low incomes (1986, p. 56). Most important, among those with preschool children, none—even those working full-time—avoided falling into poverty.

Since Arendell's study, many more women have begun to enter the workforce prior to marriage. Increasingly, young women establish well-paying careers before deciding to have children, and once they do become mothers, they are more reluctant than those in the past to abandon their careers. Many married mothers continue to work part-time, keeping up skills and marketability. Presumably these recent developments should have ameliorated the severe economic effects documented in the earlier years of the divorce revolution. Yet surprisingly, Smock (1993) found that, despite such gains for single and married women, divorced mothers remain just as vulnerable as in the 1970s and 1980s. Prior work history does not protect women with children from the cost of marital breakdown.

What about mothers with the highest levels of education? Surely, we think, they do not encounter poverty, unless there are complicating circumstances, as in Christine's case. Alarmingly, even for these mothers, the situation is not benign. While highly educated women who work full-time before divorce are certainly in a better position to support themselves and their children after separation, paradoxically, they are precisely the ones who have the most to lose. Because they tend to choose mates of similar or greater education and earning potential, their income-to-need ratios (a measure of income, including child support, relative to the poverty level) suffer the greatest declines after divorce. Although these mothers' prior employment does offer protection against subsequent slide into poverty, it does not vaccinate them against a radically lower standard of living (Bianchi et al., 1999). In Christine's case, neither a business degree from a prestigious school nor years of established success in her field immunized her against divorce's financial blight.

EFFECTS OF LOWERED INCOME
ON MOTHERS' MENTAL HEALTH

Postdivorce economic deprivation has many adverse effects on mothers. I will particularly highlight those on mental health, as without an adequate sense of well-being, mothers may be unable to recover or nurture their children as they would have desired.

Becky: Shattered Dreams

Becky, a thirty-year-old mother of two, separated from her husband Ron after three years of marriage. Our interview took place about one month later. Her first child had just turned two; her second was three months old.

Becky had known Ron since she was a high school freshman, when they first met at a rock concert in their hometown of Minneapolis. Although they never dated, they developed a lasting friendship, often confiding to each other their problems.

After Ron married his girlfriend at the time, he began to complain to Becky that his wife was cold, deprived him of sex, and did not do housework. Reading between the lines, Becky believed his wife was probably cheating on him. As a result, Becky did not feel too guilty when Ron began an affair with her and left his marriage. Only twenty-two at the time, she was young, naive, and attracted to his charisma.

Although Becky and Ron moved to Portland, Maine, and lived together for three years before marrying, they were not without problems. At one point, she considered leaving, as he was not home much and rarely looked her in the eyes. Mistrustful and frustrated, she started an affair with a man who gave her more attention, but this liaison was not very satisfying to her, as it was Ron's love she really craved. After she ended the affair and confessed, Ron forgave her and then surprised her by asking her to marry him. Not making any decision at first, she began to discuss their relationship, and as she did, Becky felt better. Her affair actually acted as a catalyst to their talking about their feelings and becoming closer. Ron, now more available and loving, told her she was so different from his first wife, so much more caring, that she need not worry they would ever divorce. Happily, they set the wedding date. At the same time, since they both wanted children, they decided to begin trying. Becky was one month pregnant on her wedding day.

After Evan's birth, their marriage went well. Ron bonded with his son during the first year; eager to return from work to play with him, he seemed truly to enjoy fatherhood. After Evan turned one, however, Ron began distancing. He seemed less involved with both his son and his wife. One problem was that Becky, soon after she weaned Evan, became unexpectedly pregnant, and Ron was not particularly excited by the prospect of being a father again so soon.

Shortly after Linda's birth, Becky had an intuition that her husband was unfaithful, but this did not become explicit until Christmas Eve, when he announced he would be spending the night out. Apparently he had met a woman, fifteen years younger than himself, to whom he was highly attracted. (By now Becky was thirty-eight, Ron thirty-seven.) Becky trimmed the tree alone, and the next morning tried to appear happy so as not to spoil Evan's Christmas. She tried to pretend it was normal for his dad not to be there while they opened presents, but all she wanted to do, she later told me, was scream and scream, take the children, and leave the house forever.

As far back as she can remember, Becky had known she wanted to be a mother. She had envisioned being able to stay at home or work part-time, so that she could devote herself to raising a family. That is why, although very intelligent and talented at writing, she had not pursued a more high-powered career. She was hoping that as her children grew older, she might have more time to work on her short stories and even publish them. These were her ambitions: to be a good mother and writer.

Since Ron left, both dreams have been seriously affected. During our interview, which took place in her home in Portland, Becky tried to pay close attention to three-month-old Linda, engaging her by responding warmly to her daughter's smile. At the height of their connection, however, she jumped up, abruptly putting her daughter down as water boiled over on the stove. In earlier months, the water would have been for herbal tea to sip while writing short stories or reading to Evan. Now it is for washing dishes, as the hot water heater has broken. Sometimes, she confessed, she also uses the stove for heat, as she cannot afford to buy oil for the furnace, and neither can she afford to have her washing machine fixed, so clothes pile up until she can find time to do them all by hand. Apologetic about the condition of her home, she also worries about the peeling lead paint, though fortunately her two children have tested negative for lead poisoning. She is thankful, for she cannot afford to move.

Emotionally, the breakup has been rough on Becky. Although very early in the relationship she had questioned her commitment to Ron, by the time they decided to marry she felt she had worked through her doubts and had pictured her vows as a promise—not necessarily to stay together if their relationship became overwhelmingly difficult—but certainly to try to work on problems before leaving. "I thought that between taking wedding vows, and then having two children, this would be permanent," she said. Not only was her marriage short-lived, but it unraveled at a speed that left her emotionally traumatized. After Ron left, she burned some wedding gifts; their charred pieces were visible as I entered the house.

Her early motherhood, Becky feels, has been stolen from her. "I'm spending what little emotional capital I have left just managing," she said. Although she is taking adequate physical care of Linda, she fears her daughter might be picking up on her depressed mood and irritability. Having little help with child care, she becomes stressed and fatigued and, for the first time in her life, has severe mood swings. She never hits her children, but she knows that Evan is seeing her fuse, shortened by fatigue and depression, blow too often. She would like just to stop doing everything and cry for a week, but knows she cannot. Grief is a luxury she feels she cannot afford.

In addition to the effects on herself, Becky has noticed those on her son. Formerly a happy, confident boy who loved spending time with Ron in his carpentry workshop, he has lost his sparkle. "Daddy workshop, Daddy workshop," Evan repeats mournfully, while searching for his father. Becky knows this is a hard time for Evan, having lost his dad at the same time his mom is busy with a new infant.

The loss, of course, is not total; Ron does spend some time with his children, but he often leaves them at his own mother's during visitation hours, so that he is free to be alone with his new girlfriend, who is understandably more interested in him than his children. Although formerly a good dad, Ron is now disengaging. When he does visit at night he turns the television up loudly, becoming absorbed in adult shows. Not paying much attention to his children, he tells Becky he does not believe divorce will affect them much.

Becky wonders what changed in Ron, for he had seemed very committed to her and Evan. She knows that her two pregnancies put a damper on their sex life, but she had tried to find time to be intimate with him, and had also tried to include him in family events. She is still in too much shock to be able to think it all through, but in retrospect she wonders if Ron needed her undivided attention.

As difficult as is her situation, Becky tries to hold on to her hopes, including her long-term dream of publishing some of her work. But unlike J. K. Rowling, she has no Harry Potter up her sleeve. As she contemplates going on welfare, as the laundry piles up and her car dies, she is pained that her children are poor and she will have little time to develop her writing skills. Although previously rarely depressed, now she struggles with frequent despair, as not only her marriage but her chances to realize her deepest personal ambitions fade into invisibility.

Before they had children, on their combined salaries Becky and Ron had been able to pay their bills, but after Evan was born, they found that their baby's extra expenses, coupled with Becky's quitting work, caused them to start falling behind. Now that they have a second child and Ron has left, it is unclear how they will manage, as rather than benefiting from Ron's full salary, Becky and the children will have to live, at best, off a fraction of it. Not only must Becky deal with the psychological trauma of her divorce, but she must also contend with economic deprivation on a scale she never anticipated.

Such financial damage initiates a cycle of poverty from which it can be difficult to escape. Considering the three ameliorating factors for mothers' economic recovery—collection of child support, remarriage, and return to work—how do we predict Becky will fare?

First, let us consider child support. These awards are made according to mathematical formulas based primarily on the two parents' relative incomes; custodial parents making over a minimum amount

($15,000 a year in Massachusetts in 1994) receive less support than if they did not work. As Becky is unemployed, the amount she receives will be unaffected by this penalty and based entirely on Ron's earnings. Although we do not know exactly what the amount will total, we do know that for two children it is usually no more than 30 percent of their father's income. Given that Becky could barely pay the bills on Ron's full salary, she will fare poorly unless she has very significant other sources of income.

Second, let us consider remarriage. This option, although not an unreasonable goal, seems remote. Becky has months, more likely years, ahead in which she must deal with the emotional sequelae of her breakup, which because of its unilateral, rejecting, and untimely nature may leave her with more than the usual scars. Even after trying to mend these wounds, she must find time as well as money to date, and she must compete with younger, unencumbered women to find a man willing to assume partial responsibility for two young children lacking financial resources. Intellectually, she knows such men do exist, but after her recent trauma, she has difficulty believing it in her heart.

Third, let us consider Becky's returning to work. She estimates that should she work full-time, the cost of day care for her two children would be $5 each, or about $10 an hour. That adds up to $400 a week, or over $20,000 a year, mostly non–tax-deductible (her child care tax credit allows a refund of just $500 a year). At her previous job as an office manager, she earned $28,000 a year before taxes. For returning to work not to be a losing game, she would have to find less expensive child care, or enter a new field. Although she has looked for "cut-rate" child care she does not care to subject her children to its compromises, which she discovered often include poorly trained staff and overcrowded facilities. Furthermore, much as she would like to enter a higher income bracket, she does not have the skills to do so—not because she lacks intelligence or ambition, but because she had thought her main "career" would be that of wife, homemaker, and mother. Of course, she could return to graduate school, but she would have to take out large loans to pay not just tuition but also child care, and she is not sure she could ever pay them back. Until her children are much older and in grade school, she suspects her working options are limited.

Accordingly, Becky may have a long road ahead before she reestablishes herself as middle income, before she hooks up her washing machine and hot-water heater. Her three ameliorating factors, as other researchers have found, initially add up, not to hot water, but to hot air.

Yet, we must remember, Becky is an unusually intelligent and creative woman. Perhaps she will overcome such obstacles through sheer talent and determination. Similar to Rowling, maybe she will be able to publish her work or develop her skills to the point she could be hired as a writer or editor. To do so, Becky needs to maintain her mental health. Exhausted, short fused, and poor, she can still push her body to write during the night hours, but if she succumbs to depression, she will be unlikely to persevere. Her mental health may be one of her most important assets, the one holding the key to unlocking her other talents.

Just as Becky's mood affects her financial prospects, so does her financial state affect her mood. There is no question that if her income were sufficient, she would be less depressed and more hopeful, yet each day as her children play amidst peeling paint, she becomes a bit more depressed, a bit less able to feel motherhood's joy, a bit less able to focus on her writing. Not only her children's opportunities, but also her own, were fuller before divorce.

Becky's case is hardly unique. Of the sixty women Arendell (1986, pp. 46-52) studied, those doing best emotionally had children of elementary school age or older at the time of divorce, were able to afford working only part-time, or had help parenting. In other words, all women doing well psychologically either had significant other sources of income, considerable help with child care, or both. While none of the nine who achieved complete economic recovery reported suffering serious emotional sequelae of divorce, forty-four of those in poverty reported frequent struggles with depression and despair. Twenty-six, in fact, contemplated suicide at some time after divorce, most citing economic hardship as the primary stress pushing them to this point. Their financial situation was much more dire than for those women less depressed, and it appeared that the former condition drove the latter.

Although some self-help books extol the opportunities divorce brings for personal growth and development, Arendell found this to be a gross misassumption for mothers, for although divorce may allow them to break free of unhappy marriages, it brings no parallel economic liberation. Instead, it often sets off a chain reaction of narrowed choices, resulting in financial meltdown. The mothers in Arendell's study did not feel more fulfilled after divorce. Most admitted that their parenting skills suffered for months, as they struggled to get through the days with inadequate resources:

> Most of these women were engaged in an ongoing struggle to make ends meet, to handle simultaneously the tasks of parenting and earning an income, and to cope with the stress brought on by the uncertainties of their lives. Rather than being liberated single women, they were socially and emotionally isolated, as well as overloaded with demands on their time and energy. (p. 155)

Arendell highlighted the devastating economic effects divorce has on women and children, and the close relationship between mothers' financial stability and emotional well-being. Indeed, the effect of financial downslide is so powerful that it may initiate clinical depression in mothers who were previously well adjusted.

CONCLUSION

> A fourth straight year of growth in real median household income made 1998 the year with the highest income levels ever recorded, as poverty dropped significantly and the children's poverty rate was lower than 20 percent for the first time since 1980. (U.S. Bureau of the Census, 1999b, p. 1)

Buried on page three of this otherwise glowing report, however, we discover the following qualifier:

> Despite the drop in child poverty, children under age 6 remained particularly vulnerable; those living in families with a female householder and no husband present experienced a poverty rate of 54.8 percent, more than five times the rate for children under 6 in married-couple families (10.1 percent).

Although these figures included never-married as well as divorced mothers, other researchers have found that about 45 percent of children of all ages raised by a divorced mother live near or below the poverty line (U.S. Bureau of the Census, 1997).

These figures hardly seem an improvement over those of fifteen years ago. How can this be true, when considerable efforts have been made to increase collection of child support, when we have witnessed an unprecedented economic boom, the benefits of which, according to the same 1999 report, have been reaped by men and women across race, class, and geographic region?

The answer appears to be that the "ameliorating" factors popularly believed to offset the financial hardships of divorced mothers—including opportunities for women to work at higher-paying jobs, increased efforts to collect child support, and the possibility of remarriage—have been inadequate to compensate for the loss of fathers' full incomes. Despite a recent radio advertisement announcing that personal wealth is no longer measured in millions, but rather billions, of dollars, over half of children in female-headed families live in poverty. As our nation has prospered, single and divorced mothers, and their children, have not.

Such statistics also indicate that the younger the children, the more likely they are to be poor. What can we conclude about the economic future of women and children who divorce at childbirth?

Divorce at this time magnifies the financial problems we have discussed in at least four ways. First, many postpartum women, such as Christine and Becky, are unprepared for divorce. Before becoming pregnant they believed they were in viable relationships. Far from having a baby to save their marriages, if they had thought divorce was imminent they either would not have had children or, at the very least, would have started planning how to manage after separating. The economics of divorce at childbirth, accordingly, do not simply reflect those of mothers with older children, nor are they similar to those of single women who decided to have babies on their own. There is an added element of surprise, a complete lack of planning, and, all too often, emotional trauma.

Second, the months around childbirth represent a time many mothers find it particularly difficult to maintain full-time jobs. Although some do return to work immediately postpartum, the emotional and economic price tags are often exorbitant. Many find that the cost of child care, coupled with the exhaustion of balancing job, commuting, homemaking, and infant night feedings, make working full-time a losing proposition.

Third, as we have seen through many of the stories in this book, divorce at childbirth may ignite extremely intense conflict. Couples do not often separate amicably during the postpartum period. Rather, something has gone very wrong, very suddenly. One partner either has an abrupt realization that the other partner is dangerously unfit for parenthood or experiences a sense of inexplicable betrayal. Unlike divorces with older children, those involving infants are less likely to be either planned or mutual. Furthermore, the timing of these break-ups means that little triadic bonding between infants and parents, and little sense of being a family has occurred. Consequently, whereas many separating couples with older children try to maintain a sense of family, even if not a traditional one, this may be difficult for those divorcing at childbirth. How, they may wonder, can they become a family if they never were? Nonresidential fathers may feel particularly alienated. With animosity high between them and their former wives, with little sense of triadification, such fathers may be less likely to pay child support regularly than those with older children to whom they have already bonded.

Fourth, few new mothers have the desire, much less leisure, to begin dating. While childless divorcées may be eager to look for new partners and remarry, divorced mothers with young children have little time or energy to devote to this. We recall Stern's (1995) notion of the motherhood constellation, in which new mothers orient toward other women to learn the necessary skills; nowhere in this constellation is there psychological room for new romantic adventures. Mothers with infants may be at risk of a long wait until remarriage offers a road out of loneliness and poverty.

As a result of these four factors, divorce at childbirth is likely to create even more financial havoc than divorce involving older children. No wonder few in my book avoided going on welfare, as well as using extensive resources of their relatives, as they began their steep uphill climb toward recovery.

This brings us to a final point. The harsh economics of divorce at childbirth force many mothers to rely heavily on their own families, essentially realigning the transfer of assets matrilinearly. It is not their former husbands who provide the missing pieces in these children's economic puzzles, but a combination of public assistance and support from the mothers' extended families. To the extent that this shift is occurring on a massive scale, an economic realignment of our society is underway (see also Furstenberg et al., 1995).

Even with help from their own families, however, these mothers remain highly vulnerable to loss of income. They also remain highly vulnerable to the psychological effects of their unexpected plunge into poverty. For many, this last event alone would be an enormous blow, even if accompanied by a supportive spouse and minus a baby, but following unexpected divorce at childbirth, such economic dives can be crippling. While some women who leave unsuitable mates at this time may be especially strong swimmers, others find their strokes inadequate for colder waters. As they lose strength, their hopes slip away. Many dreams—including lifestyle, career choice, and simply being able to spend adequate time with their children—may sink like stones. For such women, adversity is not opportunity, but just adversity.

Chapter 6

Effects of Divorce on Children

In the last two chapters, we reviewed the emotional and economic effects of divorce at childbirth on adults and noted that it may take five or more years to recover. How, we wonder, do their infants fare?

The vast literature on the effects of divorce on older children, although contradictory at times, points to some general conclusions. Little, however, has been written about the effects on infants. To address this topic, I will first review what is known about how older children react to their parents' breakups. In the next chapter, I will extrapolate these findings, as well as those of recent infant research, to the case of the very young.

How do children react to divorce? Whitehead (1997, pp. 84-102) noted two waves of research on this topic; the first, occurring in the immediate wake of the divorce revolution, minimized the recognition of any damaging sequelae, as dissatisfied couples were encouraged to separate according to a "trickle-down" theory of happiness, which stipulated that if parents were happier, so would be their children. The second wave, using more sophisticated tools, came to less sanguine conclusions.

Amato and Keith's studies (1991a,b) exemplified this second wave. Performing a meta-analysis of ninety-two studies involving over 13,000 children, they found short-term negative effects in the areas of school achievement, conduct problems, psychological well-being, social adjustment, and parent-child relations. This actually came as no great surprise, as these problems had long been observed by parents, teachers, therapists, and researchers, many of whom hoped such difficulties might only reflect children's temporary reactions. In a second meta-analysis of thirty-seven studies involving over 81,000 adults, however, Amato and Keith discovered similar results for divorce's long-term impact. Early negative effects on academic achievement, conduct, and psychological adjustment persisted to adulthood.

Of course, not all divorced children suffered such long-term sequelae, but compared to those whose families remained intact, their adjustment showed a statistical downward shift, even when socioeconomic conditions were controlled.

Tolstoy wrote that whereas happy families are all alike, every unhappy family is unhappy in its own way. Whether or not we agree with the first half of his statement, the second half rings true: each divorcing family appears uniquely stamped with its own brand of misery. Statistical findings such as Amato and Keith's represent only an average, a general drift, and do not have the resolution power to perceive the finer grains of individual difference. Some children, we know, actually do better after their parents separate—relieved, perhaps, that an unbearable level of conflict finally ended. But in spite of Tolstoy's observation, and in spite of the wide divergence among families, divorce does have some predictable effects. If we trade his high-powered lens for one with broader scope, these come into view.

Before turning to a discussion of such research, I must first backtrack, for, as a psychotherapist, I must mention one caveat: in contrast to their outward, observable behaviors, children's internal reactions to loss can be most difficult to assess fully.

DIFFICULTY ACCURATELY ASSESSING CHILDREN'S REACTIONS TO LOSS

Children are notoriously hard to read. A recent news clipping described how a school-age girl living alone with her mother reacted to discovering her death: she cuddled all night with her mother's lifeless body, then in the morning packed a lunch and went to school as usual, where she appeared sufficiently unperturbed that her teacher did not take her seriously when, chatting during recess, she let it slip that her mother had died. Later there was much outcry against the teacher, but the story illustrated how well children can hide their feelings, and how successfully they can appear to function under even the most traumatic circumstances. Perhaps because they cannot afford to be thrown developmentally offtrack, they have strong defenses against experiencing pain.

Such observations are not new. Deutsch (1937) noted the "phenomenon of indifference" that children frequently show following the death of a loved one. Her explanation was that children are not constitutionally mature enough to mourn and must protect themselves from doing so. Mourning would simply be too traumatic, too developmentally derailing.

Similar observations were made by Wolfenstein (1966), who had extensive experience with children and adolescents whose parents had died:

> Sad feelings were curtailed; there was little weeping. Immersion in the activities of everyday life continued. There was no withdrawal into preoccupation with thoughts of the lost parent. Gradually the fact emerged that overtly or covertly the child was denying the finality of the loss. The painful process of decathexis of the lost parent was put off, with the more or less conscious expectation of his return. (pp. 336-337)

Wolfenstein referred to children's "short sadness span" (p. 340) after such tragic events, and she noted how closely young children protect fantasies that their lost parents might return. Confrontation with reality, she thought, might be too painful to bear (p. 344).

Contrary to views that children do not mourn, other clinicians observed that children do—but just not obviously. Robert Furman (1968) described one of his young patients, who, after losing his mother, shared much painful mommy-missing with him. Incredibly, this boy's grief was invisible to most observers, including the boy's father, who believed his son did not miss his mother very much. Furman noted that parents, themselves in the throes of acute grief, may be too preoccupied to notice their children's sorrow. In another example, he portrayed a boy whose father had been recently murdered. According to the mother and teachers, the boy seemed to have little feeling about the tragedy, and, in fact, when he went to school, he acted as though nothing had happened. Only when interviewed by his therapist did he break down in tears, explaining that he had tried to tell his mother how he felt, but she had not been able to listen. Neither had anyone at school inquired how he was doing. Furman later verified the correctness of the boy's statements (p. 374).

Erna Furman (1974) also observed that children's grief may affect them silently. Although initially these children may appear relatively unperturbed, their superficially good early adaptations often lead to major long-term problems: the adoption of defenses that at first appear healthy but later impede growth because they are too extensive or rigid.

> For the most part these problems did not arise at once but tended to follow a long period of relatively appropriate functioning, marked by controlled behavior, subdued affective response, and little reference to the parent's death. The adults in the child's environment tended to regard this quiescent period as a sign of good adjustment, and even those who were concerned or puzzled at the child's apparent lack of reaction often welcomed it and hesitated to interfere by bringing up the subject of the dead parent. (p. 387)

Simply because children do not show immediate grief does not mean they are unaffected. Their grief-avoiding defenses, although helpful in the short run, may cause long-term damage to their ability to access important feelings. Normal childhood mourning can easily turn pathological if there is insufficient support for emotional expressiveness (Frankiel, 1994). If the surviving parent is unable to provide a suitable climate for mourning, it is likely that a young child, trying to cope alone with overwhelming sadness, will attempt to set his or her own emotional thermostat.

Many child psychotherapists similarly concluded that such "indifference" following loss of a parent may actually represent a defense, which becomes necessary when children try to manage severe grief on their own. Although most literature has focused on such reactions following parental death, however, a case par excellence of children receiving insufficient support with mourning must certainly be divorce. We know that separating couples, mired in their own turmoil, often overlook their children's sadness. Teachers, struggling to meet the demands of their classrooms with dwindling resources, may also lack time and privacy to ask the critical questions. In studying children's reactions to divorce, therefore, researchers must be careful not to mistake the mask for the reality. Studies relying on questionnaires or parental reports but, not providing in-depth interviews with children themselves, may considerably underrate negative reactions. One researcher's remarks, although lengthy, are worth repeating:

> It is because of the complexity of the issues that are unfolding that there is cause for concern if there is too single-minded a fo-

cus on a single research paradigm such as much of the current preoccupation with quantitative methods, carefully controlled samples, control groups using group-aggregated data, and statistical determination of significance. If these methods were to be adopted to the exclusion of intensive clinical methods and case studies, it might well cost the individual voice of the child. Given not only the complexity of family issues but also the vast numbers of future citizens whose lives will have been profoundly changed by divorce, it is especially important that future research gives weight to the testimony of the inner world of human experience; in this instance to the child's experience. (Wallerstein, 1991, p. 359)

In other words, Tolstoy's lens still matters. With this in mind, let us turn to how divorce affects children.

ADVERSE EFFECTS OF DIVORCE ON CHILDREN

Allison: Empathy's Flaw

Allison, an obstetrical nurse, separated in her midthirties after five years of marriage, when her daughter was eleven months old. Our interview took place two and a half years later.

Allison and Chuck became friends while attending the same college in western Massachusetts, and they began to date shortly after graduation. Even then, Chuck had a problem with alcohol, as drinking binges and long disappearances—sometimes for days at a time—characterized his party lifestyle. Allison, however, thought such behavior was more a sign of his youth than a serious problem. Indeed, many of his friends had stopped their heavy drinking after marrying and starting families. Hoping Chuck would similarly mature, Allison thought she could help him change.

Soon after they married, she accidentally became pregnant, and she miscarried at three months. She was unprepared for how sad and empty she felt afterward. To make up for her terrible loss, she felt she just had to have another baby. Chuck, although he had not felt ready for children, understood how devastating the miscarriage had been for her. He became eager to try again, and by the time they conceived a year later, he seemed to be truly looking forward to having a child.

In spite of his apparent commitment to fatherhood, Chuck continued to drink heavily. Always saying he would stop soon, he simply ignored Allison's suggestions for ways to quit. Even marriage counseling did no good, and he refused to attend Alcoholics Anonymous (AA) meetings recommended by their therapist. All this began to take a toll on Allison, who, as her pregnancy progressed, became increasingly intolerant of Chuck's drunken binges and absences, but as she began asking for more attention from him, he gave less and less. Feeling pressured, he told her he did not like her "change in attitude."

Although after Sarah's birth Chuck seemed to engage well with his daughter and enjoy fatherhood, he was unable to sustain this happy state. When Sarah was about ten months old, during a week-long family vacation he disappeared for three days. This was not the first time he had done so, but it was the first time since his daughter's birth. Now that she had a baby, Allison was less forgiving. When Chuck returned, Allison angrily told him that if he staged a similar disappearance, she would begin divorce proceedings. Telling her that she was overly emotional, he ignored her ultimatum and a few weeks later disappeared again. This time he stumbled home to discover she was kicking him out.

Chuck was enraged. In denial about the severity of his alcohol problem, he took no responsibility for his marriage's demise. Furthermore, although Allison actually encouraged visitation, he accused her of taking "his" baby away from him. Their divorce was extremely acrimonious. Allison, sleepless and emaciated, did not back down.

Allison had never liked alcohol herself, but she had been able to tolerate Chuck's drinking as long as they were childless. With only the two of them to worry about, she had told herself that he still had plenty of time to grow up; meanwhile she could live her somewhat separate life, pursuing her nursing career at the same time she ran the household. In a sense, she had functioned as a mother to Chuck. That all changed when she had a real baby. The prospect of her daughter growing up with an alcoholic father, traumatized by his drunken disappearances, became too much for Allison to bear. No longer able to live under such conditions, in spite of the enormous stress her divorce caused, she proceeded to do what she felt was best for her daughter.

After separating, Allison felt great emotional pain. Even though she had initiated the divorce, she felt Chuck had actually left her. Why, she wondered, if he loved her, was he not willing to get treatment for his alcoholism? By the time of our interview, two and a half years later, much of her anguish has burned out; most of the time she just feels numb. Nevertheless, every meeting with her ex-husband threatens to rekindle her pain.

Chuck professes to love their daughter Sarah and is reliable about weekday baby-sitting, though rarely showing up for scheduled weekend visits. But in spite of their frequent trading of child care duties, Allison has very little honest communication with Chuck. She finds him wispy, hard to pin down. He remains embittered about the divorce and continues to drink. When working he pays child support, but when unemployed—a frequent occurrence—his support checks stop. Allison's life would be much easier if she did not have to see him, yet even if she could arrange this, she would not want to deprive Sarah of a father.

Currently spending as much time as she can with her daughter, Allison is also attempting to advance her nursing career so that she can support herself and Sarah. Meanwhile money is tight, and she is not sure how she would manage if her ex-husband's relatives were not kindly, offering her low rent on one of their condos in Amherst. Of course, such favors come with emotional price tags, which in Allison's case is a frequent earful about how evil she was to divorce Chuck. Eventually she hopes to be able to support herself adequately.

Allison's other hope, to meet a man who could be a good stepfather to Sarah, seems further off in its realization. She does not have much time to date, and even if she did, she does not know any available men. Once she flipped through the personals, but as she read descriptions of the type of women for whom men were searching, it only brought tears to her eyes. Unlike Chuck, who has a new girlfriend, Allison is on her own. Neither can she turn to her family of origin, as after her parents died during her childhood, she was raised by older siblings, now all gone separate ways.

Sarah, Allison says, seems happy, or at least she appears not to have been too affected by her father's departure just before her first birthday. At three and a half, she has started asking questions about why her parents do not live together. Allison feels like telling her, "You transformed my life; you gave me the power to leave," but she does not want to undermine Sarah's love for her father.

For most of our interview, Allison maintained a bright, if slightly forced tone. She had no regrets about her divorce and, despite its hardships, felt she was the hardier and Sarah the happier for it. Yet toward the end of our talk, she let down her guard enough to reveal a painful dilemma. Like a jewel whose flaws appear only under certain beams of light, Allison's empathy for her daughter is marred by Sarah's resemblances, fading and then reappearing, to her father. Because Allison perceived the divorce as Chuck's fault, because her anger toward him never truly abated, and because she felt more trauma than grief over losing her husband, aspects of Sarah reminiscent of Chuck can trigger her anger and disgust.

For example, hardest for Allison is hearing Sarah talk like her father. Similar to many children her age, Sarah enjoys making up long, imaginative tales. Such childish fables, rich in fantasy and humor, would ordinarily delight a mother. Instead, they remind Allison of Chuck's elaborately winding lies. Worried that Sarah might have acquired her father's trait of dishonesty, Allison stiffens, feels her stomach churning, and scolds, "Sarah, don't make up stories." Other times, when Sarah draws on the wall after Allison has told her to stop, Allison's body remembers how Chuck was always testing, testing, testing. Her heart racing and her hands gripping, she leaves the room, slamming the door before she starts to scream. Allison thinks Sarah's behaviors are probably normal, but she is not entirely sure. As they trigger memories tinged with enormous pain and anger, Allison cannot resonate with such important aspects of her daughter.

It is widely believed that if divorce ameliorates overt parental conflict—the screaming, the name-calling, the frying-pan-throwing—it will act in the best interest of the child. Divorcing parents are often reassured that if they simply avoid open expression of their hostilities, all will be well. Yet Allison's story, favorable on this account, reveals a deeper problem: unless parents separate amicably, respectfully, as friends or at least as good working colleagues, they may have difficulty accepting aspects of their children that remind them of each other. Even though Sarah benefits by no longer living in a family riddled with alcoholism and frequent fighting, she still faces a major disadvantage.

Her mother has difficulty tolerating aspects of her suggestive of her father—aspects that for a child this age should be considered healthy.

But thank goodness Allison did leave her husband, my readers are probably musing. Surely Sarah is better off in a peaceful household, without a frequently drunk father, without the loud arguments, or without the long waits for him to stumble incoherently home. And I would agree, but I would also add that parents such as Allison, for whom divorce is more a trauma than a grief, may be hindered in their ability to relate to their children as effectively as they would have desired.

Allison's problem—difficulty empathizing with aspects of her child "similar" to those of her former spouse—is one of the most intractable that traumatically divorced parents face. It is, however, far from the only one with repercussions for the young. Having reviewed the effects of downward socioeconomic slide in the previous chapter, let us now consider some other effects of divorce on children. Transmission of their parents' emotional responses, internal processing of divorce, and differences in mourning parental divorce and death begin our look at the large reservoir of clinical experience; we will also discuss findings of large-scale studies on externalizing problems. I am not attempting a complete review, but simply to frame our understanding of how divorce may affect, not only older siblings, but very young infants, such as those in my study.

Transmission of Parents' Emotional Responses

Divorce, we know, involves extreme emotional upheaval. Most parents try to protect their children, putting on their bravest faces while masking the full force of their own anguish. We sometimes forget, however, that parents' emotional responses, even if not directly expressed, are often indirectly telegraphed to children, whose antennae are exquisitely attuned to such signals.

One frequent signal is a parent's depressed mood. Maternal depression itself, even in the context of a well-functioning marriage, may have profoundly negative effects on young children, but after divorce, without the backup of a second live-in parent, children may be even more vulnerable if locked into this single troubled listening channel. Although some depressed mothers are able to shield their children from their condition, others are not able to do so.

Working with adults whose mothers had been depressed many years previously, Green (1986) referred to such mothers as having been "dead" to their young children:

> I shall not be discussing here the psychical consequences of the real death of the mother, but rather that of an imago which has been constituted in the child's mind, following maternal depression, brutally transforming a figure, toneless, practically inanimate . . . the dead mother, contrary to what one might think, is a mother who remains alive but is, so to speak, psychically dead in the eyes of the young child in her care. (p. 142)

Reconstructing his patients' childhoods, Green believed that they had survived either by identifying closely with their depressed mothers or, alternatively, by finding solace in lonely, disconnected states. His findings reflected those of psychotherapists who tried to understand retrospectively the effects of maternal depression. Many researchers, in addition, are now studying children directly.

In one such study (Radke-Yarrow, 1991), children ranging in age from sixteen months to three and a half years were followed until age eight to nine. Their mothers had been diagnosed with either unipolar depression (N = 45) or no psychiatric problem (N = 45). Radke-Yarrow also included twenty-one bipolar mothers in her study. Among the children of mothers with a history of unipolar depression, the researchers found substantial manifestations of sadness, anxiety, and downcast mood. Even the youngest toddlers were already developing various means of coping; some, drawn into very tight relationships with their mothers, had the mixed consequences of enjoying the security of such closeness at the same they incorporated their mothers' anxious sadness into their own nascent self-definitions; others become avoidant, turning away from connection. The authors felt that even at this early age, compared to children with nondepressed mothers, those with depressed ones had developed disturbed emotional states. These prospective findings were similar to Green's retrospective ones.

Other attachment researchers, such as Lyons-Ruth et al. (1997), also found that a high level of maternal depression during the first five years predicted later problems in children's behavior. Greater levels of aggression and poorer academic performance were noted up to at least age seven.

Studies such as these, which included children from a variety of family types, may not reflect the even more serious situation in which clinical depression in one or both parents has been precipitated by divorce, for after this event there is no second parent at home in reserve to buffer the other's mood swings. Nor is the situation resolved, if it is the mother who is depressed, by assigning temporary custody to the father, unless this arrangement was agreed upon for other reasons, as children may feel their mother is being penalized and their own lives disrupted. Unfortunately, as we observed in Chapter 4, a very high rate of depression is present among newly divorced parents.

Depression, however, may be only the tip of the iceberg at this time. Tessman (1978), working with a population drawn from a community clinic, found that in 34 percent of divorcing families with young children, at least one parent was completely emotionally disabled—either psychotic, suicidal, in prison, or severely alcoholic. Although her figures probably reflected a sample more disturbed than the usual, they nevertheless revealed that many children must contend with their parents' extreme emotional distress at the same time they are trying to adjust to the separation.

Most important, even if parents avoid major incapacitation, Garber (1984) found they may still transmit their difficulties in mourning the loss of their marriages. For example, some mothers who felt cruelly treated by their husbands lack sufficiently positive memories either to help their children grieve or to accept aspects of their children reminding them, even obliquely, of their former partners. As in Allison's case, such mothers may discover that significant parts of their children's healthy personalities trigger strongly negative reactions, and, devastatingly, some fathers may avoid seeing their children so as not to be reminded of former spouses. Particularly those parents experiencing divorce as a trauma may have difficulty not only with their own grief but with helping their children mourn as well.

Children's Difficulty in Internally Processing Divorce

Children do not just pick up their parents' emotional signals; they also process them in their own unique ways, and the conclusions they reach may be quite different from those we might expect. On the one hand, some children from very high-conflict families may be relieved to learn their parents are separating. Older siblings, tired and traumatized from witnessing years of violence, may exclaim, "High time!" Many families, however, separate for reasons less clear to their children, who may have felt quite content with their lives. For such young ones, departure of one parent means dramatic changes in their relationships with both.

Unfortunately, these changes are often negative. Overburdened and economically strapped, custodial parents typically have less quality time to share, and noncustodial ones, even with frequent visits and overnights, may try to maximize shorter time frames by squeezing in an array of activities that, although guaranteed to make visitation pleasurable, do not substitute for a previous low-keyed, stable availability. Furthermore, as children shuttle back and forth between households, they lose the opportunity to relate to their parents as a family. Their bonds are now separate, tightly dyadic, no longer involving the complexity of the adult-adult-child triad—unless, of course, fresh partners enter the picture, and they may unwittingly create highly competitive new triads. To such children, divorce is a loss—a loss of unmeasured time with the departed parent; a loss of the family as a unit; a breaking of the triangle into two separate, often noncommunicative, pieces. What for parents is liberation, for children is often amputation.

As a result, even if such divorcing parents avoid blaming each other, their children wrestle with a difficult question. From their point of view, they ask, What went so wrong, that the exiting one's desire to live full-time with them did not prevail? Explanations such as "Neither Mom nor Dad is to blame; we just couldn't get along anymore, but we both still love you" do not suffice and may even add more confusion to the already bewildering crisis. Such explanations, particularly in those families which had little overt conflict, may read similarly to unexpected suicide notes that state, "Don't feel bad. This isn't your fault. I love you."

Their families split, given such pseudoexplanations, children search their own souls for answers. They may blame themselves, or one or both parents. In addition to trying to understand what went so wrong, they may also have a new concern: how to protect their relationship with a parent now departed. Safer to direct anger toward themselves than toward a parent no longer there, they may reason. Alternatively, they may accuse the custodial parent of driving the other away. Attempting to protect the bond that feels most fragile, they may rage at themselves and their custodial parent, while idealizing the departed.

Jacobson (1965) found that children who lose a parent to death not only idealize the deceased but also firmly expect him or her to return. The remaining parent tends to be blamed. Her findings were not limited to loss due to death but were also relevant to cases of desertion:

> In the minds of all these patients this—actual or supposed—desertion had not been the fault of the lost parent who, they were sure, had been a wonderful person. It had been caused by the surviving parent's intolerable character traits or moral worthlessness. (p. 234)

Extending these findings to children of divorce, Neubauer (1989) similarly noted much idealization of the departed parent. The need to assign responsibility, he found, is paramount in young minds, and it is rarely assigned to the noncustodial figure. Children of divorce either feel undeserving of the departed's love or believe that the remaining parent made it impossible for the other to stay. In addition to increased hostility, such children may exhibit an unusual degree of clinging, fearing that if one parent could leave, so could the other.

Similarly, Michaels (1989) studied the fantasies of preschoolers whose fathers were absent from the home due to divorce; contact varied from none to frequent, with some visiting multiple times per week. As Neubauer predicted, she found that these children had overwhelmingly good fantasies about their nonresident fathers. Only minimally recognizing the latter's negative qualities, the children lacked the mixed feelings usually characteristic of this age group. With much dyadic fantasy, but little concept of triadic relationships, they also lacked the notion of their parents as a couple. Believing that working through such triadic themes helps form the basis for more mature, realistic concepts of father as a complete person, Michaels concluded, "The existence of bad aspects of father in actuality or fantasy is perhaps more dependent on father's presence than on his absence, and a luxury that preschool children with nonresident fathers cannot afford" (p. 421).

Children's internal processing of divorce, accordingly, does not always correlate with the "facts" of the separation. In particular, children are more likely to shift blame either onto themselves or onto the parent with whom they feel more secure. Such a tendency was illustrated by Jennifer's story, which I will summarize briefly.

Jennifer, raised Catholic, did not believe in divorce. Always hoping Charlie would change, she tolerated his physical abuse for years. Besides punching her in the stomach during each of her pregnancies, he frequently subjected her to other violence—on one occasion bashing her head against a wall, on another attempting to strangle her with a phone cord—all witnessed by their young son. After the birth of their second son, Jennifer finally found the courage to divorce.

Time did not abate Charlie's fury that she had ended the marriage, however. Even several years later, he continued to express his anger by refusing to commit to a regular visitation schedule, often arriving extremely late to greet his children, who had been anxiously waiting for hours. He continued to be physically abusive toward a new girlfriend. But in spite of their frequently witnessing his violent and irresponsible behavior, his children referred to him as a "great daddy." It seemed that the worse his behavior, the more they idealized him. Jennifer, on the other hand, felt the full brunt of their anger, as after they returned from visits with Charlie, they talked back to her in an extremely derogatory style.

As Michaels (1989) pointed out, for the child desperately trying to hold onto a relationship with a departed parent, such idealization initially appears to serve a useful purpose, but later it may interfere with maturation of the ability to integrate good and bad aspects of important others. A significant distortion of reality, it may stunt a child's understanding of self and others.

Comparing Divorce to Death:
Differences in Mourning and Identification

In the past, research on the effects of parental loss focused on the circumstance of death. More recent studies (Garber, 1984; Rodgers, 1994; O'Connor et al., 1999) reveal a surprising but consistent thread: the child losing a parent to divorce may suffer even more long-term sequelae than the one losing a parent to death. Whereas the bereaved child appears on the surface sadder, more withdrawn, and preoccupied, the one whose parents have divorced is more likely to be in conflict with his or her environment. This child's anguish seems more outwardly directed, more overtly hostile. As he or she acts out through antisocial behaviors, these bring the child less comfort, more pain.

The effect of losing a parent to death, early in life, cannot be overestimated. Such untimely, irrevocable loss, coupled with the emotional and financial problems of the surviving parent, make this an extreme misfortune. Yet a number of studies show that, all else being equal, the bereaved child may have a greater chance of emotional recovery than the one of divorce. Of course, this rule does not always apply, but we should be alert to the possibility that a large number of our young (40 percent of children born to married parents, by some calculations [Furstenberg, 1994]) will suffer effects at least as severe as those we had thought reserved for the relatively small number experiencing the tragedy of premature parental death.

This finding, I admit, is startling. As we consider how differently children psychologically process the two situations of death and divorce, however, it becomes less so. Garber (1984), for instance, found that after a child loses one parent to death, identification with the deceased is often encouraged by the surviving other. A boy losing his father, for example, may be emotionally supported by his mother in mourning; as he identifies with his lost father, perhaps assuming some of his mannerisms, his mother may take comfort in these reflections. Her husband's resurrection in her son is cause for celebration, however muted by loss.

By contrast, after divorce, parents do not rejoice in being reminded of each other. As for Allison, such reminders can be most problematic if the custodial parent no longer loves, or indeed has lost respect for, the absent one. Admonishing divorced parents simply not to put the child in the middle can work only so far. If one parent is unable to mourn the divorce, it will be difficult for the child to do so. Perhaps this is why children of divorce may suffer more long-term clinical depression than those who have lost a parent to death (Rodgers, 1994).

Externalizing Problems

Studies such as Garber's (1994) involve lengthy, painstaking interviews, which both limit the sample size and add an element of subjectivity. Because of these difficulties in assessing children's internal processing, some researchers have focused on more tangible outward manifestations. More easily measured, such "externalizing" problems, as they are known, include aggression, poor academic performance, and difficulty socializing with peers.

Divorce has consistently been shown to be associated with externalizing problems. Emery (1988) reviewed several significant cross-sectional studies. In 1976, for instance, the National Survey of

Children was initiated, involving 2,258 children ages seven to eleven, who after initial assessments were followed periodically with information obtained directly from them as well as from parents and teachers. Even when economic conditions were controlled, children of divorce were found to be at increased risk for aggressive behavior. Teachers rated them as more aggressive than those whose parents remained in "very happy" or "fairly happy" marriages; only children living with the most unhappily married parents (representing a mere 2.5 percent of the married parents) were more aggressive than children of divorce (p. 50). These findings, moreover, held up at five-year follow-up (p. 52), at which point another effect became clear: children who had been under age six when their parents had separated were found to have the most adjustment problems (p. 75). As Emery noted, other researchers, using different databases, arrived at similar results. Wadsworth et al. (1985), in their study of 12,743 British families, found increased antisocial behavior among five-year-olds living with only one parent, and, similarly, Hetherington et al. (1978), studying a nonclinical sample, found children of divorce to be more disobedient, aggressive, demanding, and lacking in self-control.

Emery (1988) also found agreement that children reared in single-parent families perform more poorly on a variety of cognitive and academic measures than do those from two-parent homes. Although single-parent families represent a heterogeneous group consisting of divorced as well as never-married mothers and fathers, test scores of children of divorce are generally lower than those of children raised by unmarried single parents. Although these differences are small, when other measures such as teacher ratings, grade point averages, school attendance, and number of years of school are factored in, they become considerably larger (p. 59).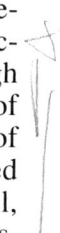

Such findings have withstood time. Amato and Keith (1991a,b), as mentioned earlier, came to similar conclusions regarding externalizing problems, and, more recently, Hetherington and Stanley-Hagan (1999) reviewed a number of studies tracking the effects of divorce. As expected, she confirmed earlier findings that immediately after their parents' separation, children show decreased cognitive ability and academic achievement, as well as increased aggressive behavior, lack of self-regulation, anxiety, depression, and problems in social relationships.

Whereas some researchers reported the size of such differences to be small—Amato and Keith (1991b), for instance, found only 0.14 of a standard deviation—in her own research, Hetherington found between one-half and one full standard deviation of difference between divorced and nondivorced children's externalizing problems. Looked at another way, 20 to 30 percent of divorced children score above the clinical cutoff for behavior problems on the Child Behavior Checklist (a standardized measure of behavioral problems), compared to 10 percent of nondivorced ones. Nevertheless, Hetherington did not conclude that divorce is always harmful for children. If they move from extremely conflicted, abusive, or neglectful family situations to more harmonious ones, she believed they may actually benefit.

LONG-TERM EFFECTS OF DIVORCE ON CHILDREN: WHAT HAPPENS WHEN THEY ENTER ADULTHOOD?

Hetherington and Stanley-Hagan (1999) also reviewed the expanding body of research on how divorced children fare as they grow into adults. She found that although initial negative effects decrease over time, on average, these children remain less socially, emotionally, and academically well-adjusted. Adolescents from divorced households are two to four times more likely to drop out of high school, engage in antisocial behavior, associate with delinquent peers, or be referred for clinical treatment than those from intact families. Furthermore, adolescence may trigger problems in some teenagers who had seemed previously well-adjusted to their parents' divorce; growing into adults, they have more problems with close relationships, more difficulty completing college, and often flounder as they attempt to build careers. Perhaps this is the "sleeper effect" noted by Wallerstein and Blakeslee (1989, pp. 56-64).

Other researchers have looked even more specifically at the effects of divorce on children's long-term adjustment. Such repercussions are, of course, difficult to tease out due to the many confounding intervening events. Nevertheless, some problems appear with increased frequency, including negative effects on mental health as well as on the ability to form satisfying adult romantic relationships.

Effects on Mental Health: Dissatisfaction, Depression, Anxiety

Common sequelae of loss in general, mental health problems had previously been known to affect children in divorce's immediate wake, but as these children were followed into adulthood, they were found to continue to suffer from an increased frequency of psychological problems, such as depression, anxiety, and general life dissatisfaction (Amato and Keith, 1991a). Rubenstein et al. (1998) noted that parental divorce and, even more dramatically, remarriage increased the risk of teenage suicidal behavior in their particular sample from 9 percent for children of intact families, to 20 percent for those of separated or divorced families, to 38 percent for those from remarried families. Rodgers (1994), analyzing a large British data-base, found that whereas children who experienced parental *death* in childhood were not more likely, as adults, to develop clinical depression, women (not men) who had experienced parental *divorce* in childhood were at significant increased risk, and these effects held up across socioeconomic class.

Although he found inconsistent evidence for increased incidence of a clinical level of depression, Emery (1988, pp. 66-67) reviewed researchers' other measures of mental health effects and concluded that as children of divorce grow into adults, they show more unhappiness, less satisfaction with their family, friends, and communities, and higher levels of anxiety than those from intact families. They more frequently feel that bad things happen to them. Similar to other researchers, Emery concluded that, among women, parental divorce was more predictive of adult unhappiness than early death of a parent. Although such effects were small, they were nonetheless significant.

Problems with Relationships

Compared to those from intact families, children of divorce have more problems with adult love relationships. They are five to twelve times more likely themselves to divorce, a figure consistent across race, gender, and socioeconomic class (as reviewed by Emery, 1988, p. 67). Daughters of divorce are more likely to become pregnant as teenagers, and more likely to have problems finding stable, happy relationships (Hetherington and Stanley-Hagan, 1999). One study (Wallerstein and Blakeslee, 1989, pp. 54-70) referred to this as the difficulty these young adults have playing their "queen of hearts."

Wallerstein (1991) followed 131 children, ages three to eighteen at the time of their parents' separation, and found that ten years later about one-half were still troubled—drifting, angry, self-deprecating, and showing significant problems with close relationships. Although boys exhibited problems earlier, by adolescence girls had caught up, demonstrating a "sleeper effect" whereby young women who had previously appeared well-adjusted became troubled as they entered unusually destructive romantic relationships. To explain her findings, Wallerstein noted that children internalize not only their relationship with each individual parent but also the one they perceive operating between their parents. In this regard, children of divorce carry an internal template of failure:

> The failure of the marital relationship is thus likely to have a lasting impact on the young person's inner developmental course. The developmental task of establishing intimacy and trust in relationship with the opposite sex is felt to be persistently burdened to a greater or lesser degree by the template of the failed man-woman relationship that these youngsters carry within them. (p. 358)

Although Wallerstein's study had limitations—it was not a random sample, but a self-selected one of divorcing middle-class families offered situational counseling—it did not represent a particularly disturbed population. In fact, Wallerstein and colleagues screened her subjects carefully, excluding children who were already showing significant emotional problems before their parents separated. Furthermore, in her most recent work (Wallerstein et al., 2000), she included a control group from intact families and came to similar conclusions: many children of divorce have considerably greater difficulty being able to risk love.

Internal Working Models

What causes these children to have such problems with adult romantic relationships, and why do some studies, occasionally, contradict these findings? Contrary to the general consensus that children of divorce have more pessimistic assessments of their romantic attachments, some researchers claim that, later in life, these adults are just as happy, committed, trusting, and optimistic about their partners as those from intact families.

To sort all this out, Henry and Holmes (1998) designed a longitudinal study of introductory college psychology students (mean age 19.7 years). During initial interviews, the students were categorized as coming from divorced families (101 students), intact happy families

(98 students), or intact families with very high conflict (65 students). They were also classified as having generally secure or insecure attachment styles. In addition, they were asked how happy they were in their current relationships. (To qualify for the study, all students had to be involved in a serious dating relationship; on average, they had been dating their partners for twenty months.) The students were then followed over six months. We will confine our discussion to the results for women, as those for men did not reach statistical significance.

Relative to daughters from happy intact families, those of divorce were much more likely to be generally "insecurely preoccupied"— defined as having negative views of themselves, yet positive ones of important others in their lives. They worried about abandonment and feared future partners would leave them for more attractive women. Moreover, this was not simply a reflection of their general low self-esteem. These daughters of divorce actually felt good about themselves in other domains, such as social skills, academic ability, physical appearance, and overall self-worth; only their images of themselves as romantic partners were tarnished. The clouds in their crystal balls were specific to reading their future in love.

These women, accordingly, had developed internal working models of heterosexual relationships involving low worth for women, with men at the controls. Perhaps, the authors speculated, their fathers' departures may have telegraphed a specific message: neither you as a girl nor your mother as a woman are worth staying with. But did these daughters' internal working models, based on years of observing their parents' interactions, actually affect their happiness in their current relationships?

At the beginning of the study, it seemed they did not. Relative to daughters from happy intact families, daughters of divorce claimed to be just as satisfied, committed, trusting, and in love with their current partners, and they were just as optimistic about their futures. Based on these reports, the authors initially believed that these daughters could overcome their old, dysfunctional internal working models if they found current healthy, supportive partners. The present, it seemed, held the advantage over the past.

They were mistaken. Although at the start of the study, daughters of divorce had been as pleased with their boyfriends as daughters from intact families, at the six-month mark the former had a dramatically higher breakup rate. Moreover, their breakups seemed unrelated to the degree of satisfaction they had experienced earlier. Whereas intact-family daughters' breakups did correlate with their lower levels of satisfaction at the beginning of the study, by contrast, the breakups of daughters of divorce were not predicted by how happy they had earlier been, but rather by their areas of psychological vulnerability. Those with a "preoccupied" attachment style were most likely to end relationships, even if they had previously felt very content with them.

In summary, the authors believed that at the beginning of the study powerful defense mechanisms, such as compartmentalization and denial, separated divorced-family daughters' old internal working models of relationships from their current conscious feelings about their boyfriends. The negative models, however, continued to operate. To protect themselves from once again being rejected by men they loved, they tended to strike preemptively. Their abandonment concerns did not appear to be based in reality, but in fantasies engendered by their negative internal models.*

If these women had been asked at only one time about their level of satisfaction with their partners, we would have missed these important findings. Simply asking grown children of divorce how happy they are with their current relationships—in fact, asking a series of questions similar to those on standard interviews to assess relationship or marital quality—may obscure disavowed internal working models, which over time make their presence known. These are divorce's true ghosts.

CAUSE OR EFFECT?
OR WHAT SHOULD PARENTS DO?

The studies mentioned earlier represent only a few of the many documenting the association of divorce with children's poorer adjust-

---

*The authors also compared daughters of divorce to daughters from intact families with high conflict. Instead of being "insecurely preoccupied," the high-conflict-family daughters' attachment styles clustered within two avoidant categories: either "fearful," with negative models of both self and other, or "dismissing," with negative models of others but positive models of themselves (p. 299). These daughters worried about getting too close and became anxious when their partners made intimacy demands. Similar to the daughters of divorce, they also found ways to insulate their feelings about ongoing relationships from their negative general models (p. 299). Over time, they tended to stay with their partners, even though these relationships tended to be very conflictual.

ments. Across a broad spectrum of measures—from behavior problems to academic achievement, from childhood self-esteem to adult depression—children of divorce are at a disadvantage, and these problems may be only the tip of the iceberg. Because so many emotional effects are difficult to measure, and because children are so adept at hiding their most troubled feelings, the damage may be more extensive even than these studies indicate. Many therapists today, I believe, are impressed with how overrepresented children of divorce are in their practices.

But are such problems caused by divorce, or did they exist prior to separation, simply reflecting the accumulated effect of conditions predating the demise of the parents' marriages? After all, in addition to years of conflict and unhappiness, these children may have also experienced significant parental dysfunction, such as drug addiction, alcoholism, or violence.

Cause or Effect?

Much attention has focused on trying to sort out these complex factors. So far, results are mixed. Some studies show little effect of divorce per se; of these, Block et al.'s work (1986, 1988) is often cited as suggesting that boys' externalizing problems actually precede divorce by many years. (Interestingly, this study also showed that many years before separating, fathers disengage from their sons.) Similarly, analyses of the National Survey of Children in this country, as well as of the British National Child Development Study, reveal sharply reduced effects of divorce once children's prior behavior problems are taken into account (Cherlin et al., 1991). Such research supports the notion that, in many cases, divorce does not initiate difficulties but, rather, exacerbates them.

Other research, however, suggests that factors related to divorce itself may cause children's downward slide; even if their previous adjustment is taken into account, their parents' breakups may still have a negative impact. Pagani et al. (1997), for instance, prospectively examined the effects of divorce and remarriage on children who were first assessed in kindergarten and then followed until age twelve. Her results: divorce caused problems above and beyond those predicted from their prior adjustments. Compared to their predivorce baselines, these children showed increased disobedience and defiance, anxiety, and attention deficit hyperactivity disorder (ADHD). Early divorce (before age eight) was found to have especially enduring negative consequences for ADHD. Furthermore, some discrepancies between the divorced and intact groups, such as those relating to anxiety and ADHD, actually increased over time. Thus, Pagani et al. found that divorce not only *predates* behavioral problems in many children but also causes a steady increase afterward in anxiety and ADHD. Although remarriage helps moderate ADHD, it does not help reduce children's anger or anxiety.

Similarly, Kasen et al. (1996), analyzing data from 805 families followed over eight years, found no baseline differences between children from families that remained intact and those which later divorced. Yet by adolescence, youths in divorced families (with single custodial mothers) showed three times the risk for conduct disorder, three times the risk for oppositional defiant disorder, and two times the risk for anxiety disorders. Alarmingly, those whose mothers had remarried had four times the risk for conduct disorder. Unlike Block et al., (1986, 1988) who used a small nonrandomly selected group of families, Kasen et al.'s (1996) study involved a large, randomly selected community sample.

Shaw et al. (1993), in reanalyzing data from the New York Longitudinal Study, also found no baseline differences in behavior between children from soon-to-be divorced families and those in families who stayed intact, but they did notice less adequate parenting in the former, which for boys predicted a downward adjustment after divorce.

When Should Parents Divorce?

What should we make of these findings? First, divorce is not a single event, like a simple fracture, with which children cope for a short time before healing. It is an ongoing process that, like loss of a limb, is repeatedly reworked during different developmental stages. Children may initially appear to do well but later show problems when they hit adolescence's obstacle course. Divorce is a condition that affects children the rest of their lives.

Second, we may ask, from the standpoint of children, when should parents stay together? Reviewing numerous studies, Hetherington and Stanley-Hagan (1999) found that children of happily married parents are better adjusted, overall, than those of divorced ones, who in turn are better off than those remaining in intact, but highly conflicted families. Although children assessed during the immediate aftermath of the breakups show the most problems of all, over time these dissipate, provided animosity between their parents declines. In other words, when divorce brings about a change to more harmonious, less stressful circumstances, children do almost as well as those in happily married families. By contrast, when it brings long-term increases in parental stress, animosity, or other adversity, children show even more problems than those remaining in high-conflict families.

Hetherington and Stanley-Hagan's findings (1999) are so important, I will repeat them: continued high levels of parental conflict have even more adverse effects on children *after* divorce than *before*. Unless divorce acts to mitigate parental animosity, children may be better off if their parents stay married.

Yet, my readers may ask, is that not divorce's purpose? To end the fighting? To give all members of a family a second chance at enjoying a calm, relatively conflict-free environment?

According to Hetherington et al. (1999), it is a questionable assumption that this end can be easily attained. Rarely does conflict decline after divorce. In fact, it often increases. Some couples who had maintained calm, if unsatisfactory marriages may become much more overtly hostile during and after divorce. Others, already fighting for years, may now escalate their battles as the stakes rise. No longer bickering over grocery money and vacation destinations, they may declare open warfare over child support and visitation. Research, Hetherington notes, suggests that lowering parental conflict is not easy to achieve by ending marriages. One-fourth of divorced parents continue to have long-term, extremely high conflict, with the child in the middle; one-fourth have cooperative, mutually supportive relationships; and the other one-half develop a style of parallel parenting—disengaged, rarely communicating, with anger in many cases simmering just below the surface.

But what about remarriage? Will not children's problems be ameliorated by this event, which should lessen bitter feelings between former spouses as they "move on" emotionally and enjoy economic relief? Unfortunately, similar to other researchers, Hetherington and Stanley-Hagan (1999) note that children raised in stepfamilies show no emotional or behavioral improvement over those remaining with single parents, despite improved economic circumstances. Although divorce may benefit children if it ameliorates conflict and their custodial parents can cope with single parenting's hardships, Hetherington concludes:

> These conditions may be difficult to attain. The stresses encountered during and following divorce should not be minimized and for some parents and children they are pervasive and persistent. Moreover, the few systematic studies of interventions for divorced parents and their children suggest that when adverse outcomes occur they may be difficult to modify through educational or short-term therapeutic interventions. (1999, p. 137)

CONCLUSION

Divorce is not a one-time event, but rather an ongoing, complex process. Although it is difficult to predict how an individual child will fare, overall, children of divorce have an increased frequency of behavioral problems, poor academic achievement, depression, anxiety, and relationship difficulties. If their parents' marriages had been characterized by very high levels of conflict or abuse, divorce may act positively for children, but with at least three provisions: the level of overt conflict must substantially diminish, the mental health of the primary caretakers must remain intact, and there must be enough money to go around.

In a recent *Time* magazine article, in a rebuttal to Wallerstein's latest findings regarding the long-term negative consequences of divorce for children, columnist Katha Pollit (2000) mused:

> We've learned a lot about how to divorce since 1971. When Mom has enough money and Dad stays connected, when parents stay civil and don't bad-mouth each other, kids do all right. The 'good enough' divorce—why isn't *that* ever the cover story? (p. 82)

Perhaps that is not the cover story because these conditions are so difficult to achieve. Often parents continue to fight just as much, or even more so, after separating—the only difference being they now do it between two households and over issues with higher stakes, engendering even more anger than before. Although levels of such conflict after divorce are important predictors of children's adjustment (perhaps more important than other ameliorating factors, such as frequency of visitation by the noncustodial parent (Emery, 1988; Hetherington and Stanley-Hagan, 1999), many parents continue to engage in subtle or not so subtle battles, and as we saw in Allison's story, even if they do not show such overt hostility toward each other, they may telegraph damaging messages to their children, messages that may include, "I have difficulty accepting parts of you reminding me of your father (or mother)."

Often parents are blamed for not being able to get over their anger, to bury their hatchets, to rejoin the world of the psychologically fit. I am not convinced that this is always possible, however. To the extent that divorce is not a mutually desired solution, it does not diminish conflict and, in many cases, actually ignites it: parents traumatized by divorce may have extreme difficulty grieving and letting go of their anger. They may also have trouble reestablishing psychological health, as they are plagued by a sense of emotional numbness. To the extent our society sanctions unilateral divorce on demand, it condones a process virtually guaranteed to cause emotional shock, difficulty grieving, and ongoing conflict between partners, whose children partake in their misery. Although we might hope that the use of this legal privilege be reserved for extreme cases such as Allison's, in practice it is not.

Having reviewed the effects of divorce on older children, now let us turn to how infants may be affected, for divorce at childbirth, often unwanted and unanticipated, is most unlikely to be a "good enough" divorce.

Chapter 7

When the Bough Breaks: Effect of Divorce on Infants

Given divorce's impact on older children, how might it affect those under the age of one? Several findings of the previous two chapters, such as communication of parental stress and repercussions of downward socioeconomic slide, may be presumed to apply. In other ways, however, infants represent a special case. Too young to have acquired language, they express their distress differently than older children.

Before discussing the special case of infants, we must realize that when attempting to assess divorce's long-term effects on them, the many intervening years make retrospective analysis complex. My interview of Jason, now in his late twenties, exemplifies how early adversity becomes interwoven with the child's internal processing of his or her parents' divorce, as well as with later events.

JASON: SEARCHING FOR A FATHER

Jason's father returned from Vietnam suffering from severe post-traumatic stress disorder. As a result, even though his wife soon became pregnant, he was unable to enjoy this happy event. Reexperiencing ambushes in which many of his buddies had been brutally killed, he felt disconnected from ordinary life and became increasingly dysfunctional, alternating between states of numbness and extreme irritability. Although he had never previously been abusive, he now became violent toward his wife, to the point that even though she was pregnant, she asked him to leave. Angry at first, he later agreed to a divorce, as he felt the responsibility of fatherhood was more than he could handle. He stayed involved with his son initially but then gradually tapered off visits, sometimes disappearing for a year or two. Even though his father's presence was sporadic, Jason looked forward to spending occasional summers with him.

With only a little family help available, Jason's mother went on welfare. She had many legal battles with her ex-husband over child support, which, even when she received it, was grossly insufficient. Eventually she was able to finish school and find employment, but all those hard years took a toll: tired, stressed, and working two jobs, even though she loved her son, she had trouble finding sufficient time for him. She also had difficulty disciplining Jason, who now admits he was a "terror," frequently testing his mother's limits. Looking back, he believes he was searching for a father figure.

When Jason was ten, his mother remarried. Although their economic situation improved, it quickly became clear that his stepfather was not interested in him. In fact, Jason felt ignored. At the same time, he felt the further loss of his mother's attention. Alienated from his stepfather, angry at his biological father, and feeling rejected by his mother, he developed more severe behavior problems. Nevertheless, he did well academically throughout grade school. Several teachers noticed he was smart and helped him to take pride in his academic performance.

This was not to last. Although he now lived in a fashionable Chicago suburb with his mother and stepfather, as Jason entered high school he began associating with a group of boys who, similar to himself, felt angry and alienated; this crowd introduced him to alcohol and drugs, which consumed his teenage years. When upsetting events occurred, he felt he had no one in whom he could confide, as by now he had sufficiently disappointed his mother that he felt too ashamed to reveal to her the extent of his problems. His father had drifted out of the picture. Eventually Jason dropped out of high school.

Remarkably, he was later able to turn his life around. In his early twenties, he stopped drinking and using drugs, obtained his GED, and enrolled in college. He mended his relationship with his mom. Finally, he reconciled with his father, for whom he began to have compassion. Although while Jason was growing up his father had not been available, once Jason no longer needed him as a parent, he could accept his father as a supportive friend and relinquish some of his anger.

So far, Jason's story is one of resilience. Nevertheless, he still has one major problem: he greatly fears intimacy. Even though he would like to meet a woman, marry, and have a family, he has difficulty even dating. When asked why he remains single, he admits it is not from lack of opportunity. A handsome, articulate young man, he is frequently approached by women. Rather, he is unsure of his own capacity to be a good husband or father and remains frightened to try.

Jason's story shows how complex are the effects of parental divorce when it occurs at life's beginning. There are so many intervening variables, including, in his case, the emotional and economic stress on his mother, the transmission of that stress to her son, and his internal processing of it over many years. Other effects arose from his mother's remarriage, his encouraging teachers, his peer group, and alienation from and eventual reconciliation with his father. Jason's story illustrates how divorce is not a single event, but a process that continues well into adulthood. Even though he was unborn when his parents separated, their divorce remains alive for him.

RESEARCH ON HOW DIVORCE AFFECTS INFANTS

Given the complexity of retrospective analysis, it would seem that prospective studies could more easily tease apart, both immediately and at later developmental stages, the effects of divorce on infants. However, little such research focuses on this young age group. Most studies involve families with older children.

Although not specifically focusing on infants, one prospective study (Bretherton et al., 1997) did explore how divorcing families with very young children adapt. The authors followed fifty mothers, identified through public court records, who had been legally separated or divorced at least two years. All were middle-class, with an average income of $24,000 including child support. All either worked outside the home or attended school. Their children's average age at time of permanent separation was sixteen months.

Bretherton et al. found that at an average of three to four years after the final breakup, only one-third of mothers felt they communicated reasonably well with their ex-husbands; the other two-thirds reported ongoing acrimony and disappointment, the reasons for which included difficulty communicating and coparenting, low levels of trust, competition for their children's love, and low regard for the fathers' parenting. Consequently 84 percent of the mothers, while continuing to raise children with their ex-husbands, relied more heavily on their own parents for emotional as well as practical help. These very young children of divorce became much more involved with their maternal grandparents, and much less so with their fathers and their paternal relatives, than typical for intact families.

The authors concluded that insufficient attention has been given to the difficulties faced by such divorcing parents, who at the same time they are trying to resolve grief and anger over failed marriages, must renegotiate the task of coparenting children still at vulnerable and dependent ages. Although the effects of divorce on these very young ones were not directly assessed, we can predict that their parents' high degree of unresolved anger might affect them adversely.

These findings, I believe, are particularly relevant to divorce at childbirth, a time when few couples separate amicably. As in Bretherton's sample, animosity runs high, making the job of coparenting more difficult than peace negotiations between the most rancorous enemies. Few divorced mothers, moreover, have the resources to raise an infant solo, even with child support. As a result, grandparents may play a much more pivotal role than previously, as the family reorients matrilinearly.

Although few studies focus directly on the consequences of divorce for infants, we do have some notion of what these might be. Let us turn to the field of infant research, which in the past twenty years has revolutionized our understanding of the first months of life.

ATTACHMENT THEORY: THE IMPORTANCE OF THE FIRST YEAR OF LIFE

Of all the ways divorce affects infants, we conjecture that among the most profound must be the transmission of enormous parental stress. But do infants absorb their parents' emotional states, and, if so, how important is the first year of life? Is parental dysfunction more harmful at this time than subsequently? Although there are a few dissenting voices (see Bruer, 1999), most infant researchers believe the first year of life is very important indeed—to the degree that later events, although in some cases ameliorating earlier adversity, must work uphill to do so.

Attachment theory is one branch of research underscoring the importance of the first year. In brief, this theory (see summary by Rutter, 1995) developed from Bowlby's (1963, 1969, 1973) conviction that children have built-in, biologically based systems modulating attachment with significant caregivers. Whereas Bowlby initially focused on children's reactions to major types of loss, later researchers extended these observations to include children's reactions to more minor separations, such as frequently occur in the course of an ordinary day.

The "Strange Situation"

Some of Bowlby's followers (Ainsworth et al., 1978) developed an experiment called the "strange situation," in which a one-year-old toddler is observed during the following series of events: First, the mother (or father, if he is the primary caretaker; I will refer here to the mother for simplicity) brings the child into a strange room, where they play in the presence of an observer. Second, the mother leaves the room, and the toddler's separation response is observed. Third, upon the mother's return, the quality of the reunited relationship is assessed. After observing many mother-toddler pairs, Ainsworth et al. (1978) classified one-year-olds' attachment styles into two types, "secure" and "insecure." Insecurely attached toddlers were further subcategorized as "ambivalent" or "avoidant." Main and Solomon (1990) added an additional type of insecure attachment, which they referred to as "disorganized."

Securely attached toddlers showed obvious distress on departure of their mothers and were able to be comforted by them on return. After hugging their mothers and being soothed, they returned to play. They and their mothers communicated easily and effectively.

Insecurely attached toddlers, on the other hand, displayed several varieties of difficulty with this process. Ambivalent ones, although upset by their mothers' departures, had difficulty being comforted upon return; at the same time that they seemed to desire holding and soothing, they also were unable easily to accept these offerings, sometimes arching away in anger. Remaining preoccupied, they had difficulty returning to play. Avoidant toddlers, by contrast, did not seem to mind when their mothers left, nor did they notice them much upon return, as they continued to play unperturbed; of importance, although such independence made avoidant toddlers appear superficially well adapted, physiological markers such as heart rate indicated they were actually more stressed than ambivalent ones, as they appeared already to have developed a defensive sense of self-sufficiency to deal with their extreme anxiety. Finally, disorganized toddlers showed no clear strategies for coping with maternal separation and return. Darting toward their mothers and then running away, they were unable to organize an effective response. They remained unsoothed, unable to play.

So far, attachment researchers had simply given names to observed patterns. There was no indication that avoidant toddlers, for example, would eventually adjust less well than those labeled as secure. It was clear, however, that by their first birthdays, children had established stable attachment styles, repeatedly reproducible in the laboratory— styles that were the signatures of their relationships with their primary caretakers.

This finding alone would have been interesting, but over the next twenty years, as these children were followed from age one through grade school and into adolescence, an extraordinary trend emerged. Attachment style toward the primary caretaker (usually the mother, but sometimes the father) at age one was highly correlated with later adjustment, within as well as outside the home.

What Does Attachment Style Predict?

Before discussing the correlates of attachment style as measured in the strange situation, we must understand that it may differ toward different parents. A one-year-old may appear secure with father but insecure with mother, or vice versa. As such classifications tend to remain stable within each parent-child dyad over time, it is the attachment style toward the primary caretaker that becomes the predominate one later, influencing relationships with teachers and peers. A number of points are significant:

- Children classified as secure at age one have the best prognosis. During preschool and grade school, they tend to adjust fairly easily. They are well liked, even tempered, and inclined to do well academically.
- Children classified as ambivalent at age one tend to develop less secure peer relationships. They are more anxious in the classroom and less at ease socially.
- Children classified as avoidant at age one tend to develop later problems with anger and aggression. Some may become bullies, while others may develop disruptive behavioral patterns in class. They tend to perform less well academically.
- Finally, disorganized one-year-olds have the worst prognosis. These children often come from homes with violence or abuse and develop more severe levels of aggression and cognitive difficulties than those in the other groups.

In families in which the mother is the primary caretaker, a child's attachment style can be predicted on the basis of independent ratings of maternal empathy and sensitivity, even when measured prenatally (see Chapter 2). Pregnant mothers who present coherent narratives of their own childhoods, narratives that are internally consistent even if including hardship or trauma, tend to have children who are securely attached, while those who still feel much unresolved anger toward their own parents tend to have children with ambivalent attachment patterns. Alternatively, pregnant mothers who idealize their childhoods but provide few supporting memories tend to have children with avoidant attachment. These findings argue against attachment style being innate and suggest instead that it is significantly influenced by the psychological makeup of the mother, as measured before her child is even born.

Attachment Research: What Does It Mean?

So striking are the previous findings that many researchers find them hard to believe, much less explain. How could the quality of infant bonding in the first year of life predict later adjustment so well?

We can approach this question in at least three ways . We could hypothesize, for instance, that the first year of life represents a critical time frame, and that relationship patterns established within this window become hard-wired, accurately forecasting later development. Less drastically, we could suppose that while patterns in the first year are important in setting the stage for later development, they do only that—set the stage. Perhaps subsequent events modify, even reverse, the initial course. Finally, and most liberally, we could argue that secure attachment status simply marks a confluence of positive forces, such as parental temperament and sensitivity, which tend to remain constant. Secure children do well, according to this last explanation, not because their first year of life is particularly consequential, but because their caretakers continue to provide a nurturing environment.

Although it is not entirely clear which of these hypotheses holds, many attachment researchers subscribe to the second approach. Rutter (1995), for example, states, "There is a sensitive period during which it is highly desirable that selective attachments develop, but the time frame is probably somewhat broader than initially envisaged and the effects are not as fixed and irreversible as once thought" (p. 551). He also notes that although associations between infant insecure attachment status and later behavioral and emotional problems are significant, they are of only moderate strength and not entirely consistent across studies. Nevertheless, he states that there is abundant evidence linking parenting quality and attachment status. Maltreated or depressed mothers' children, he notes, are often highly insecure.

Some attachment researchers have tried further to assess the degree to which attachment shows plasticity over time. Beckwith et al. (1999) found that although maternal sensitivity during infancy has long-lasting influences, it does not always overcome subsequent life events, particularly adverse ones. On the one hand, infants who received relatively *insensitive* maternal care generally continued their initial maladaptive styles when followed to age eighteen; subsequent positive life events, including in some cases their mothers becoming more emotionally available, did not alter their course. By contrast, *sensitive* care during infancy failed to protect completely against the effect of later adversity, as even some eighteen-year-olds who had experienced much positive infant care developed an increased rate of insecure attachment (ambivalent type), as measured by the AAI, after experiencing parental divorce. Intervening adverse life events, accordingly, we were able to override children's initial favorable starts. Nevertheless, Beckwith et al. found that when maternal sensitivity altered dramatically over time, children's early experience remained most salient, in spite of later changes in their caretakers' mood or behavior.

Studies such as Beckwith et al.'s suggest that while secure attachment at age one is a moderate predictor of future well-being, this arrow may be bent by subsequent adversity. In spite of occasional changes in later course, the earlier years point the bow.

How Does Attachment Style Develop?

Given that attachment style at one year is an important predictor of future adjustment, we wonder, how does it develop? What are its precursors? To observe in finer detail the first few months of life, Beebe et al. (1997) videotaped mother-infant interactions and played them back at slow speed. Among healthy mother-infant pairs, they discovered a mutuality of interaction, a bidirectionality that was not always predictable. Mother-infant systems, they found, are emergent and complexly creative.

More specifically, Beebe and Jaffe (1992) studied the vocal interactions of four-month-olds, who as they gaze and smile at their mothers, engage in a complex type of "conversation," which, similar to adult language, has rules for turn taking and pauses. These four-month-olds are already learning the organization, not just of language, but of human relationships: the syntax of turn taking, sharing, and taking space, the grammar of influence as well as how to avoid being known. Interestingly, mother-infant pairs showing the most complex patterns of vocal matching—those sometimes in tune with each other and sometimes not—become the most securely attached by one year. By contrast, those whose vocal rhythms at four months are either very tightly matched or very desynchronized later develop insecure attachments—the former group an ambivalent subtype, the latter an avoidant one. The most desynchronized babies, who at four months not only avoid matching maternal vocalizations but also avoid meeting maternal gaze, appear "cocked for escape" from human interactions.

Beebe et al.'s work has at least two important take-home points: First, mother-infant pairs most likely later to develop secure attachment patterns can already be identified by four months. Second, their interactions are complex, creative, and not tightly determined. An observer does not always know what they are going to do next, as they already appear to be comfortable playing.

Their own work, Beebe et al. (1997) state, is only part of a large literature documenting that variations in early mother-infant interactions, including those in mutual gazing, smiling, vocalizing, and play, do correlate with later cognitive development and attachment status. Studies demonstrate that infants identified as secure at one year had shown more looking, smiling, and excitement in social play at two to four months, while those identified as insecurely attached at one year had earlier shown more gaze aversion, fussing, and unresponsiveness. Cohn et al. (1992) also found that by six months an infant's method of coping with the still-face situation, in which the mother is instructed to look at her baby without changing facial expression, has become characteristic, predicting later attachment status. If the infant attempts to engage the still-faced mother, to elicit a response from her with behaviors such as smiling, cooing, and even fussing, attachment is likely to be secure at one year. Conversely, if the infant does not attempt to elicit a response, if he or she appears to have given up, attachment is likely later to be insecure.

A sizable body of evidence indicates such infant responses do not primarily reflect inborn temperament but are largely reactive to primary caretakers' signals (Beebe et al., 1997). Although attachment style is not thought to be genetically determined, it has been found to have biological correlates. Gunnar (1998), for example, suggested that children are born with a highly reactive hypothalamus-pituitary-adrenal (HPA) axis. This hormonal system modulates the secretion of cortisol, which under normal conditions rises during morning hours and ebbs in the late evening; in addition, cortisol is released in response to acute stress. Gunnar noted that children reared in Romanian orphanages, who exhibit a high rate of insecure attachment, have very high cortisol levels throughout the day and evening—a markedly abnormal response. Secure, responsive caregiver relationships, Gunnar hypothesized, may serve to buffer the HPA system's reactivity to everyday stresses, which to the newborn infant may otherwise feel enormous. Children growing up without the ready availability of sensitive, comforting caretakers may experience repeated unbuffered stress responses, eventually leading to chronically elevated levels of cortisol, which have been associated with a variety of psychiatric problems such as clinical depression and lowered volume of areas of the brain involved with memory.

EMOTIONAL COMMUNICATION IN THE FIRST YEAR OF LIFE

Attachment researchers are not the only ones underlining the importance of early development; investigators from many other schools have generally concluded that newborns are much more sophisticated than previously thought. Even though they do not walk or talk, they rapidly know what is going on around them.

How Infants and Parents Tune In to Each Other

Murray and Trevarthen (1985) observed that shortly after birth infants correctly express and interpret emotions. As early as one to two months, they begin imitating adults' expressions, and this is no idle mimicry. Murray and Trevarthen thought that infants, by mirroring (sometimes subtly) the facial expressions of their caretakers, begin to share the same feeling states, through a release of inherited links between muscular and endocrine responses. In the parent-infant forcefield, emotions are permeable, hard to avoid.

The youngest infants, accordingly, can tell the difference between joy, sadness, and anger in their mother's faces. They also know when their mothers are not resonating with them. "Clearly," writes Tronick, "the emotional state of others is of fundamental importance to the infant's emotional state" (1989, p. 114). Similar to Murray and Trevarthen (1985), he notes that this importance is not simply the result of a passive process but rather results from infants' active use of their mothers' emotional signals to guide their own behavior (Tronic, 1989).

By three months, mother and baby are exploring each other's faces, engaging in a musical dance that can escalate into a burst of shared laughter or decelerate if one partner looks away. The baby is learning how to connect and disconnect, how to share but also protect himself or herself should the infant feel overly stimulated. Much of this learning depends on the infant's partner, who, like a good receiver, tunes in to the baby's emotional state, and then by raising or lowering the volume or changing the channel slightly, alters the baby's experience. In a largely unconscious effort to bring her infant more in line with her own preferences, a mother may tune in just slightly off the dial. This is a normal process. If she is very depressed or preoccupied, however, she may lower the volume on her baby's joyful states, while raising it on his or her quiet, nondemanding ones (Stern, 1985). At the most severe end of the spectrum, when mother is so depressed that she never smiles back—if she just takes adequate care of her infant but remains emotionally flat—the baby's distress may escalate. The infant will try to connect but, after repeated failure, lose hope.

Still-faced experiments have a predictable result among healthy infants: rapidly increasing distress, disorganization, disintegration, and ultimately withdrawal into a depressedlike state (Tronick, 1989). Confronted with this situation, most three-month-olds try to reengage their mothers through vocalizing, facial signaling, and gesturing. When they fail, they become distressed and then appear despondent and withdrawn, averting their gaze as they attempt to comfort themselves. These reactions occur even if the mothers are still-faced for only a few seconds.

What happens when a mother remains psychologically dead, not for seconds, but for months or years? We know that after divorce depression is frequent.

Consequences of Maternal Depression on Infant Development

Depression covers a broad spectrum. Mild varieties commonly affect new mothers, many of whom are successfully able to shield their babies from their moods, as they put aside upsetting feelings to engage with their children. Moderately depressed mothers may still be able to participate in their children's play but not share their more joyful moments; eventually their children learn to turn down the volume on their exuberance, as their joyful sides go underground. Although even these moderately depressed mothers may be able to stay connected with their infants, not all mothers, particularly those more seriously depressed and without adequate support, are able to do so.

In observations of mother-infant facial mirroring, for instance, researchers have seen how infants of severely depressed mothers show distress, and sometimes despair, over trying to elicit the needed cues from their mothers' faces, whose ordinary flux of spontaneous emotions may have been replaced by a sluggish or even frozen mask. The mutual delight characteristic of mother-infant facial play collapses, in these cases, into a one-person project. Like a ballerina without a partner, the baby's dance on the interpersonal stage folds into stilted solo exercises.

No mother-infant relationships are perfect, nor should they be. All involve multiple, frequent moments of misattunement and incoordination. Ordinarily, such "mistakes" are easily repaired, and this very ability to repair sets a standard for hope and confidence that, in spite of occasional missteps, good relationships can be sustained. By contrast, when a mother is significantly depressed, she may teach her infant that if he or she stumbles once, the dance ends.

Studies of depressed mothers and their infants, in fact, show that this capacity for repair is often critically disturbed (Beebe et al., 1997). Citing several researchers (Tronick, 1989; Cohn et al., 1990; Field et al., 1990), Beebe et al. (1997) concluded that failure of interactive repair, forcing the infant back on his or her own self-regulatory abilities, can be a major source of psychopathology in the first year. As Tronick stated:

> My interpretation is that depressed mothers, in different ways for different mothers, fail to appropriately facilitate their infant's goal directed activities. Their interactive behaviors and affect are poorly timed or often intrusive. Their affective displays are negative (e.g., anger, sadness, irritability), conveying the message that the infant should change what he or she is doing . . . the participants are stuck in affectively negative miscoordinated interactive states, and their messages calling for change are disregarded. (1989, p. 116)

When mothers are significantly depressed, as they often are after unwanted divorce, they may be unable to hear or respond to such messages.

In addition to these psychological effects on infants, Beebe et al. (1997) noted that several researchers have discovered biological responses to maternal depression. For instance, Field et al. (1988) demonstrated that six-month-old infants of depressed mothers have elevated heart rates and cortisol levels, indicative of a state of heightened arousal and distress. By ten months, infants' brains reflect maternal depression by showing altered electroencephalograph (EEG) patterns (Dawson, 1992a,b). Although there may be room for later repair, studies such as these provide a biological dimension to what clinicians have long known: when primary caretakers are seriously depressed, very young children may suffer consequences not easily reversed.

Of the women in my study, over one-half reported a state of serious depression after their breakups. Many were unable to sleep or eat, and a few considered suicide. Although counseling and antidepressants were helpful, not all women were able quickly to receive treatment, and of those who did, few responded rapidly. The stresses on them were simply too enormous to be countered quickly by short-term therapy or medication. Eventually, however, most did respond to treatment, as well as to the new lives they had brought into the world. How, we wonder, did their infants fare?

MIMI: DEPRESSION'S SHADOW

Mimi, a thirty-two-year-old teacher, was six months pregnant at the time of our first interview. She had separated from her husband three months previously. Speaking slowly and tearfully, she told me her story.

When Mimi first met Jack, she had just broken up a long-term relationship with a man whose children she had helped raise. Saddened by the breakup and wishing to marry and start a family of her own, she had been thrilled to meet Jack, a charming, considerate man. Discussing marriage and children only a few weeks after they met, he was equally enamored of her. Even though his pace was fast, when he asked her to marry him, she did not hesitate, as she felt she had met the right man at last.

Soon after their wedding, they spoke more about their mutual desire to have children. Mimi was thirty, Jack a few years older. Although they began trying to conceive, they did not have quick results. Months later, after consulting a fertility specialist, they decided that Mimi should try Clomid. A full participant in this decision, Jack was very supportive and hopeful that she would conceive.

Mimi had just ecstatically confirmed her positive pregnancy test when Jack began to act strangely distant. Several days later, he told her he had met another woman, was not happy with Mimi anymore, and wanted to move out. In the turmoil of the arguments that followed, he shoved her against a wall and injured her arm. Five weeks pregnant, Mimi fled to her father's house, where she did not give up but called Jack, begging him to reconsider. "Not interested," he replied.

Two weeks later, he moved in with his new girlfriend. Wanting to be free to remarry, he pressured Mimi for a quick divorce. When she begged him to wait at least until after the birth of their child, so that she could complete her pregnancy with less emotional upheaval, he made light of her distress. "It's not that hard to get divorced," he explained and he proceeded to file.

Six months pregnant, Mimi worries how she will survive. Although still working full-time, she cannot afford child care even on her present full salary. How will she manage after delivery, she wonders? Fortunately, she will be able to live temporarily with her uncle, and although she had never thought she would need it, she has applied for public assistance. Jack has given her no money. Her happiness shattered by his sudden turning on her, a betrayal that she cannot understand, she speaks slowly, seems numb, and is in shock. Her pregnancy is darkened by the shadow of approaching depression.

I spoke with Mimi again two years later, when her daughter Alexis, was eighteen months old.

Mimi had developed toxemia toward the end of her pregnancy, delivered five weeks early, and returned to the hospital for emergency surgery with her daughter in tow, as no one was at home to watch her during the day. Postpartum, Mimi had become severely depressed. Constantly crying, her weight below 100 pounds, she had felt exhausted and had had no time for herself. This state lasted about one year. Only in the past few months has she been feeling better, as counseling and antidepressant medication began to take effect. It was particularly useful for her to learn that Jack, who had been addicted to cocaine many years before they met, recently relapsed. Evidently, she mused, his recovery was not as solid as she had supposed. With this partial explanation for his departure, Mimi found some meaning in her story and started to heal. She gradually began to go out again, socialize with friends from whom she had withdrawn, and make play dates with other mothers and their children. Suddenly, she noticed, she felt interested in life again.

Although she had tried hard to be a good mother during the early months, Mimi remembered what an ordeal that time had been. Often she had been so depressed that she could hold her infant only for a few minutes before breaking down into tears, as she kept thinking that Jack should be with her rather than partying with his new girlfriend. She had simply been unable to imagine that he did not want to raise their daughter together. Sobbing, Mimi would place Alexis in her crib, where she would wail while Mimi paced the floors or tried to comfort herself by going to bed—not that she could sleep, but she did have a white-noise machine that provided soothing background static that helped numb her pain. When he did not have to work, her uncle helped out, but most of the days Mimi and her baby were alone.

The amazing thing, in Mimi's view, is that Alexis's development seems on course. She is now walking and utters a few words. Mimi just hopes that during the first year, when she felt so dead, Alexis knew that inside Mimi was an alive mother who wanted to love her. As Mimi starts to recover from her ordeal, she is optimistic that she is still young, and her life and Alexis's are just beginning.

Although what Mimi said is heartening, it is not entirely true. Alexis's life is not just beginning—in fact, her infancy is now over. Similar to Mimi, we hope that she will recuperate from her difficult first year, as her mother continues to work so hard to heal, and we hope that together they will be able to repair their relationship. We suspect, however, that both will have to work hard to achieve this, for, young as she is, Alexis already has internalized a template of a mother crying too much herself to be able to comfort Alexis's tears. While the trajectory of his first year may be reversed, we wish that she had not become a test case.

Mimi is a very dedicated mother. A schoolteacher with much love and knowledge of young children, she has a repair kit probably better stocked than the average. Consequently, I do believe that eventually Alexis may bear no scar from her earlier trauma. In the larger arena of divorce at childbirth, however, all bets are off, as couples gamble on the plasticity of their infants' brains.

CONCLUSION

Although studies have not yet focused on how infants react to divorce, we predict their adjustment will show a downward shift similar to that of older children. Although they do not express distress through adult language, they do exhibit complex reactions to parental dysfunction. These, designed to make the best of early impaired relationships, may themselves later distort social development.

Despite sharing many common features with those involving older children, divorces within a year of childbirth are also a special case. Some researchers may argue that as infants are too young to recall their non-resident parents living with them, they may not grieve their loss from the home. The first year of life, according to this argument, may represent a relatively optimal time for children to experience parental divorce.

This reasoning fails on at least three accounts, however. First, infants do rapidly become attached to their caregivers, so that marital separation would have to occur extremely early, perhaps within the first few weeks, to bypass this effect. Second, even if it were possible for infants not to miss their nonresidential parents, the result would be failure to form close, optimal bonds between them. Third, and most important, due to the extreme stress of divorce on adults at this juncture—stress that may be accentuated by a lack of psychological or practical preparation—infants must contend with their parents' transmission of emotional trauma at a time of their own biological vulnerability.

No time of life may be quite as critical as the first year. Recent research demonstrates that infants are exquisitely sensitive to their parents' emotional signals. It also suggests that the first year of life represents a critical time frame for fine-tuning parental empathy as well as its repair—a fine-tuning that, in turn, significantly predicts toddlers' attachment status and subsequent adjustment to school and peers. The quality of parent-infant interaction in the first year of life sets the stage for later development. The actors may change, but the script remains the same, changed only through luck and labor.

In Chapter 4, we saw that in the case of traumatic divorce, parents may take many years to recover, to understand the event, to integrate it into meaningful life narratives. In this chapter, we learned how parents' unresolved grief and trauma may be linked to their children's subsequent development of insecure attachment status (see also Fonagy, Steele, and Steele, 1991; Fonagy, Steele, Steele, et al. 1991; Main and Hesse, 1990). We also saw that maternal depression, extremely common after divorce, can seriously affect young children. These findings alert us to the possibility that, if occurring at childbirth, unexpected, traumatic divorce may have even more dire consequences than if occurring later. How, we wonder, are such parents to resolve their feelings in time to be emotionally available to their infants? Although there is always room for repair, this space may be constricted by the velocity of divorce, and the time taken to recover comes out of the baby's biological clock.

PART III:
CONCLUSION

We have reviewed both the causes and effects of divorce at child-birth. Drawn from a number of disciplines, including sociology, academic psychology, clinical psychology, and psychoanalysis, a wide range of research suggests that, for many couples, transition to parenthood is more difficult than anticipated. Sleepless nights, conflict over downtime, and adjustment to a baby stress many marriages, no matter how previously happy. As couples open their dyadic bonds to incorporate their newborn, no wonder some less resilient marriages crumble, and when they do, each member of the mother-father-child triangle must pick up the emotional pieces, which do not easily fit into stable new structures. We have portrayed much about difficult transition to parenthood, and much about divorce's loose ends.

While confirming such findings, the stories told by the women in my study also point to two further conclusions. First, a few of the women or their husbands experienced transitions so difficult that they left marriages in which they had felt previously content. The problem was not so much that stresses added up linearly to overwhelm such couples as that one parent experienced quantumlike activation of internal issues, leading to a state of personal crisis. These new parents underwent more of a transformation than a transition to parenthood.

Second, an immense difference exists between women able to grieve the end of their marriages and those unable to do so. While the former group could hold on to at least some good internal representations of their former spouses, those unable to grieve exhibited more of a trauma response, characterized by a walling off of such positive memories, resulting in emotional numbness. I do not believe that these two models—grief versus trauma—have been systematically applied to divorce recovery.

With these two findings in mind, we turn in Chapter 8 to discussing the full results of my study. Since much of this material has been already presented, I will be succinct. Nevertheless, I hope that organizing the information in this way may be useful for further research.

In Chapter 9, I summarize similarities and differences between my findings and those of other researchers, and I make some brief recommendations for clinicians. These are meant only to be initial guidelines and not to replace the wisdom resulting from close work with an individual or couple over time, but I hope some clinicians as well as their clients will find even these rough signposts useful.

For those of my readers who have experienced divorce at childbirth firsthand, I regret that I am unable to provide a succinct self-help guide to recovery. Although I did consider including such a chapter, I feared its brevity might suggest that such trauma is easy to overcome. Nevertheless, I did summarize what factors the women in my study felt were most helpful for their healing. Perhaps a full discussion of this subject awaits another book.

Chapter 8

Discussion

In this chapter I will summarize my study, which although limited by its small size and the subjective nature of its reports, nevertheless illustrates several important aspects of divorce at childbirth. As a pilot effort, it may also point to directions for further research. So let us return to my original six questions:

1. What did these women think caused their marriages to end? Were there any common themes?
2. How did they react to their breakups, both immediately and later? What was most difficult?
3. How did they feel their breakups affected their mothering capacities? Did they notice any effects on their children?
4. How have their relationships with their ex-husbands evolved following separation?
5. Reflecting on their own family histories, did these women discover any relevant information?
6. What helped them cope with this difficult time in their lives? How did they attempt to heal?

In discussing these questions, at times I will divide the women into two groups, those who were "leavers" and those who were "left." This distinction is important for at least two reasons. First, women who initiated separation were able directly to reveal why their marriages ended so shortly after childbirth. Their reports may reflect a more accurate understanding of such breakups than the more subjective accounts of those on the receiving end of the divorce decision. Second, I was interested in whether there were any differences between these two groups. Did women who desired divorce fare any better than those who did not believe it was a reasonable alternative?

WHAT DID THESE WOMEN THINK
CAUSED THEIR MARRIAGES TO END?

Women Who Initiated Separation

Of the seven mothers who initiated separation, six were in marriages made intolerable by a partner's chronic drug addiction, physical abuse, or emotional maltreatment. Before becoming pregnant, most of these women had been aware of their husbands' faults but were hoping that, in spite of them, their husbands would make adequate, if not perfect, fathers. Perhaps they also hoped that their husbands would mature into new roles. After going through childbirth's transformation, however, these women changed their outlooks radically: realizing they could not subject their newborns to such environments, they left their marriages. Only one of the seven who initiated divorce did so for reasons other than her partner's severe dysfunction, and after working through internal issues triggered by childbirth, she reunited with her husband. In this sample, women did not often initiate separation or divorce at childbirth unless they felt desperate—desperate that their children's emotional or physical lives were at stake.

Women Whose Husbands Initiated Separation

Of the ten mothers whose husbands initiated separation, four were not entirely shocked; their marriages, after all, had been troubled for years. As a result, although these women had not foreseen divorce, once it occurred, they could understand it in a context of ongoing conflict. The other six, however, were taken completely off guard. As they had truly believed they were in happy marriages with loving partners, their stories are more puzzling.

On the one hand, we might think this second group of women simply ignored warning signs that their marriages were failing. Perhaps their surprise upon finding themselves divorced reflected their difficulties in facing the deep cracks in their marriages. Indeed, family therapists often use the word "mystification" to refer to such disavowal of unmistakable marital problems.

Although this is a frequent explanation, I do not believe it applies to these particular women. All six, each of whom I interviewed at length, appeared psychologically insightful and resourceful. None were abusing alcohol or other substances that could have clouded their judgments. None were financially dependent on their husbands prior to childbirth. None seemed adverse to examining their own psychological processes, even when doing so was painful. So how did they make sense of their husbands' sudden departures?

Five of the six learned, after separating, that their husbands had had hidden problems. These included dormant character traits, such as a history of abusive behavior, a need for frequent sexual novelty, or a pattern of pathological lying, as well as hidden issues, such as identification with an impaired father or a fear of narcissistic needs being unmet. Wives had not been earlier aware of such problems for two reasons. Some of the husbands had deliberately kept these sides of their personalities under wraps; perhaps they had truly wanted to reform their lives but later found they were unable to do so. Other husbands had so deeply buried their past problems that they themselves were unaware of their continued potency. Only after undergoing fatherhood's upheaval did these men reexperience the eruption of previously dormant issues, now rising to the foreground.

DID COMMON THEMES EMERGE?

As I listened to the seventeen women tell me why they believed their marriages ended, I noticed four main themes. First, some thought parenthood had been a transforming event either for themselves or their partners. Second, their stories confirmed earlier research (see Chapter 3) that the decision to separate or divorce is often unilateral. Third, not all separations could have been easily predicted, and, fourth, for some women, divorce at childbirth is experienced as a form of emotional abuse.

Parenthood As a Transformative Event

For some people, parenthood shifts values, behavior, lifestyle, or choice of partner in a sudden, quantum-leap way. This can occur either in a direction toward parenthood, as in the case of Winnicott's (1956) primary maternal preoccupation, or in an opposite direction, as in the case of those fleeing such absorption. At its most extreme, this shift may cause a person to appear metamorphosed, with little continuity between the old and the new.

For example, when asked what caused the sudden transformation of love into hate, spouses exiting at childbirth may deny that love ever existed, thereby avoiding the dilemma of reconciling past and present. According to their wives, several husbands had been unable to account for unanticipated departures, except by disconnecting themselves from their pasts; they either minimized their earlier love and commitment by saying they had never loved their wives in the "right" way, or they denied having been active participants in the project of having a child. While these men seemed to believe their explanations, their wives, who had experienced the contrary, did not. With new sets of values, often quite opposite to those held before, the men seemed to rewrite the history of their marriages to support their current actions. One new father exulted in his transformation, giving it a quasi-religious spin, as if in casting off the "shoulds" of society he had arrived at a deeper, more spiritual plane, while another spoke of finding his true self, renaming as "false" the self who had loved and committed to his partner, now discarded.

Several recent popular books extol the virtues of such quantum leaps of the soul, which are, of course, not limited to men: inexplicably and miraculously as a Wagnerian moment, grace is thought to embrace a person, as a truer self is found—often with a new partner. Along these lines, Thomas Moore (1994) wrote:

> A modern way of making sense of former relationships is to learn from them not to make the same mistakes again, but this utilitarian approach has little soul in it, and in any case most of our own histories prove that we will continue to make similar mistakes. The point is not to learn from our supposed failures, but to be initiated into soul through them. By embracing the feelings that come at times of ending, as well as the thoughts and feelings that linger for a very long time afterward, we become renewed persons. The soul never learns, but it does metamorphose, like worm to butterfly, to use Emerson's image. The soul makes these "ascensions of state," undergoes its initiations by means of life experiences, including relationships and their endings. (p. 203)

William James (1902), in *The Varieties of Religious Experience,* thought otherwise. Examining apparent sudden religious conversions, he discovered that such rapid psychological transformations actually represent the final step in a long chain of internal events, events of which a person is not always fully aware. One of the fathers of modern psychology, James believed in the unconscious. It was observations such as his, as well as those of many later clinicians, that were supported by my interviews: although a number of women in my study initially experienced their husbands' changes as sudden, subsequent exploration revealed that, in most cases, new fathers' quantumlike metamorphoses were neither spiritual in nature nor signified "true" versus "false" selves, but rather they represented activation of deeply buried, split-off issues.

Fathers were not the only ones who appeared to transform in this way. Several of the mothers dramatically changed certain habits, such as alcohol or drug use, while at the same time reappraising their marriages. Some had been troubled by lifestyles that were tolerable before having a child but became rapidly intolerable afterward. For each of these women, rediscovery and activation of her protective maternal ideal allowed her to leave a marriage she knew would be harmful to her child.

Only one mother initiated separation for reasons other than severe dysfunction of her husband. As with several of the men in the stories, she also appeared to undergo a sudden transformation; developing a new independence and defiance, she triumphantly fled a husband and home she had cared for deeply. Yet after she left, rather than be initiated into a new transcendent state, she became more lonely and depressed. In retrospect, she realized she had been responding to issues and fears that had long haunted her, even though most had remained outside her immediate awareness. Her capacity to understand herself, to connect her old self to the new, allowed her to return to her husband and renew her marriage.

Unilateral Nature of the Decision to Separate

Most women described the decision to separate, whether made by themselves or their partners, as unilateral. On the one hand, the majority of women initiating divorce felt so hopeless about their marriages that although they had previously given their husbands multiple chances to change, they did not specifically discuss divorce prior to departing. Perhaps they even feared that such communications might escalate the violence at home. Several husbands on the receiving end of this decision "didn't get it" that their addictions or abuse had ended their marriages and became enraged that their wives were spurning them—from their point of view, for no good reason.

Neither did the women who were left, whether surprised or not, recall any previous conversations about the possibility of divorce. Although some agreed after the fact that it was a reasonable solution to their problems, others who had thought they were in happy marriages experienced their husbands' sudden departures as traumatic.

In only one of the seventeen marriages was the decision to separate or divorce, within a year of having a child, truly mutual. This finding supported those of other researchers that many divorces—perhaps a larger proportion than commonly realized—are forced upon nonconsenting spouses. Sometimes the latter are in deep denial about the extent of their own problems; other times they are the victims of their partners' inner turmoil, triggered by issues other than problems with the marital relationship. In either case, if a spouse does not agree with the necessity of the breakup, a state of trauma may result.

Could These Divorces Have Been Predicted?

Can any danger signals alert couples to the possibility that their marriages will not survive childbirth? Reassuringly, many mothers in my study were well aware of serious difficulties long before they separated. Slightly over one-half (nine of the seventeen) had known their marriages were riddled with manifest problems such as substance abuse, physical abuse, or infidelity. Even though few of these mothers thought divorce was imminent, in retrospect, they were not too surprised it had occurred.

The other eight, however, were in marriages that they had thought happy. While two of these women abruptly left their husbands after childbirth (one in response to her husband's sudden escalation of cocaine use, the other in response to activation of her own internal issues), another six were themselves unexpectedly left. This did not reflect their particular blind spots. Rather, their husbands had either deliberately hidden significant levels of dissatisfaction or had experienced sudden activation of dormant issues concerning fatherhood.

A number of exiting partners, accordingly, were not considering divorce before they conceived a child; it is unlikely that either they or their partners could have predicted the suddenness with which their marriages broke down. Understandable in retrospect, such apparent transformations in love are exceedingly difficult to predict prospectively. For although parents' reactions to childbirth are at least partially determined by their prior psychological makeup, the latter is not so easy to define. As in chaos theory, the difficulty of accurately knowing the parameters of a person's unconscious makes predicting a course difficult.

Divorce As Emotional Abuse Under Some Circumstances

Emotional and physical abuse were frequent themes in these stories. A number of women *already* experiencing abuse noted escalation of maltreatment after conception; it seemed that pregnancy and early motherhood, rather than bringing out their husbands' protective instincts, further activated sadistic trends. In several marriages such abuse escalated to the point that either the wife fled, or, alternatively, her husband stormed out in a final show of cruelty. Some such "decisions" to separate seemed to involve a need to exert power over wives who now represented the men's own disavowed faults.

These stories portrayed how a departing partner can turn angrily on the other, even when the latter has not behaved poorly. This conduct can be puzzling, as ordinarily we expect a person to feel guilty upon hurting another, and to use that guilt as a signal to moderate action.

Melanie Klein's (1935) ideas are helpful in this regard. As reviewed earlier, her notions of the "paranoid" versus the "depressive" positions differ in terms of how one handles guilt. In the depressive position, one is able to tolerate taking responsibility for hurt caused others and to bear feeling sad about it. In the paranoid position, one is unable to tolerate these feelings, so instead projects blame outward.

Often the leaving parties in divorce are in the so-called paranoid position. Unable to tolerate the full force of their guilt, as they would then have to take some responsibility for having caused enormous, perhaps irrevocable emotional pain, they project accountability back onto their already hurt partners. Particularly those exiting for questionable reasons may use this defense, as they flee former loved ones who seem suddenly riddled with flaws. Perceiving the latter as very angry and punitive, they may turn on them vindictively—while themselves escaping guilt's full blast.

THE EFFECTS OF SEPARATION/DIVORCE
ON THESE WOMEN: WHAT WAS MOST DIFFICULT?

Women Whose Husbands Initiated Separation

Almost all of the ten women whose husbands initiated separation were emotionally devastated. Although divorce at this vulnerable time was difficult for all who did not desire it, especially affected were those taken completely by surprise.

As predicted by attachment theory, most women not anticipating their husbands' departures went through similar phases in coming to terms with the end of their marriages: initial shock and sense of unreality, followed by protest and then despair. Five of the six who were most surprised experienced a prolonged period of severe depression. For some, the turning point came when they recognized they were not to blame for their husbands' departures. For others, particularly those unable to make meaning out of their husbands' sudden changes of heart, emotional numbness continued for months or years.

Women Who Initiated Separation

Compared to women totally unprepared for divorce, those initiating it generally fared better. Whereas the former reported more shock, disorientation, and dysfunction, the latter tended to experience the less detrimental feelings of sadness, grief, and guilt. Of importance, even though most felt psychologically "left" by their husbands, those women who did the actual leaving had some control over the process: six of the seven initiating divorce felt they had already been emotionally deserted by abusive or addicted husbands, but only two felt truly traumatized. The other four, feeling less victimized, were able to grieve.

Trauma versus Grief Responses

Contrary to the view that in a failing marriage it is rather arbitrary which partner initiates separation and divorce, these stories suggest that even in one riddled by severe infidelity, drug addiction, or physical abuse, being the spouse who decides to separate confers a significant advantage. Among women whose marriages were already very troubled, those who took the initiative to leave generally felt more grief than trauma. By contrast, the majority (seven of ten) of women whose husbands left them exhibited trauma responses, as did all wives who were very unexpectedly abandoned. This trend may partly reflect the greater capacity of women with more resources to exit troubled marriages, but it also reflects the healing nature of taking control. Although it is sometimes said that it is as hard to leave a relationship as to be left, these stories do not support that notion. Particularly for women in the postpartum period, it is much harder to be left.

What Was Most Difficult?

When asked what had been most difficult about the breakup of their marriages, women often mentioned factors related to single parenthood, such as fatigue, lack of adequate backup or child care, and economic stress. Exhaustion and burnout were mentioned by all as a problem in the first year after separation. The difficulty they had finding time to go out on a social occasion or even to take a shower alone were mentioned as among the most trying aspects of their new lives.

Linked to these difficulties was economic deprivation. Few former husbands paid the minimum mandated child support, and of those mothers who did receive it, most found it grossly inadequate. Eight of the seventeen women in the study were forced to move back in with their own families, putting into effect the matrilineal shift in assets noted by some researchers.

One important finding of my study was that even women with higher-paying jobs prior to childbirth experienced economic difficulty after divorce. Most were resourceful and eventually able to make ends meet, but few were able to do so on the basis of only their salary plus child support. Most eventually relied on a combination of their own earned income, child support, financial help and babysitting from relatives, and state and federal subsidies. Even in this group of middle-income, well-educated mothers, most of whom had previously held professional jobs, few were able to manage without significant adjunctive economic help following their divorces—help that did not come from their husbands.

Yet of all these problems, for new mothers left unexpectedly, managing their own emotional trauma was the most difficult. Alternating between rage and severe self-doubt, many blamed themselves for not having been more attentive to their husbands' needs. The experience of their formerly loving spouses turning on them so cruelly left this group shattered and traumatized; several said they would rather have been physically abused than to have gone through what they did. The further complication that these men were the fathers of their children—carrying half of their genes, sharing half of their names, and being forever linked together—made recovery very difficult. As a result, several women described divorce's most difficult aftermath as being forced to coparent with men they now hated. Struggling to turn anger to pity, some women were successful, but others, no matter how hard they tried, continued to feel unbearable hurt and anger.

HOW DID THE BREAKUPS AFFECT THEIR MOTHERING CAPACITY?

It is painful to admit impairment in one's capacity to parent. Particularly if the failure is major, facing it may be a most difficult task. Therapists working with clients recalling unequivocal parental neglect, for example, notice how rarely these clients receive an apology, even though one would be quite healing. Perhaps much shame and guilt stand in the way.

Such feelings may explain why many people have difficulty objectively evaluating the effects of divorce on their children. More sanguine than outside observers or their children's own reports, parents generally underestimate divorce's aftermath. Perhaps they are preoccupied with their own turmoil, or perhaps they are exhibiting a natural difficulty facing the distressing truth that children's and adults' interests are only partially congruent. Pursuit of parental needs, even those keenly desired, sometimes occurs at the expense of the young.

With these thoughts, I expected few of the women to acknowledge any impairment in their mothering capacities. I was surprised, therefore, when most openly admitted significant dysfunction during the first year after separation. Although all were able to meet adequately their infants' basic physical needs, most described a state of numbness, shock, preoccupation, or depression that interfered with being fully tuned in to their infants' emotional states. This is not to say that these mothers did not love or ever enjoy their babies—after all, they had been looking forward to this time as one of the best in their lives—but in spite of such happy anticipations, intrusive emotions related to the divorce trauma interfered with their bonding. Overwhelmed and depressed after their breakups, more irritable than they would like to be, they knew their babies were not receiving optimal starts. Although the duration of their distress varied, for several women it lasted at least a year, and in some cases two or three years. Looking back, they felt sad that both they and their children had lost so much time.

As their babies grew into preschoolers, most mothers no longer had the same sense of acute impairment. Indeed, they consistently placed parenting as a priority over other areas of their lives, with motherhood being the area about which they felt most positive. Nevertheless, long after their divorces, they continued to struggle with accepting aspects of their children reminding them of their ex-husbands, particularly if the latter had been abusive or sadistic.

Compared to mothers who had separation forced on them, those who initiated it felt their parenting skills were somewhat less impaired. Although they had to contend with much sadness and economic hardship, they believed they had done the right thing by leaving partners unsuited for fatherhood. As a result, they tended to feel grief rather than trauma. Compared to trauma—a condition of disorganized, alternating states of emotional hyperarousal and numbness—grief is a state of relatively organized sadness, a state that may also have allowed mothers to resonate more easily with aspects of their children reminding them of their former husbands.

When asked how they thought their children were doing, most mothers felt they had got on track with their babies after the first year or two, and they believed that their children now appeared developmentally normal. Since the breakups had occurred in the first, preverbal year of their children's lives, mothers often wondered if events had been harder on older siblings, who were more vocal about their distress. (Several of these, in fact, were noticed to have "lost their sparkle," or to have developed cognitive or behavioral problems not apparent prior to separation.) Most mothers, despite remaining worried about how their emotional states had affected their infants, reported no outward signs of harm. However, as I did not systematically interview these young children, and as their average age at the time of my study was only 2.9 years, we must regard these reports with caution.

HOW HAVE RELATIONSHIPS WITH EX-HUSBANDS EVOLVED?

When childless couples separate, they may decide to go their separate ways. By stark contrast, when parents split, their relationships do not end. In spite of a plethora of popular books proclaiming otherwise, there may be no such thing as true divorce among those who continue to share the raising of their young. Although these couples may no longer live together, cooperate financially, or have a sexual relationship, and although they may have both found new romantic partners, they nevertheless remain bound together in an endeavor more emotionally demanding than any of these factors. Many parents would say the most important part of their lives—the most meaningful, permanent, and transcendent of individual existence—is the raising of their children. Truly divorcing their spouses, in the sense of being able to start afresh without the other's presence in their minds and hearts, is a faulty prospect. Even in cases in which one parent abnegates visitation entirely, he or she lives on in the child.

Divorced parents, accordingly, often remain more emotionally entangled than they had anticipated. In some cases, their relationships continue to resemble marriages gone sour, with divorce just one more battle in an ongoing war. Unfortunately, such combat does not necessarily abate following separation. Couples engaged in high conflict often continue to do so, just with greater stakes, while those previously enjoying calm, if troubled, relationships may find their fragile peace evaporating after divorce.

How did the women I interviewed experience their relationships with their ex-spouses changing, for better or for worse, after divorce?

Women Whose Husbands Did Not Visit Regularly

Six of the seventeen fathers removed themselves from regular visitation, severing themselves from any type of ordinary participation in their children's lives. Only one of these regularly paid child support.

These six fathers' lack of participation in their children's lives did not reflect a choice on the part of the mothers. In five of the cases, the fathers had been the ones unilaterally to end their marriages. None were discouraged from visiting; in fact, all were encouraged to do so by their former wives, one of whom placed her husband's framed picture above her baby's crib. Rather, it appeared that these men had priorities other than fatherhood. At the time of their departures, four admitted they had already begun affairs. Perhaps these new involvements had become more important than bonding with their newborns.

Deserted and bewildered, their former wives yearned for more contact—not for themselves, but for their children, for whom they longed to have fathers. At the same time, these women were thankful they did not have to cope with the trauma of seeing their ex-husbands frequently, although they did have to cope with their ghosts, living on in their children.

In addition to the six fathers who actively removed themselves from their families, another two would have preferred to remain involved but were unable to sustain regular visits because their former wives felt forced, for financial reasons, to move back in with parents or relatives who happened to live in distant cities (neither father paid regular child support). These mothers did not discourage visits, but the practicalities of long-distance travel compounded by the severe dysfunction of the fathers made regular visitation difficult.

Women Whose Husbands Remained Involved As Fathers

Unlike the previous eight mothers, the other nine struggled with ongoing relationships with ex-husbands who remained actively involved in child rearing. Few of these postdivorce relationships were amicable. In fact, several mothers reported that their relationships had further deteriorated *after* separation: for those women fleeing physical abuse, a high level of conflict continued, played out in the courts at great expense, while for those left against their will, intense hurt followed encounters with their former partners—encounters that could occur as frequently as several times a week. Sometimes persisting for years, pain did not easily fade. Time, perhaps, healed only those wounds not continually reopened.

Overall, did these women consider their former husbands' visits a plus?

Women Who Would Have Preferred Their Husbands Not to Have Been Involved

Almost half of these women (four of the nine) whose husbands remained involved admitted they would have preferred otherwise, yet to survive economically, they needed child support. Mindful of their financial dependence, they reluctantly allowed visitation—but at great emotional cost. Financial desperation sometimes overrode concerns, not just about their own ability to cope with such repeated interactions, but also about their husbands' abilities to parent appropriately.

Most important, even if not worried about direct harm to their children, these mothers felt that their own distress at being forced into ongoing relationships with cruel ex-husbands impaired their ability to parent. They were not hesitant about visitation out of spitefulness, but rather out of an accurate assessment: being handcuffed into parenting partnerships with men who had treated them brutally was likely adversely to affect their mothering. Furthermore, as in most cases infants had had little contact with their fathers before separation, some mothers felt there was more to gain by preserving their own mental health than by striking up relationships between newborns and departing fathers. Afraid if they made waves their already meager child support would be cut, however, they did not challenge their husband's visitation rights.

Women for Whom Their Ex-Husbands' Involvement
Was a Plus

Slightly over one-half of the women (five of the nine) expressed more mixed feelings about their ex-husbands' continued participation. Overall, they felt the positive aspects of continued connection outweighed the negative ones. Two reasons explain why these mothers took this more benign position.

First, some had older children already attached to their fathers. These women had a history of being part of a family with their spouses and could not easily conceive of breaking ties, already strong, between father and child.

Second, none of the women with a more benign attitude toward visitation had been unexpectedly left. They had either been the ones to initiate separation or had been not very surprised when their husbands left them. As a result, this group experienced less anger and could more easily cope with seeing former partners and attempting to coparent with them.

DID THEIR CHILDHOODS HOLD
ANY RELEVANT INFORMATION?

Over one-third (six of the seventeen women) reported a history of losing at least one parent, to either death or divorce, during their childhood or early teenage years, and two more women described major dysfunction at home, such as parental psychiatric illness or sexual abuse. Almost half the women, accordingly, reported early loss—either physical or psychological—of at least one parent.

Interestingly, two of the women who themselves had not suffered such losses told me that their *husbands'* childhoods were marked by such. One husband's parents had divorced when he was age three; subsequently he became estranged from his violent father. Another one's father had had numerous affairs, repeatedly leaving home to live with other women.

In at least ten of the seventeen couples divorcing at childbirth, accordingly, at least one spouse had a history of loss, early in life, of a parent as an effective role model. This finding supported other research highlighting the intergenerational transmission of parental loss. It is well-known, for example, that children of divorce have a higher statistical chance of themselves divorcing (see Chapter 6), and it has also been suggested that losing one's mother early in life may be a risk factor, at least for women, for later adjustment problems. Perhaps having two well-functioning parents provides a protective buffer against later adversity; an internal template of a healthy family triangle may help guide them through parenthood's gates.

SURVIVING THIS DIFFICULT TIME: HOW DID THESE WOMEN ATTEMPT TO HEAL?

Not only did these newly separated mothers have to contend with challenges such as economic difficulties, finding child care, and moving, but they also had to cope with extreme inner turmoil. Furthermore, they had to do so while simultaneously learning how to care for their infants. They used a variety of coping strategies, including eliciting support from family and friends, returning to work, and attempting to find new partners. Additionally, they called on inner resources, as they tried to make meaning of events, reestablish self-esteem, and focus on the wonderful new experience of motherhood. How successful were they?

Family Support

As noted previously, most of the women turned to their own families for economic and emotional aid. Eight of the seventeen simply moved back in with their families. Although not always happy with this arrangement, they felt that in the short term they needed the shelter, economic aid, available baby-sitting, and emotional support that only their families could provide. Prior to separation, none of these women had been economically deprived; several, in fact, had been quite well-off, benefiting from dual incomes, substantial personal savings, and assorted financial investments. Yet after separation, with the unrelenting responsibility of caring for their infants, few escaped economic hardship. Unable to work full-time at their previous salaries, burdened with the expense of child care for the hours they did work, and saddled with expensive legal fees and in some cases their former husbands' debts, they became unable to make ends meet. Emotionally and physically exhausted, no wonder they returned to live with their families.

Support from Friends

Mothers actively sought emotional support from friends, who because they had different interests and perspective than family, provided a balanced outlook. One pregnant woman asked a friend to be her labor coach, while others sought out the company of single mothers in similar predicaments, whose advice and support was helpful.

Returning to Work

Despite wishing to do so, eight of the seventeen were unable to return to work during the first year after separation. Most felt so upset that they could not focus on preparing for job interviews, much less the demands of the workplace. Even if they could overcome this obstacle, however, they were then faced with the difficulty of finding work both flexible in hours and with a sufficient salary to cover the cost of child care.

Well-educated professionals, most hoped that they would be able to return to work and become self-supporting once their children were older. Meanwhile, their previous career experiences helped them hold on to identities other than those of wives. Maintaining these other identities was especially helpful for women left by their husbands, as it preserved an area of self-experience relatively uncontaminated by rejection.

Finding New Partners

By the time I interviewed them (on average 2.5 years after their final separations), several women had begun to date. While this process seemed helpful for their emotional recovery, it did not usually occur in the first year after separation. In contrast to the fathers, most of whom quickly found new female partners, few mothers had the time, let alone inclination, to enter the single's world while caring for infants. Furthermore, although several women were interviewed many years after their breakups, only one in the entire sample had remarried.

Among this group of women, remarriage as a solution to the problems of single motherhood did not occur quickly. Nonetheless, most were hopeful that at some point they would remarry or at least find stable new relationships. This vision helped pull them through the difficult years, during which the ability to hold on to hope, even in the face of poor immediate odds, was an important coping mechanism.

Finding Meaning in the Events

One way we try to heal from trauma is by attempting to understand it, and we may go about this in at least two ways (see review by Tedeschi and Calhoun, 1995). On the one hand, interpretations that help explain *why* an event occurred, that explicate its *causes,* help us feel less victimized. If reasonable explanations can be found, even if they involve self-blame, we feel less vulnerable to future traumas. There is a sense of having learned something useful, of being the wiser, of being once again in control.

Unfortunately, this poses a dilemma for those recovering from such trauma as unexpected divorce, for, in this case, if a person blames himself or herself, he or she can regain a sense of control over his or her life, but at a great price: if self-blame is not particularly warranted, this person is left none the wiser, and much the poorer in self-esteem. Exactly this struggle was apparent in a number of the women I interviewed, as they alternated between blaming themselves, thereby achieving an illusion of control, or deciding their husbands had inexplicably changed character—raising the fear that love relationships, even the most committed ones, cannot be trusted. Nonetheless, they continued to seek this type of understanding. Perhaps they knew that finding plausible causes for their husbands' departures would help convert their own traumas to more manageable griefs.

The other type of meaning we may seek has less to do with the cause of traumatic events, and more with how these changed our lives. Adversity, we know, can be seen either as a hopeless stacking of forces against us, or as a challenge to be met. After a storm a tree can be broken, or it can twist to grow in a new, unexpected direction. Many women in this study struggled to so bend.

Some turned to religion to help them find this second type of meaning. Those who strongly believed that God had a plan for their lives found this faith helped them accept their fates; others felt that religion gave them strength to overcome their hardships. In addition, several women entered counseling, while still others read books on philosophy and spirituality, as they sought not just the causes of their divorces but also their emergent meanings.

Despite the value of this second emergent type of meaning, it was my impression that, by itself, it was insufficient; those women able to identify plausible causes for the ends of their marriages fared better than those who remained bewildered. Without an understanding of why their marriages collapsed, of why their husbands suddenly left, new mothers felt more traumatized than bereft, more rage than grief, more part of a sadistic farce than of a meaningful tragedy. Even though forests may regenerate after a tornado, as humans, we would like to know how to predict the storm.

Regaining Self-Esteem

Many women believed that the most decisive factor for their recovery was regaining self-esteem. For most of those initiating separation, this sense remained relatively intact. We recall that almost all of these women were in marriages riddled with alcohol, drugs, or physical abuse; realizing they had made poor choices of husbands, they proactively cut their losses before their children were adversely affected. By saving their little ones from much suffering, they boosted their own sense of competency; being able to leave a partner, even an abusive one, at such a vulnerable moment as childbirth required a certain amount of intelligence, character, and creativity—and these women knew it. Although they grieved the loss of their marriages and felt angry their husbands had not tried to change, self-esteem was generally strengthened.

This was not the case for new mothers whose husbands left unexpectedly. Many initially blamed themselves, taking to heart the accusations that they had not been attentive, attractive, or alluring enough. (Their husbands certainly knew the Achilles' heels in their postpartum wives' otherwise healthy self-regard.) Overcome with confusion and self-doubt, these women took months, sometimes years, to reorient themselves to who they were, as well as to the usual boundaries of decent behavior, but when they were able to organize their thoughts sufficiently to reflect that, after all, they had not been at fault in their husbands' departures, their recoveries took a right-angle bend. Traumatic shock, numbness, and a sense of inner chaos gave way to rage, which united their fragmented selves into a whole again.

Further healing occurred when anger turned to pity toward their ex-husbands, some of whom showed, over time, a downward spiral. These women were then able to convert their initial trauma responses to ones of grief. For others, however, particularly those left unexpectedly at this time, rage could not be overcome, no matter how hard they tried—and try they did, for rage is a most unpleasant state. Yet its frequently recommended antidote, forgiveness, may be most user friendly within an ordinary range of experience. Outside those limits, its accessibility fades.

Focusing on Their Babies

Perhaps the most important factor sustaining these women was their babies. By engaging with these wonderfully fresh new lives, mothers gathered emotional strength. Not only did focusing on their newborns help divert attention from the turmoil in their own lives, but it enhanced self-esteem, for although it took some mothers many months to do so, when they were finally able to tune in to their babies, they began to feel alive, beautiful, and lovable again. Opening doors that had just seemed forever snapped shut, their newborns showed them again what love is.

SUMMARY

In summary, separation and divorce within a year of childbirth, particularly if not anticipated, were often devastating to women's lives. Only those fortunate to have generous families avoided significant financial struggles. Only those who could understand why their marriages ended avoided trauma and despair.

Although women react very differently to initiating divorce at childbirth and having it forced upon them, even those in the second group fare better if they can form some coherent understanding of why their marriages ended. Understanding engenders grief, and those able to grieve, rather than experiencing divorce as only a trauma, are at a significant advantage, as are their children.

Yet for even the most traumatized women in my study, the will to survive adversity predominated. Remarkably, they protected their babies from the wide range of overt harm that could have easily occurred during this chaotic time, and as they painstakingly regained hope, they became involved, capable mothers. As Dylan Thomas described the force that through the green fuse drives the flower, so through motherhood's transformative fuse were these women empowered to overcome their not-good-enough divorces.

Chapter 9

Conclusion

At a recent psychotherapy conference, a case was presented of a father in treatment many years after leaving his first marriage. Although he had dutifully paid monthly child support, over time he had lost contact with his son, who had been an infant during the separation. Burdened at first by much self-blame, this father was later able to work through his guilt and happily remarry. But now, many years later, he was again encountering marital difficulties emerging after his second wife became pregnant. Taking his client's lead, the therapist focused on problems in the two marital relationships—how perhaps this man had not felt sufficiently connected to his first wife, and how that dynamic might now be replaying. The client, who was considering leaving his second wife, felt much relief of his guilt.

Although such understandings are important, they may not be sufficient to explain why many people become so completely disillusioned with their partners at the particular time of pregnancy and childbirth. What leads them to such a drastic decision as divorce with a one-year-old infant involved? Questions such as these often generate answers which assume that the marriages must have already been very strained, but if as therapists we collude with such explanations too easily—or worse, if we initiate them ourselves—we may miss the opportunity to help our clients overcome shame and guilt in a way that they ultimately might find more useful.

To conclude, I will summarize similarities and differences between my findings and those of other researchers. I will also make some brief recommendations for clinicians, which are meant only to initiate discussion, as they are necessarily incomplete.

FINDINGS RELEVANT TO RESEARCH
ON TRANSITION TO PARENTHOOD

Before becoming pregnant, over one-half of the women in my study were in marriages already riddled with problems, including a partner's physical abuse, chronic alcoholism, or other serious addiction. In a few cases, the women were abusing substances themselves. Such problems, along with the conflict they engendered, had predated divorce by many years; the baby simply represented one more stress, perhaps the one breaking the marriage's back. These findings support the notion, common in sociological research, that when couples experience increased conflict after childbirth, it is not the baby that is to blame, but preexisting dynamics.

My research also supports a second conclusion, one less prominent in the literature. For a few couples, transition to parenthood is difficult, not because their marriages were already in trouble, but because childbirth activates powerful issues, internal representations, or character traits that were previously dormant. New parents may then experience extreme anxiety, leading to flight from marriages in which they had been previously happy.

As a result of activation of such issues, some new parents may appear to undergo radical personality transformations, which need not always be negative, as many people move toward nurturing and protecting the newborn. Now responsible for not just their own happiness but also that of their children, they may decide that a partner's previously tolerable dysfunction is so no longer.

FINDINGS RELEVANT TO RESEARCH ON DIVORCE

My study supported three major previous findings regarding divorce: the unilateral nature of many decisions to separate, the severe economic downslide that frequently follows, and the distressing psychological sequelae that may take years to resolve. Although these themes were already prominent in the literature, they seemed further amplified by the timing at childbirth.

First, the women in my study reported that their divorce decisions were almost always made unilaterally; seldom did spouses discuss the possibility of separation prior to one of their departures. While previous research suggested that divorce represents a mutual decision less often than we think (see Chapter 2), my study revealed that child-birth is a time when couples are particularly unlikely to agree about the necessity of ending their marriages. Consequently, an unusual de-gree of animosity may ensue.

Second, separation and divorce caused significant economic down-slide for almost all mothers in my study. Although these effects have been well documented for divorced women and children in general, they seemed especially poignant in my sample, where, remarkably, even highly educated women who had previously enjoyed quite com-fortable lifestyles were initiated into poverty. The dual tasks of nur-turing their infants and coming to terms with the ends of their mar-riages—which in some cases occurred quite suddenly—eclipsed these mothers' ability to sustain their previous career performances. Those who attempted to stay in high gear were faced with another ob-stacle: unless they could afford to pay child care's "tax," returning to work became a rough uphill ride.

Third, the emotional effects of divorce at childbirth were often se-vere and prolonged. Some women took many years to recover. Partic-ularly hard hit were those who had considered themselves in good marriages, yet even those who had left their husbands, if they felt forced to do so because of the latter's dysfunction, went through a time of great strain. Similar to other researchers, I found that women in both groups were vulnerable to developing significant depression, but I also noticed another theme, one previously less discussed: a number of women also exhibited a trauma response.

COMPARING TRAUMA AND GRIEF REACTIONS

My study highlighted the difference between trauma and grief re-, actions. Although these distinctions have been made in other con-texts, I do not believe they have been systematically applied to di-vorce.

Trauma has many definitions. For therapists most interested in the subjective world, it is often sufficient that clients feel traumatized in order to offer validation of their inner states; researchers, on the other hand, may require more objective criteria, including the nature of the traumatic event as well as its particular emotional sequelae. In this book, I have defined trauma as a reaction to an event so painful that its memory cannot be integrated with related emotions into a coherent narrative. Such representations remain walled off, relatively inaccessible but nevertheless active, as they continue to work underground. They become the black hole of a life story. Often circumstances surrounding the event lie outside the ordinary range of human experience and may include an unusual degree of surprise, lack of control, or cruelty. The women in my study who had thought they were in happy marriages but who were shocked to find their husbands leaving shortly after childbirth were severely traumatized.

Trauma creates alternating states of emotional numbness and physiological hyperarousal, which, vacillating unpredictably, lead to a sense of inner disorganization. As the mind tries to cope with such confusion by defensively walling off painful memories and feelings, it dissociates much else that is valuable. For people undergoing traumatic divorce, what is lost may be not only representations pertaining to the immediate divorce period but also those from many years earlier. The ability to reflect on happy times in the marriage and on good qualities of the former spouse may be forfeited, as it may be too painful to remember love shared after it has been devalued.

Of course, spouses frequently do break up; probably most find it painful to remember their previous happiness together, once it is lost. Is every divorce, then, traumatic? Surely the majority of people who have gone through one list it as one of the most difficult times in their lives.

According to the more restrictive definition I am using, not all divorces are traumatic. Most involve a long period of mutual recognition that the marriage is failing. Consequently, neither party is too surprised; neither experiences the complete lack of control felt by those upon whom divorce is unexpectedly forced. Neither has to wrestle, perhaps for the rest of their lives, with the unresolved question, "What did I do that was so wrong, to deserve such treatment?" Under ordinary circumstances, divorcing couples are able to grieve the end of their marriages.

Grieving couples have an easier time remembering and then gradually relinquishing ties with their former spouses. They experience a state of relatively organized sadness, rather than one of disorganized numbness and hyperarousal. They retain more access to memories of their former partners' positive qualities. Most important, they have a sense of control over the process and mutually agree that divorce, after all, is a reasonable solution.

Traumatized partners, by contrast, feel divorce is being inflicted upon them. Vacillating between rage and crippling self-doubt (for what is better guaranteed to knock even the most self-assured off their feet than a spouse's sudden departure?), they attempt to reestablish emotional equilibrium by dissociating from feelings about their former loved ones. In the process, they become numb not only to their ex-mates but also to much of their own inner worlds. Tragically, they lose the access keys to accepting many parts of their children.

GUIDELINES FOR CLINICIANS

As clinicians, we may be called upon to help with divorce at childbirth's immediate upheaval as well as its aftershocks. Although an adequate discussion of this subject might require another book, I will briefly outline how my findings may guide us. Although my research has been psychoanalytically informed, my remarks are directed toward psychotherapists from a variety of schools, who may be attempting to help both individuals and couples overcome divorce's trauma.

Expanded Understanding of Divorce at Childbirth

First, as clinicians we may need to expand our notion of what causes couples to divorce at childbirth. Earlier models explaining difficult transition to parenthood as a paradigm of additive stress must be augmented with the finding that many marriages—in my sample almost one-half—did not appear markedly strained before pregnancy. Whereas some involved a shared illusion that no underlying problems existed, others represented two people who, to the best of their knowledge, were happy together before conceiving a child. As discussed in Chapter 3, this second "transformation" model provides additional insight into why some spouses previously content with their partners undertake, quite rapidly, a flight from parenthood.

Second, when treating such parents "in flight," we must recognize that initially they may rewrite the history of their marriages. Some will tell us that they never loved their partners, or that they never loved them in the right way. They may hint that their spouses were riddled with all kinds of faults, which elicits our secret sympathy for our clients. Of course, we should not entirely disregard such claims, but neither should we take them at face value, for parents divorcing at childbirth may be experiencing such profound anxiety concerning activation of internal issues that they defensively project the blame on to their partners. Their turmoil may be so disorganizing that they grasp on to pseudoexplanations to achieve an illusion of coherence. Their shame and guilt over fleeing may be so enormous that they cannot face the meaning of their actions.

Parents in flight may be using strong defenses to avoid looking at issues that are painful and terrifying. We may need to work patiently, gradually creating a therapeutic relationship in which they are comfortable exploring these difficult issues, while we help them bear much anxiety, shame, and guilt, before underlying problems can be fully addressed.

If appropriate, parents divorcing at childbirth should be seen not only in individual therapy but also in couples counseling, as the other partner often provides information that facilitates our understanding of why the marriage is ending. Meeting with the couple, we may be able to more quickly assess whether the marriage does indeed have major flaws and, if so, whether these can be addressed.

Containment

As parents divorcing at childbirth often present in a state of extreme emotional turmoil, we should, if possible, encourage them to delay divorce until they have had sufficient time to understand the reasons for their sudden wishes to exit. I recommend this with one obvious caveat, however: if any member of the family is in imminent danger, our first goal is not containment, but safety. In situations involving violence, severe substance abuse, or other impending harm, protecting the parties at risk takes precedence, and although this may involve recommendations for hospitalization of one spouse, it may also involve supporting the other's decision to separate—no matter how untimely. On the other hand, in situations less dire, I do believe we should strongly consider advising our clients to delay action.

Some of my readers may feel uncomfortable with this suggestion. After all, as psychotherapists we belong to a tradition long adverse to advice giving. We do not wish to sway our clients with our notions of right and wrong, or with our ideas of how we might act in similar circumstances. Instead, we wish to help them clarify their own thoughts, access their own desires. Yet we also belong to a tradition of providing emotional containment for those in crisis. For clients temporarily overwhelmed by anxiety generated by issues that they may not fully apprehend, many therapists do suggest that they delay action until there has been adequate time to consider.

When treating parents on the brink of separating at childbirth, accordingly, we may suggest that they postpone this action, without recommending whether they ultimately proceed. As part of our therapeutic containment, when appropriate, we may tell them that we believe they are experiencing activation of issues that may take time to elucidate. We may also inquire, in a supportive way, if they have realistically weighed the advantages and disadvantages of divorce, not only for themselves, but for their infants. Have they acquainted themselves with the wide literature on the effects of divorce on children and attempted to apply it to their own situations? Have they absorbed recent findings on the importance of the first year of life? Are they aware of the long-term effects of divorce on adults, too? Interestingly, although I believe many parents divorcing at childbirth ponder such questions from their own subjective standpoints, few have time in the middle of such personal crises to do any systematic research, beyond reading a self-help book or two. When all is told, they may be distressed to find that they have put more diligent research into the last model of car they bought than in considering the road ahead, should they divorce, for their infants and families.

The Divorce Decision

Our initial goal is to help clients clarify both the problems in their marriages and their internal anxieties concerning parenthood before making a divorce decision, but sometimes one spouse is strongly bent on leaving, even when such "work" does not appear to have been done. We are then faced with trying to help those in the throes of divorce at childbirth achieve the best possible adjustment.

Although many ways to approach this exist, I will focus here on a most important finding: the advantages of divorce being a mutually agreed upon solution, rather than one unilaterally imposed, are enormous. Nor are the benefits limited to the immediate time around separation. Recovery for both parties, recovery that may continue, in many respects, for the rest of their lives, will be much facilitated if they both feel divorce is a reasonable solution, if both have some control over its process. If these conditions are met, parents will more easily grieve the loss of their marriages and, by so doing, will greatly assist their children's recovery.

When working with couples considering divorce at childbirth, accordingly, we may try to help them achieve a mutual decision. We may even consider advising them that unless they both agree that dissolving their marriage is reasonable, they may face long-term negative consequences for them and their children. (I am, of course, referring to situations not involving violence or imminent danger.) Yet we must also be aware of a major pitfall, one that I believe has inadvertently injured some clients: in our own wish for couples to achieve this equitable result, in our own distaste for witnessing divorce thrust unilaterally upon one party—in perhaps our own horror of such emotional violence taking place in our offices—we may suggest to spouses truly not wanting divorce that perhaps deep down they really do. "If the marriage is over for your partner, it must be over for you," we may suggest. And this pronouncement, if incorrect, can cause harm.

When working with individuals, we are less able directly to assess the degree of mutuality of the divorce decision, yet the same principles apply as when working with couples. As we exercise our "containing" function, we may consider advising those unexpectedly and unilaterally leaving their marriages that their legal right to do so does not imply that they are, necessarily, doing the right thing for themselves or their families.

Finding Meaning

Trauma responses may be ameliorated if divorcing couples arrive at their decisions in a truly mutual manner. Unfortunately, this is not always possible. We may be seeing clients for whom it appears inevitable that one partner will leave against the other's will, or perhaps such a divorce has already occurred, and we are being consulted for help with its aftermath. In either case, we can facilitate our clients' recovery by helping them find meaning in the events. Through this process, trauma may be converted to grief.

As discussed in the last chapter, the search for meaning can take at least two forms: understanding the causes of an event—the reasons it occurred—and understanding its results—its creation of emergent opportunities for new growth and direction. As important as is this second endeavor, I believe it is most successfully accomplished after the first has been addressed. As anchored ships can only drift in circles, so may people charting only this second course of meaning initiate, not new growth, but recurrent cycles of failure.

For those left at childbirth against their will, understanding what led to their partners' departures may be very helpful. If a new mother recognizes that her husband's severe alcoholism led to his flight, for example, she may feel less trauma and more grief than if she remained perplexed about the reasons for his exit. By contrast, if she had been the one suffering such dysfunction, she may benefit from the knowledge that it hastened her marriage's end. Only then will she be able to unfetter her future course from past problems.

Unilateral "leavers" may also benefit from a review, even long afterward, of their reasons for their actions, for although they may not have experienced the same degree of shock, numbness, and rage as their former traumatized spouses, they did not get off lightly. Many carried a burden of guilt, a burden they may have unsuccessfully tried to shed, however clumsily and at whatever cost to themselves, their children, and society. To truly release this anchor, they do not need to be reassured that they have created expanded opportunities for themselves. Nor do they need their therapists' acceptance that their divorce decisions were right and reasonable. What they need is to identify, in as clear and consistent a way as possible, why they left their spouses at childbirth. Although in some cases these reasons may be already clear, in others they are not, for it is particularly those people who remain troubled by their decisions who may consult us many years later. We can help them tolerate anxiety concerning finding truer meanings, ones that will free them, not just from guilt's full weight, but from cycles of repetitive disappointment.

Divorce at childbirth epitomizes our conflict concerning our society's most basic principles. We wish to ensure that people have the freedom to make reasonable choices for their lives, but we also wish to ensure that they do not have the freedom impulsively to hurt others. The ease with which our current legal system offers unilateral divorce on demand—no questions asked, no fault assigned—highlights this dilemma for us.

Take, for example, the case of a mother fleeing a violent husband and in imminent danger of losing her life, as were several of the women in this book. For such divorces, we would hardly want to slow down our current legal process, nor would we wish to prevent such a husband, should he initiate separation, from doing so quickly.

But if that same mother were to leave a caring, responsible husband, taking with her their new baby, depriving both father and child of living together, and if her primary motivation was to pursue a new romantic relationship that she found more thrilling than the worn one with her husband, might we question the ease with which she can obtain no-fault divorce without first working on her dissatisfactions? Comparing her case with that of a father abruptly leaving his postpartum wife to pursue a similar goal, is justice done when the child support he owes is the same in both situations? We wonder whether our laws do justice, not only to divorcing couples, but to the notion of marriage vows themselves.

In many circumstances, we would wish for no legal roadblocks, but at other times, perhaps the privilege of unilateral divorce on demand, designed for conditions of danger or extreme dysfunction of one partner, is being abused by those who use it to divert attention from their own internal problems. For such people, we should seek to slow down their decisions, often hasty and destructive.

Perhaps we cannot do both. Given a choice, it is probably easier to guarantee that spouses in imminent danger can easily exit their marriages than to ensure that those experiencing activation of internal issues behave decently. Although we cannot prevent the baby from rocking the cradle, as a society we can facilitate the cradle being safe, and as therapists we can provide a protected place for our clients to tell us how their babies, unexpectedly, rocked them.

References

Ainsworth, M.D.S., Blehar, M., Waters, E., and Wall, S. (1978). *Patterns of attachment*. Hillsdale, NJ: Erlbaum.

Amato, P.R. and Keith, B. (1991a). Parental divorce and adult well-being: A meta-analysis. *Journal of Marriage and the Family*, 53, 43-58.

Amato, P.R. and Keith, B. (1991b). Parental divorce and the well-being of children: A meta-analysis. *Psychological Bulletin*, 110(1), 26-46.

Arendell, T. (1986). *Mothers and divorce: Legal, economic, and social dilemmas*. Berkeley, CA: University of California Press.

Arendell, T. (1995). *Fathers and divorce*. California: Sage.

Atkins, R.N. (1989). Divorce and fathers, some intrapsychic factors affecting outcome. In S.H. Cath, A. Gurwitt, and L. Gunsberg (Eds.), *Fathers and their families* (pp. 431-458). Hillsdale, NJ: The Analytic Press.

Beckwith, L., Cohen, S.E., and Hamilton, C.E. (1999). Maternal sensitivity during infancy and subsequent life events relate to attachment representation at early adulthood. *Developmental Psychology*, 35(3), 693-700.

Beebe, B. and Jaffe, J. (1992). Mother-infant vocal dialogue. *Infant Behavior and Development*, 15, 48. ICIS Abstracts Issue, May.

Beebe, B., Lachmann, F., and Jaffe, J. (1997). Mother-infant interaction structures and presymbolic self and object representations. *Psychoanalytic Dialogues*, 7(2), 133-182.

Benedek, T. (1959). Parenthood as a developmental phase. *Journal of the American Psychoanalytic Association*, 7, 389-417.

Bianchi, S.M., Subaiya, L., and Kahn, J.R. (1999). The gender gap in the economic well-being of nonresident fathers and custodial mothers. *Demography*, 36(2), 195-203.

Bibring, G. (1959). Some considerations of the psychological processes in pregnancy. *This Annual*, XIV, 113-121.

Bibring, G.L., Dwyer, T.F., Huntington, D.S., and Valenstein, A.F. (1961). A study of the psychological processes in pregnancy and of the earliest mother-child relationship. *The psychoanalytic study of the child*, 16, 9-44. New York: International Universities Press.

Block, J.H., Block, J., and Gjerde, P.F. (1986). The personality of children prior to divorce. *Child Development*, 57, 827-840.

Block, J., Block, J.H., and Gjerde, P.F. (1988). Parental functioning and the home environment in families of divorce: Prospective and concurrent analyses. *Journal of the American Academy of Child Adolescent Psychiatry*, 27(2), 207-213.

Bollas, C. (1987). The transformational object. In *The shadow of the object: Psychoanalysis of the unthought known* (pp. 13-29). New York: Columbia University Press.

Bowlby, J. (1963). Pathological mourning and childhood mourning. *Journal of the American Psychoanalytical Association,* 11, 500-541.

Bowlby, J. (1969). *Attachment and loss, Volume 1. Attachment.* (2nd edition 1982.) New York: Basic Books.

Bowlby, J. (1973). *Attachment and loss, Volume 2. Separation, anxiety, and anger.* London: Hogarth Press.

Bretherton, I., Walsh, R., Lependorf, M., and Georgeson, H. (1997). Attachment networks in postdivorce families: The maternal perspective. In L. Atkinson and K. J. Zucker (Eds.), *Attachment and psychopathology* (pp. 97-134). New York: Guilford.

Bruer, John T. (1999). *The myth of the first three years.* New York: The Free Press.

Cherlin, A.J., Furstenberg, F.F., Jr., Chase-Lansdale, L., Kiernan, K.E., Robins, P.K., Morrison, D.R., and Teitler, J.O. (1991). Longitudinal studies of effects of divorce on children in Great Britain and the United States. *Science,* June 7, 252, 1386-1389.

Cheung, Y.B. (1998). Can marital selection explain the differences in health between married and divorced people? From a longitudinal study of a British birth cohort. *Public Health,* 112, 113-117.

Chodorow, N. (1978). *The reproduction of mothering: Psychoanalysis and the sociology of gender.* Berkeley, CA: University of California Press.

Clarke, S. (1995). *Monthly Vital Statistics Report,* July 14, 43(125), Table 6.

Cohn, J., Campbell, S., Matias, R., and Hopkins, J. (1990). Face-to-face interactions of post-partum depressed and nondepressed mother-infant pairs at 2 months. *Developmental Psychology,* 26, 15-23.

Cohn, J., Campbell, S., and Ross, S. (1992). Infant response in the still-face paradigm at 6 months predicts avoidant and secure attachment at 12 months. *Development and Psychopathy,* 3, 367-376.

Corboz-Warnery, A., Fivaz-Depeursinge, E., Bettens, C.G., and Favez, N. (1993). Systemic analysis of father-mother-baby interactions: The Lausanne triadic play. *Infant Mental Health Journal,* 14(4), 298-316.

Cowan, P.A. and Cowan, C.P. (1988). Changes in marriage during the transition to parenthood: Must we blame the baby? In G.Y. Michaels and W.A. Goldberg (Eds.), *The transition to parenthood: Current theory and research* (pp. 114-154). New York: Cambridge University Press.

Dawson, G. (1992a). Frontal lobe activity and affective behavior of infants of mothers with depressive symptoms. *Child Development,* 63, 725-737.

Dawson, G. (1992b). Infants of mothers with depressive symptoms: Neurophysiological and behavioral findings related to attachment status. *Infant Behavior and Development Abstracts,* 15, 117.

Deutsch, H. (1937). Absence of grief. *The Psychoanalytic Quarterly,* 6, 12-22.

Edelman, G.M. (1989). *The remembered present: A biological theory of consciousness.* New York: Basic Books.

Emery, R. (1988). Marriage, divorce, and children's adjustment. Newbury Park, CA: Sage.

Erikson, E.H. (1980). Growth and crises of the healthy personality. In *Identity and the life cycle* (pp. 52-107). New York: W.W. Norton and Company.

Fast, I. (1993). Aspects of early gender development: A psychodynamic perspective. In A.E. Beall and R.J. Sternberg (Eds.), *The psychology of gender* (pp. 173-193). New York: Guilford Press.

Fedele, N.M., Golding, E.R., Grossman, F.K., and Pollack, W.S. (1988). Psychological issues in adjustment to first parenthood. In G.Y. Michaels and W.A. Goldberg (Eds.), *The transition to parenthood: Current theory and research* (pp. 85-113). New York: Cambridge University Press.

Fenwick, R. and Barresi, C.M. (1981). Health consequences of marital status change among the elderly. *Journal of Health and Social Behavior,* 22(2), 106-116.

Field, T., Goldstein, S., and Guthertz, M. (1990). Behavior-state matching and synchrony in mother-infant interactions of depressed and nondepressed dyads. *Developmental Psychology,* 26, 7-14.

Field, T., Healy, B., Goldstein, S., Perry, D., Bendell, D., Schanberg, S., Simmerman, E., and Kuhn, D. (1988). Infants of depressed mothers show "depressed" behavior even with nondepressed adults. *Child Development,* 59, 1569-1579.

Finkbeiner, A. (1996). *After the death of a child: Living with loss through the years.* New York: The Free Press.

Fonagy, P. (1999). Memory and therapeutic action. *International Journal of Psychoanalysis,* 80, 215-223.

Fonagy, P., Steele, M., Moran, G., Steele, H., and Higgitt, A. (1993). Measuring the ghost in the nursery: An empirical study of the relation between parents' mental representations of childhood experiences and their infants' security of attachment. *Journal of the American Psychoanalytic Association,* 41(4), 957-989.

Fonagy, P., Steele, H., and Steele, M. (1991). Maternal representations of attachment during pregnancy predict the organization of infant-mother attachment at one year of age. *Child Development,* 62, 891-905.

Fonagy, P., Steele, M., Steele, H., Moran, G.S., and Higgitt, A.C. (1991). The capacity for understanding mental states: The reflective self in parent and child and its significance for security of attachment. *Infant Mental Health Journal,* 12(3), 201-218.

Fraiberg, S., Adelson, E., and Shapiro, V. (1975). Ghosts in the nursery. *Journal of the American Academy of Child Psychiatry,* 14, 387-421.

Frankiel, R. (1994). Introductory notes to chapters 18, 19, 20, 21, and 22: Do children mourn? In R. Frankiel (Ed.), *Essential papers on object loss* (pp. 331-332). New York: New York University Press.

Freud, A. (1965). The concept of developmental lines. In *Normality and pathology in childhood: Assessments of development 1965* (writings of Anna Freud, Volume 6, 1974). New York: International Universities Press.

Freud, S. (1915). Mourning and melancholia. In J. Strachey (Trans. and Ed.), *The standard edition of the complete psychological works of Sigmund Freud,* Volume 14 (pp. 237-258). London: Hogarth Press, 1947.

Furman, E. (1974). Some effects of the parent's death on the child's personality development. Reprinted by permission of Yale University Press in R. Frankiel (Ed.), *Essential papers on object loss* (pp. 382-402). New York: New York University Press, 1994.

Furman, R. (1968). Additional remarks on mourning and the young child. Reprinted with permission of the Philadelphia Association for Psychoanalysis in R. Frankiel (Ed.), *Essential papers on object loss* (pp. 363-375). New York: New York University Press, 1994.

Furstenberg, F. F., Jr. (1994). History and current status of divorce in the United States. *The Future of Children: Children and Divorce,* 4(1), 29-42.

Furstenberg, F. F., Jr., Hoffman, S.D., and Shrestha, L. (1995). The effect of divorce on intergenerational transfers: New evidence. *Demography,* 3, 319-333.

Gabbard, G. and Westen, D. Toward a clinically and empirically sensible theory of thinking. Part III: Implications for theories of therapeutic action. Unpublished manuscript.

Garber, B. (1984). Parenting responses in divorce and bereavement of a spouse. In R.S. Cohen, B.J. Cohler, and S.H. Weissman (Eds.), *Parenthood: A psychodynamic perspective* (pp. 183-203). New York: The Guilford Press.

Garfinkle, I., McLanahan, S.S., and Hanson, T.L. (1998). A patchwork portrait of nonresident fathers. In I. Garfinkle, S.S. McLanahan, D.R. Meyer, and J.A. Seltzer (Eds.), *Fathers under fire* (pp. 31-60). New York: Russell Sage Foundation.

George, C., Kaplan, N., and Main, M. (1985). The adult attachment interview. Unpublished manuscript, Department of Psychology, University of California, Berkeley.

Goldberg, W.A. (1988). Introduction: Perspectives on the transition to parenthood, In G.Y. Michaels and W.A. Goldberg (Eds.), *The transition to parenthood: Current theory and research* (pp. 1-20). New York: Cambridge University Press.

Goldberg, W.A. and Michaels, G.Y. (1988). Conclusion: The transition to parenthood: Synthesis and future directions. In G.Y. Michaels and W.A. Goldberg (Eds.), *The transition to parenthood: Current theory and research* (pp. 342-360). New York: Cambridge University Press.

Green, A. (1986). The dead mother. K. Aubertin (Trans.). In A. Green, *On private madness* (pp. 142-173). Madison, CT: International Universities Press.

Greenson, R.R. (1968). Dis-identifying from mother: Its special importance for the boy. *International Journal of Psychoanalysis,* 49, 370-373.

Grossman, T.B. (1986). *Mothers and children facing divorce.* Ann Arbor, MI: University of Michigan Research Press.

Gunnar, M. (1998). Quality of early care and buffering of neuroendocrine stress reactions: Potential effects on the developing human brain. *Preventive Medicine,* 27(2), 208-211.

Gurwitt, A. (1982). Aspects of prospective fatherhood. In S.H. Cath, A.R. Gurwitt, and J.M. Ross (Eds.), *Father and child, developmental and clinical perspectives* (pp. 275-299). Boston, MA: Little, Brown, and Company.

Gurwitt, A. (1989). Flight from fatherhood. In S.H. Cath, A. Gurwitt, and L. Gunsberg (Eds.), *Fathers and their families* (pp. 167-188). Hillsdale, NJ: The Analytic Press.

Henry, K. and Holmes, J.G. (1998). Childhood revisited: The intimate relationships of individuals from divorced and conflict-ridden families. In J.A. Simpson and W.S. Rholes (Eds.), *Attachment theory and close relationships* (pp. 280-316). New York: Guilford.

Herzog, J. (1982). Patterns of expectant fatherhood. In S.H. Cath, A.R. Gurwitt, and J.M. Ross (Eds.), *Father and child, developmental and clinical perspectives* (pp. 301-314). Boston, MA: Little, Brown, and Company.

Hetherington, E.M., Cox, M., and Cox, R. (1978). The aftermath of divorce. In J.H. Stevens, Jr. and M. Mathews (Eds.), *Mother-child, father-child relations* (pp. 149-176). Washington, DC: National Association for the Education of Young Children.

Hetherington, E.M., and Stanley-Hagan, M. (1999). The adjustment of children with divorced parents: A risk and resiliency perspective. *Journal of Child Psychology and Psychiatry,* 40(1), 129-140.

Hope, S., Rodgers, B., and Power, C. (1999). Marital status transitions and psychological distress: Longitudinal evidence from a national population sample. *Psychological Medicine,* 29, 381-389.

Huntington, D.S. (1986). Fathers: The forgotten figures in divorce. In J. Jacobs (Ed.), *Divorce and fatherhood: The struggle for parental identity* (pp. 53-81). Washington, DC: American Psychiatric Association Press.

Jacobs, J. (1986). Fatherhood and divorce: A review of the psychiatric literature. In J. Jacobs (Ed.), *Divorce and fatherhood: The struggle for parental identity* (pp. 1-23). Washington, DC: American Psychiatric Association Press.

Jacobson, E. (1965). The return of the lost parent. Reprinted with permission of International Universities Press in R.V. Frankiel (Ed.), *Essential papers on object loss* (pp. 233-250). New York: New York University Press, 1994.

James, W. (1902). *The Varieties of religious experience.* New York: Penguin Books, 1982.

Jarvis, W. (1962). Some effects of pregnancy and childbirth on men. *Journal of the American Psychoanalytic Association,* 10, 689-700.

Jessner, L., Weigert, E., Foy, J.L. (1970). The development of parental attitudes during pregnancy. In E. J. Anthony and T. Benedek (Eds.), *Parenthood: Its psychology and psychopathology.* Boston, MA: Little, Brown and Company.

Kasen, S., Cohen, P., Brook, J.S., and Hartmark, C. (1996). A multiple-risk interaction model: Effects of temperament and divorce on psychiatric disorders in children. *Journal of Abnormal Child Psychology*, 24(2), 121-150.

Kestenberg, J. S. (1980). Maternity and paternity in the developmental context. *Psychiatric Clinics of North America*, 3(1), 61-79.

Kestenberg, J.S., Marcus, H., Sossin, M.K., and Stevenson, R., Jr. (1982). The development of paternal attitudes. In S.H. Cath, A.R. Gurwitt, and J.M. Ross (Eds.), *Father and child: Developmental and clinical perspectives* (pp. 205-218). Boston, MA: Little, Brown, and Company.

Klein, M. (1935). A contribution to the psychogenesis of manic-depressive states. *International Journal of Psycho-Analysis*, 16, 145-174.

Klein, M. (1940). Mourning and its relation to manic-depressive states. *International Journal of Psycho-Analysis*, 21, 125-153.

Klinnert, M.D., Gavin, L.A., Wamboldt, F.S., and Mrazek, D.A. (1992). Marriages with children at medical risk: The transition to parenthood. *Journal of the American Academy of Child Adolescent Psychiatry*, 31(2), 334-342.

Klitzing, K.V., Simoni, H., and Burgin, D. (1999). Child development and early triadic relationships. *International Journal of Psycho-Analysis*, 80, 71-89.

L'Hommedieu, T. (1984). Conclusion. In *The divorce experience of working and middle class women* (pp. 97-123). Ann Arbor, MI: University of Michigan Research Press.

LaCoursiere, R.B. (1972). Fatherhood and mental illness. *Psychiatric Quarterly*, 46, 109-124.

Lansky, M.R. (1989). The Paternal Imago. In S.H. Cath, A. Gurwitt, and L. Gunsberg (Eds.), *Fathers and their families* (pp. 27-45). Hillsdale, NJ: The Analytic Press.

LaRossa, R. and LaRossa, M.M. (1981). *Transition to parenthood: How infants change families*. Newbury Park, CA: Sage.

Lehman, D.R., Wortman, C.B., and Williams, A.F. (1987). Long term effects of losing a spouse or child in a motor vehicle crash. *Journal of Personality and Social Psychology*, 52(1), 218-31.

Lester, E.P. and Notman, M.T. (1986). Pregnancy, developmental crisis and object relations: Psychoanalytic considerations. *International Journal of Psycho-Analysis*, 67, 357-366.

Lewis, J.M. (1988). The transition to parenthood, II. Stability and change in marital structure. *Family Process*, 27, 273-283.

Lewis, J.M., Owen, M.T., and Cox, M.J. (1988). The transition to parenthood, III. Incorporation of the child into the family. *Family Process*, 27, 411-421.

Lindemann, E. (1944). Symptomatology and management of acute grief. *American Journal of Psychiatry*, 101, 141-148.

Lyons-Ruth, K., Easterbrooks, M.A., and Cibelli, C.D. (1997). Infant attachment strategies, infant mental lag, and maternal depressive symptoms: Predictors of internalizing and externalizing problems at age 7. *Developmental Psychology,* 33, 681-692.

Mahler, M., Pine, F., and Bergman, A. (1975). *The psychological birth of the human infant.* New York: Basic Books.

Main, M. and Goldwyn, R. (1990). Adult attachment rating and classification system. In M. Main (Ed.), *A typology of human attachment organization assessed in discourse, drawings and interviews.* New York: Cambridge University Press.

Main, M. and Hesse, E. (1990). Parents' unresolved traumatic experiences are related to infant disorganized attachment status. In M. Greenberg, D. Cicchetti, and E.M. Cummings (Eds.), *Attachment in the preschool years*: *Theory, research and intervention* (pp. 161-182). Chicago, IL: University of Chicago Press.

Main, M. and Solomon, J. (1990). Procedures for identifying infants as disorganized/disoriented during the Ainsworth strange situation. In M. Greenberg, D. Cicchetti, and E.M. Cummings (Eds.), *Attachment in the preschool years: Theory, research and intervention* (pp. 121-160). Chicago, IL: University of Chicago Press.

Michaels, C.S. (1989). So near and yet so far: The nonresident father. In S.H. Cath, A. Gurwitt, and L. Gunsberg (Eds.), *Fathers and their families* (pp. 409-423). Hillsdale, NJ: The Analytic Press.

Moore, T. (1994). Soulmates: Honoring the mysteries of love and relationship. New York: HarperCollins.

Murray, L. and Trevarthen, C. (1985). Emotional regulation of interactions between two-month-olds and their mothers. In T.M. Field and N.A. Fox (Eds.), *Social perception in infants.* Norwood, NJ: Ablex Publishing.

Nadelson, C., Polonsky, D.C., and Mathews, M.A. (1984). Marriage as a developmental process. In C. Nadelson and D. Polonsky (Eds.), *Marriage and Divorce: A Contemporary Perspective.* New York: Guilford Press.

Neubauer, P.B. (1989). Fathers as single parents. In S.H. Cath, A. Gurwitt, and L. Gunsberg (Eds.), *Fathers and their families* (pp. 63-75). Hillsdale, NJ: The Analytic Press.

Nichols-Casebolt, A. (1986). The economic impact of child support reform on the poverty status of custodial and noncustodial parents. *Journal of Marriage and the Family,* 48, 875-880.

O'Connor, T.G., Thorpe, K., Dunn, J., and Golding, J. (1999). Parental divorce and adjustment in adulthood: Findings from a community sample. *Journal of Child Psychology and Psychiatry,* 40(5), 777-789.

Osofsky, H.J. and Culp, R.E. (1989). Risk factors in the transition to fatherhood. In S.H. Cath, A. Gurwitt, and L. Gunsberg (Eds.), *Fathers and their families* (pp. 145- 165). Hillsdale, NJ: The Analytic Press.

Pagani, L., Boulerice, B., Tremblay, R.E., and Vitaro, F.J. (1997). Behavior development in children of divorce and remarriage. *Child Psychology and Psychiatry,* 38(7), 769-781.

Parens, H. (1974). *Parenthood as a developmental phase.* Report at the Annual Meeting of the American Psychoanalytic Association in Denver, Colorado, May 8.

Pollit, K. (2000). Is divorce getting a bum rap? *Time* magazine, September 25, p. 82.

Radke-Yarrow, M. (1991). Attachment patterns in children of depressed mothers. In C.M. Parkes, J. Stevenson-Hinde, and P. Marris (Eds.), *Attachment across the life cycle* (pp. 115-126). London: Routledge.

Rodgers, B.J. (1994). Pathways between parental divorce and adult depression. *Journal of Child Psychology and Psychiatry,* 35(7), 1289-1308.

Rubenstein, J.L., Halton, A., Kasten, L., Rubin, C., and Stechler, G. (1998). Suicidal behavior in adolescents: Stress and protection in different family contexts. *American Journal of Orthopsychiatry,* 68(2), 274-284.

Russell, P. (1998). The role of paradox in the repetition compulsion. In J.G. Teicholz and D. Kriegman (Eds.), *Trauma, repetition, and affect regulation: The work of Paul Russell* (pp. 1-22). New York: The Other Press.

Rutter, M. (1995). Clinical implications of attachment concepts: Retrospect and prospect. *Journal of Child Psychology and Psychiatry,* 30(4), 549-571.

Segraves, R.T. (1980). Marriage and mental health. *Journal of Sex and Marital Therapy,* 6(3), 187-198.

Shaw, D.S., Emery, R.E., and Tuer, M.D. (1993). Parental functioning and children's adjustment in families of divorce; a prospective study. *Journal of Abnormal Child Psychology,* 21(1), 119-134.

Smock, P.J. (1993). The economic costs of marital disruption for young women over the past two decades. *Demography,* 30, 353-371.

Spanier, G.B. and Thompson, L. (1987). *Parting: The aftermath of separation and divorce.* Newbury Park, CA: Sage.

Steiner, J. (1996). The aim of psychoanalysis in theory and practice. *International Journal of Psycho-Analysis,* 77, 1073-1083.

Stern, D.N. (1985). *The interpersonal world of the infant.* New York: Basic Books.

Stern, D.N. (1995). *The motherhood constellation.* New York: Basic Books.

Stoller, R. (1976). Primary femininity. *Journal of the American Psychoanalytic Association,* 24, 59-78.

Teachman, J.D. and Paasch, K.M. (1994). Financial impact of divorce on children and their families. *The Future of Children: Children and Divorce,* 4(1), 63-83.

Tedeschi, R.G. and Calhoun, L.G.(1995). *Trauma and transformation: Growing in the aftermath of suffering.* Newbury Park, CA: Sage.

Tessman, L.H. (1978). *Children of parting parents.* New York: Jason Aronson.

Thompson, R.A. (1994). The role of the father after divorce. *The Future of Children: Children and Divorce,* 4(1), 210- 235.

Tronick, E.Z. (1989). Emotions and emotional communication in infants. *American Psychologist,* 44(2), 112-119.

U.S. Bureau of the Census (1995). Who receives child support? *Statistical brief* 95-16, June, 1-2.

U.S. Bureau of the Census (1997). Children with single parents—How they fare. *Census brief 97-1,* September, 1-2.

U.S. Bureau of the Census (1999a). One in three custodial parents without child support are poor, Census Bureau reports. *Statistical brief 99-77,* April 23, 1-2.

U.S. Bureau of the Census (1999b). Household income at record high. *Census brief 99-188,* September 30, 1.

van IJzendoorn, M.H. (1995). Adult attachment representations, parental responsiveness and infant attachment: A meta-analysis on the predictive validity of the Adult Attachment Interview. *Psychological Bulletin,* 117(3), 387-403.

Verbrugge, L.M. (1979). Marital status and health. *Journal of Marriage and the Family,* 41, 267-286.

Wadsworth, J., Burnell, T.B., and Butler, N. (1985). The influence of family type on children's behavior and development at five years. *Journal of Child Psychology and Psychiatry,* 26(2), 245-254.

Wainwright, W.H. (1966). Fatherhood as a precipitant of mental illness. *American Journal of Psychiatry,* 123(1), 40-44.

Wallerstein, J.S. (1991). The long-term effects of divorce on children: A review. *Journal of the American Academy of Child Adolescent Psychiatry,* 30(3), 349-360.

Wallerstein, J.S. and Blakeslee, S. (1989). *Second chances: Men, women, and children a decade after divorce.* New York: Ticknor and Fields.

Wallerstein, J.S. and Kelly, J.B. (1980). Effects of divorce on the visiting father-child relationship. *American Journal of Psychiatry,* 137(12), 1534-1539.

Wallerstein, J., Lewis, J., and Blakeslee, S. (2000). *The unexpected legacy of divorce.* New York: Hyperion.

Weiss, R. (1975). *Marital separation.* New York: Basic Books.

Weitzman, L. (1981). Economics of divorce: Social and economic consequences of property, alimony and child support awards. *UCLA Law Review,* 28, 1181-1268.

Weitzman, L. (1985). *The divorce revolution: The unexpected social and economic consequences for women and children in America.* New York: Free Press.

Westen, D. and Gabbard, G. (in press). Toward a clinically and empirically sensible theory of thinking. Part I: From cognitive neuroscience and connectionism to conflict and compromise. *Journal of the American Psychoanalytical Association.*

Whitehead, B.D. (1997). *The divorce culture.* New York: Alfred Knopf.

Winnicott, D.W. (1956). Primary maternal preoccupation. In *Through paediatrics to psycho-analysis, collected papers* (pp. 300-305). New York: Basic Books, 1958.

Wolfenstein, M. (1966). How is mourning possible? Reprinted with permission from International Universities Press in R. Frankiel (Ed.), *Essential papers on object loss* (pp. 334-362). New York: New York University Press, 1994.

Index